OTHER BOOKS BY

Stanley Schuler

America's Great Private Gardens
Gardening from the Ground Up
Gardening in the East

GARDENING WITH EASE

GARDENING

A Minimum

WITH EASE

Maintenance Manual

by Stanley Schuler

THE MACMILLAN COMPANY
COLLIER-MACMILLAN LTD., LONDON

Many of the photographs in this book were
taken by the author for his earlier book
America's Great Private Gardens

The Macmillan Company
866 Third Avenue, New York, N.Y. 10022
Collier-Macmillan Canada Ltd., Toronto, Ontario

Library of Congress Catalog Card Number: 74-90225

First Printing

Printed in the United States of America

CONTENTS

 GARDENING
WITH EASE

1  You, Work, and Your Garden

Without any question, the biggest trend in gardening today is the trend to *save work*. The phrase more commonly used—probably because saving work carries an implication of slothfulness—is "to minimize maintenance" or sometimes "to reduce upkeep." But I prefer "saving work" because gardening work is not limited to the maintenance of the garden; it also is involved in the creation and construction of the garden, and I am sure you would just as soon save work in this area as in the upkeep area.

Be that as it may—this book is concerned with saving work in the garden. All kinds of work. But if the emphasis seems to be on garden maintenance, that is simply because this is the phase of gardening that demands the most, continuous work.

Why this trend to saving work has grown so fast since World War II and grows even faster today is rather obvious.

In the first place, people now have wider interests than they used to have. And since they also have more money, time, automobiles, and so on to indulge these interests, they have less desire to spend so much time on their gardens. I don't believe they want any less attractive gardens; on the contrary, current tastes in gardens appear to be considerably better than our mothers' and grandmothers'. But today people simply do not want to be slaves to their gardens. As an editor friend said to me a few months ago: "Sure I want a pretty place, but my wife and kids and I have a lot of things we like to do, and if it means giving some of them up in order to have a big garden—well, what's wrong with having a 20-foot flower bed instead of the 80-foot perennial border my mother had?"

The second reason for the trend to reduce garden work is that gardening help is disappearing. The boys who mowed your lawn for 50 cents are gone completely. The old-timers who had the greenest of thumbs and the strength of 10 oxen—that wonderful old Scottish Mac, or Pietro from the Po Valley, or Masato from Japan—if they're not quite gone, they are going. The plain truth is that gardening help today is not only scarce but fiendishly expensive. Worse, it's often incompetent. So is it any wonder that even the people who have plenty of money for gardeners are slowly, reluctantly, but inevitably redesigning their gardens so that they require less maintenance?

To anyone who thrills to really beautiful gardens—the kind of gardens I tried to find for my book *America's Great Private Gardens*—it's all a little sad.

Let's pause an instant to think wistfully of the past.

Now for the present. Our aim: to save work in the garden. Onward.

What is work? Work is: (1) a matter of personal opinion; (2) a reflection of the individual's physical condition and mental outlook at the time a task is undertaken, in progress, and completed; and (3) a reaction to the results achieved. Garden work is no different.

My wife, being a tidy soul, rather likes to weed and

therefore does not think of it as work unless it tires her. I think it's dull business and call it work although it makes no impression on me physically.

I once asked a college boy who did part-time work for me to rake the hay in our meadow, and he was in a state of collapse after raking less than a quarter acre. I raked an acre in the same length of time and was still going strong. I simply was in better shape than the boy. (My interest in the job was also different, of course.)

This spring I plowed a new vegetable garden in a section of the meadow. The grass was old and thick; the soil, which is dense clay, was sopping; and the rotary tiller was a rented brute. But at the end of an hour—which was all the job took—I was feeling on top of the world. By contrast, several weeks earlier, I chopped out a patch of bittersweet less than half the size of the vegetable garden. The work also took about an hour and was not nearly so exhausting; but I felt dragged out. Plowing the garden was *not* work because I anticipated the tasty results; removing bittersweet *was* work because it was dull, routine, and there was little to show for it in the end.

So it goes. There is no universally applicable definition for garden work. Each person must be his own Webster. And that simply means that, when it comes to saving work in the garden, each gardener must go about it in his own way.

Another reason why reducing garden work is an everyman-for-himself proposition is that garden work varies as much with the garden as it does with the gardener. It's one thing in a garden that is primarily a lawn area; another thing in a garden crammed with flowers. It's one thing in a garden by the sea; another in a garden on a mountaintop. It's one thing in a northern garden; another thing in a southern garden.

To be sure, if we were to hold a nationwide poll to determine which gardening chore is the most widely disliked, lawn maintenance would undoubtedly come out on top. However, this would simply be a reflection of the fact that more gardens include lawns than any other single feature. It would not, I am convinced, mean that the majority of gardeners today think lawn maintenance is the most demanding gardening chore, because the real work was taken out of the operation when power mowers became popular.

No, gardening entails many kinds of jobs; and undoubtedly each of them is a special problem for some one. But how widespread they are and what they represent in hours and ergs no one knows. I thought I might get some clue by asking an assortment of public parks commissioners and semipublic gardens superintendents for their experience. But even though all of them are doing their best to find ways to reduce maintenance operations, few apparently have analyzed their crews' work sufficiently to say which jobs are most time-consuming. The best answer came from Alden R. Eaton, director of landscape construction and maintenance for Colonial Williamsburg (where the gardens are very similar to home gardens). He ranked maintenance operations that take the most time at Williamsburg as follows:

1. Pruning (year-round operation)
   a. Trees
   b. Shrubs
   c. Hedges
   d. Ground covers
   e. Certain perennials
2. Grass cutting (seasonal operation)
3. Cultivating (seasonal operation)
4. Planting (almost year-round)
   a. New planting
   b. Replacement planting
5. Pest control

Many gardeners—especially those in semitropical climates—may agree about Mr. Eaton's high ranking of pruning. But those in arid climates would certainly want to add watering high on the list. And I can speak for two people—an acquaintance in Southern California and myself—who would put cleanup at the top.

My inability to give a precise list of the chores that bother most American gardeners is symptomatic of the difficulties of finding a concrete answer to the much larger question: "How can I save work without robbing my garden of all its appeal?"

The truth is that there is no concrete answer (any more than there is a concrete answer for reducing maintenance work in a factory or on a railroad). It takes five sentences to summarize the problem of saving work in the garden:

1. In the average garden, you can make a big work-saving only by making a number of small work-savings. 2. The savings you make rarely represent a 100 percent gain (for example, substituting paving for grass usually saves work; but the paving itself makes work). 3. Some work-savings are achieved only with a considerable outlay of money (for example, a garden tractor with a small complement of attachments costs in the neighborhood of a thousand dollars). 4. Some gardening work has defied simplification to this date (but in view of the major strides that have been made in simplifying other garden tasks, this situation should not continue indefinitely).

5. But despite the somewhat negative aspect of the four preceding statements, any gardener can easily reduce his work load 25 percent; and with planning, he should be able to reduce it a great deal more. At the same time, although he may change the appearance of his garden materially, he should not detract from its appeal.

The chapters that follow give many suggestions for achieving these results. They boil down to a few basic points:

To save work in the garden, determine what is really work (as opposed to work which does not strike you as work).

Use tools and materials that make light work of tedious chores or eliminate them entirely.

Improve the efficiency of your garden layout.

Switch to plant materials and plant substitutes that require little attention.

Don't try to change nature; live with it as you find it.

II  Off to a Good Start

How successful you are in reducing garden work depends in large part on what you do when your lot is still undeveloped to protect land and plants against people and the elements and to provide conditions that promote strong, healthy growth. This is a large order.

Some months ago I was talking with John Watson, of Dallas, the country's foremost outdoor lighting expert. I happened to mention my interest in garden maintenance, and instantly he remarked that maintenance has become his primary concern in garden lighting. Fully 40 percent of the time he spends on a lighting project, he said, is devoted to the problem of designing a system that will demand a minimum amount of attention through the year. "This often means," he said, "that the installation costs more initially than it used to. But the time and money put into it at the start are time and a great deal of money saved in later years."

So it is with the garden proper. The more time you spend on the early development of the garden (it should not cost a great deal of money), the more work you will save in later years.

Developing the Land

Preventing water erosion. Run-off water from rain and snow can cut sloping land to ribbons unless you grade it properly, provide waterways to funnel off the excess water, and protect the bare soil with a sturdy covering of some sort.

Grading. Grading is usually done with a front-end loader, which resembles a bulldozer. The first step always consists of stripping off the topsoil and piling it to one side. Then the subsoil is brought to the proper grade. Finally the topsoil is spread back over the subsoil in an even layer.

One objective of grading is to soften steep slopes so that water flows over the ground more slowly. This is best done by alternating flat terraces with planted banks or walls. On small lots, the terraces and banks are usually at right angles to the slope; but on large properties with an undulating terrain, they should follow the contours of the land.

To develop level contoured terraces (or contoured rows of flowers or vegetables in a garden), you need a helper and a carpenter's spirit level mounted on a long pole. First, find the point on your helper's body that is level with your own eyes when you are standing straight. Then when your line of sight along the carpenter's level strikes that point, you are both standing at the same elevation.

To establish a level line across a hillside drive a stake where you are standing and send your helper on about 50 feet across the hillside. Set your carpenter's level in front of you at eye level; then, sighting along it, direct your helper to move up or down the hill until the previously determined point on his body is level with your eyes. He then drives a stake where he is standing and moves on another 50 feet. Meanwhile, you move up to his stake and repeat the sighting process. Continue in this fashion until you have set a line of stakes across the hillside. If you have done your job carefully, all the stakes will be at the same level.

There is no rule about how wide terraces should be. But it is obvious that the wider they are, the more they will slow the run-off of water and the more useful flat space you will have. Similarly, there is no rule about how wide or how high banks should be (except in the front yard; see Chapter XI). But note that if you want to mow a bank, it should have a pitch of not more than 1 foot vertically in 3 feet horizontally (see Chapter III).

The second objective of grading is to direct runoff water away from where you don't want it to where it will do no harm. A typical problem is to keep water from pelting down a hillside into the house. One possible solution on a large property is to round off the hillside so that the water runs off in several directions instead of straight at the house (the way water runs off a rubber ball, for example). A second solution—usually simpler—is to cut the hill away from the house, thus leaving a more or less level space between the house and the hill. The level space should now be sloped slightly away from the house so that water coming off the hill is caught in the shallow V at the very foot of the hill. From there it can be shunted around the ends of the house in a grass waterway or paved ditch, or it can be funneled into catch basins leading into storm drains.

Waterways and diversions. Waterways are ditches used to carry concentrations of water safely through your property; but they differ from ditches in that there is nothing ugly about them. Many small waterways, in fact, do not look like anything at all. You can walk across a lawn without even noticing them. What's the secret?

To prevent erosion of hillside at left, homeowner built a small ridge, or diversion, along the top to guide surface runoff to a safe outlet. (U.S. Department of Agriculture)

A good waterway is simply a wide, shallow, ribbonlike depression carpeted with grass. It should be located so that water flows into it readily from the surrounding land and is then channeled slowly downhill into a storm sewer, pond, or stream.

A diversion is a rather low, grass-covered, man-made ridge across a hillside (usually following the contours). It has a shallow, grass-lined channel, or waterway, on the uphill side. The purpose is to catch the water running down the hill and shunt it to the side and then lead it gradually down to an outlet.

Diversions, in other words, serve the same purpose as terraces, because they slow the movement of water rushing off a hill. But diversions do not alter the natural shape of the hill as terraces do, and they can be built with less work.

Protecting bare soil. Diversions and waterways must be covered with sturdy sod if they are to carry water even in a hard storm. Similarly, all sloping soil surfaces must be carpeted either with grass or other durable material if they are to resist erosion.

The type of carpeting material you use depends on the location of the slope, its steepness, the appearance you want to achieve, and so forth. For instance, if the slope is exposed to full sunlight and has a pitch not exceeding 1 foot vertically in 3 feet horizontally, grass is an excellent covering. But on steeper slopes and in shady areas where grass will not grow, you need to use a woody or evergreen ground cover. And on slopes with a 1:1 or 1:1½ pitch, you should cover the ground with rocks or heavy timbers. Chapter XI discusses these matters at length.

Preventing damage by wind. Strong winds make work for you by eroding dry soil and by battering and breaking plants.

Soil erosion is most easily prevented by keeping the ground carpeted with plants or paving. Plants that can be damaged by wind need the protection of a windbreak.

Surprisingly, the best windbreak is not a solid wall or fence. Wind goes over these like a hurdler—up, over, and immediately down. Only the plants close behind are protected.

If you use a wall or fence to protect plants, it should be latticed or louvered. This allows the wind to pass through, but breaks its strength and reduces eddying. The area protected extends well back of the wall.

Fairly dense trees and shrubs are equally effective as windbreaks and much more practical if you have a large area to protect. Among the best plants for this purpose are the coniferous trees and shrubs—privet, barberry, iron-wood, and Russian olive. The trees should be planted close enough together so that the branches become slightly interlaced. If space is limited, a single row of trees will do; but if you live out in the open country, the usual practice is to plant two or three rows with the trees staggered in each row. In either case, the windbreak will provide wind protection over an area about 20 times as deep as the trees are high (that is, if the trees are 20 feet high, they give some protection to the garden for up to about 400 feet behind them).

Getting rid of excess water. Nationally, excess water is not so much of a problem as too little water, but the former cannot be ignored. Here are just four ways it can be a nuisance: (1) One of my former neighbors had a low, swampy area where nothing that he planted would grow because the roots were more or less constantly in water or excessively soggy soil. (2) One of the Boston area's most beautiful gardens is marred by a land pocket in which the winter rains and snows collect to a depth of about 2 feet. Nothing grows in the pocket except grass and some swamp iris. (3) The little houses in a new development several miles from me are built on filled land only 3 feet above a creek bed that has been hemmed in by rough rock walls. One of these days the creek will rise out of its channel and tear the bordering yards apart. (4) A friend who lives in a charming place on the shore of Long Island Sound is inundated by high tides three or four times every decade.

What can be done to prevent or at least minimize the often devastating damage too much water can do to a garden?

Draining low spots. The Boston garden owner mentioned above has a peculiar problem and neither she nor her landscape architect have come up with a satisfactory answer. Even the enormous dry well they dug in the land pocket does not hold the water that collects at that point. Their only solution would be to pump the water up out of the pocket into a storm drain or neighboring pond or stream; but none of these things is available.

Many low spots can be easily drained by putting in ditches that lead to a nearby stream or other outlet. My former neighbor did this in one of the slightly higher parts of his swamp, and it worked fine, because water always seeks the lowest point in the landscape.

Another way to grow small plants in low, wet areas is to do the reverse of ditching: build up the soil into broad ridges separated by ditches, and establish your plants on these. The ridges, or beds, can be made with new soil that you truck in; or you may be able to get enough out of the ditches.

In cases where ditching or bedding (as the above practice is called) are not adequate because of a very high water table, you should install underground drains that lead off to a storm sewer, dry well, and so forth. Use 4-inch-diameter, perforated composition drain pipes that come in lightweight 8-foot lengths. Lay the pipes with the perforations facing down, and make sure all pipes are pitched slightly in the same direction (a 1-inch drop in 20 feet is enough). A single line of pipe can drain an area 6 to 10 feet wide, depending on the porosity of the soil. Ideally, the pipes should be at least 2 feet below the surface, because most of the roots of most plants lie above this level. However, if you are planting nothing more than grass, flowers, or vegetables—which have more restricted root systems—you need not bury the drains more than 1 foot deep.

Protecting against flooding. If a stream cuts through your property or along its borders, you can do a great deal to minimize the danger of its overflowing by widening and straightening the channel and protecting the banks with stone riprap, railroad ties, willow poles laid close together as in a sapling fence, or mats of woven brush. Thus you create a sluiceway that carries the water safely by. However, construction of such a channel is not always so easy as it appears, and it may create downstream problems for which the builder would be held responsible; consequently, you would be well advised to hire a hydraulic engineer to advise you about what should and can be done.

Dikes, levees, and flood walls are rarely built until a succession of floods or high tides leaves no alternative. These solutions are obviously expensive—the more so because, to be fully effective, they must not only border the waterfront but must also be extended around all low-lying edges of the property (thus keeping the water away from the back door as well as the front). However, short sections of wall or dike are extremely useful in breaking the force of rampaging streams and storm-tossed waves.

Protecting the Garden Against Other Problems

Salt damage. The salt used on northern streets and highways to melt ice and snow has become one of the nation's worst maimers and killers of trees, shrubs, and grass. Ocean salt is equally injurious, although the number of gardens exposed to it is comparatively small.

The best way to cope with the problem—and thus to avoid the unnecessary work it makes—is not to plant anything within the area reached by the salt water and slush splashed up by passing vehicles (or waves). Pave the area instead. For instance, in Florida, the George Zahms (she is a landscape architect) live on the Intracoastal Waterway. Though their lawn is above the high-water mark, they discovered several years ago that when large power boats went by at high tide the wash often splashed up on the edges of the lawn. This killed the grass; and in addition, there was considerable erosion. So the Zahms eventually laid a 5-foot strip of white gravel between the sea wall and the lawn. This same idea would work equally well in protecting lawns and smaller grass strips along busy streets in the North.

Five-foot strip of white gravel behind seawall protects the George Zahms' fine lawn from water splashed up by boats speeding down the Intracoastal Waterway.

If a property already has good trees or shrubs close to the street, deciduous species can be protected fairly well by sloping the soil away from the trunks so that the salt water will run off quickly instead of sinking in. To improve the runoff, you might even pour a concrete apron around the street side (but only the street side) of the tree.

Evergreens can be protected in the same way. However, those with low-hanging branches are damaged not so much by salt water reaching the roots as by salt splashed on the leaves. Consequently, the best way to protect them is to erect screens of heavy polyethylene film between them and the street.

Damage by roof drip. If a house does not have gutters, rain or snow water dripping from the eaves eventually mutilates almost anything planted directly beneath. In fact, it is not at all unusual to find around contemporary houses a handsome bed of pachysandra or other ground cover cut in two by a strip of bare earth—the product of dripping water.

The obvious way to prevent the problem is to install gutters. If you and your architect object to them, the only other answer is not to plant under the eaves but to cover the ground from the foundation wall to 6 inches beyond the drip line with gravel or other paving material.

Damage caused by drip when it freezes into giant icicles occurs when a roof is without gutters and also when it has gutters that are not kept clean. A partial solution is to lay electric soil-heating cable in a zigzag pattern along the roof edge. This cuts channels through the ice and snow and encourages the water to run off too rapidly for it to freeze.

Winter damage to trees. There are no long-range measures you can take to prevent killing of trees and other plants when temperatures drop lower than usual and stay there for several days. (Even emergency measures are not very good.) But in areas where snow and ice pile high, you can and should see to it that trees with Y-shaped crotches are braced against breakage under loads. This type of crotch is weaker than more open crotches; and as a rule, it is advisable to eliminate it by cutting off one of the branches. If this is not possible, the branches forming the Y should be tied together with steel rods or cables. These should be installed by professional tree men.

(Protecting outspreading branches on trees with old or weak wood—old apple trees, for example—is an annual chore. It is best accomplished by bracing the limbs from the ground with 2 by 4s. Limbs that are too high to be braced should be knocked free of snow with a broom or long pole immediately following heavy storms, or even during them.)

Animal damage. On the whole, dogs are the worst offenders—and there is nothing humane that can be done when you start a garden to keep them from killing plants ever after. In fact, there is not too much you can do to protect plants from dogs at any time: Just wield a big stick and try to drench them with a bucket of water when they are off guard.

Raccoons are equally difficult to guard against. Deer are, too, unless you are willing to erect an 8-foot fence or will settle for plants that animals are not particularly fond of (see Chapter VI).

Rabbits and mice can be kept from girdling young fruit and nut trees by wrapping ½-inch wire mesh loosely around the trunk and sinking the bottom edge in the soil a couple of inches. The top of the mesh should be about 18 inches above the ground unless you are really overrun with rabbits—in which case, it should be 18 inches above the highest normal accumulation of snow.

A 3-foot chicken-wire fence embedded in the soil keeps rabbits out of a vegetable or flower garden, but the job of keeping weeds and vines out of the mesh is a nuisance.

Moles and armadillos are easily discouraged from burrowing under the lawn by dusting the grass in the spring with chlordane. This kills the grubs on which the animals feed and forces them to look elsewhere for sustenance.

Pocket gophers (which are known in the South as salamanders) must be controlled by trapping or poisoning. The only good traps are those especially designed for gophers. To use them, dig a narrow trench between two mounds newly made by gophers and at right angles to the burrow between them. As a rule, a trench 1 foot deep and 3 to 4 feet long will cut the burrow. To be sure of catching a gopher, place one trap in the burrow on one side of the trench and another trap in the burrow on the opposite side of the trench. Attach the traps by wires to stakes above ground; otherwise gophers that are not immediately killed may carry them off. Leave the trench open but cover it with a board to keep out dogs. The light and air entering

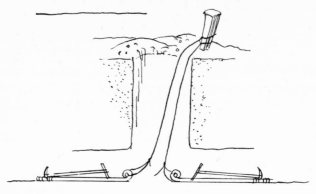

Traps placed in gopher burrow must be anchored securely at the surface to keep the little pests from carrying them off if not instantly killed.

the burrow should attract the gopher—we hope to his doom.

Baits used in poison control of gophers are sweet potatoes, white potatoes, carrots, turnips, and beets. If one bait does not work, try another. Cut the vegetables into pieces about ½ inch across and 1 inch long, and dust each piece with powdered strychnine alkaloid or thallium sulfate. Then open the burrow as when using traps, and place a few baits well back in the hole on both sides of the trench. Refill the trench.

Improving Soil

Good soil makes for easy gardening. Why? Because plants grow better with less attention. You don't have to fertilize as often, apply lime as often, perhaps not even water as often. Is there any better argument for taking extra pains to make your soil fertile, friable, and moisture-retentive before you plant your lawn and garden?

Remove foreign matter. Many properties today appear to have good soil; but if you were to dig down a few inches, you would find that some of the topsoil has mysteriously disappeared and that the rest is mixed with nails, bricks, cement, scraps of wood, insulation, and the like.

If you want plants to grow well, all such material must be dug up and taken to the dump.

If the soil contains too many baseball-size and larger stones—as if a load of coarse gravel had been mixed into it—these, too, should be removed. Small stones, however, do no harm and in fact may do a great deal of good by making the soil more porous.

Large rocks that lurk within 10 inches of the soil surface should be dug up if they lie in what is to be a lawn area, because in periods of drought the soil above them will dry out rapidly, causing the grass to die. I admit, however, that excavating boulders is easier said than done. If you have a bulldozer, fine. Or you can try breaking rocks into smaller pieces with a sledgehammer. Failing to do this, you might as well resign yourself to the idea that extra-heavy watering in the vicinity of the rocks will be necessary.

What to do about filled land. More and more homes today are being built on land that has been filled with boulders, tree stumps, and a thin covering of what passes for topsoil. In this situation, a good, relatively work-free garden is an impossibility unless you do three things: (1) Increase the topsoil to at least 12 inches in depth in those areas where you plan a lawn, flower beds, and shrubbery borders. (2) Dig out the rocks wherever trees and large shrubs are to be planted. The planting holes for trees should be at least 4 feet wide and 3 feet deep and filled with the best soil you can find. Planting holes for shrubs can be slightly smaller. (3) Pave as much of the lot as you can.

Land underlaid with ledge rock. This situation occurs in some parts of the country; to handle it, follow the directions for filled land. In this case, however, the planting holes for trees and shrubs may have to be dug with jackhammers and dynamite.

Good soil. Soil varies widely throughout the United States, and the "good soils" found in one region are often quite different from those found in another region. Yet despite these differences, all good soils are made up of a mixture of loam, humus, and gritty matter (usually sand). They are sufficiently porous to allow water and air to penetrate; and at the same time they have the ability to hold moisture. They are reasonably rich in the elements necessary for plant growth—nitrogen, phosphorus, and potassium plus iron, zinc, copper, manganese, and the other minor nutrients. And good soils are neither too acid nor too alkaline.

Increasing soil porosity. This is what experienced gardeners mean when they talk about "lightening" soil. You need to do this when soil is so dense that water and roots have difficulty in penetrating it.

To improve matters, as a rule, all you have to do is mix in coarse builder's sand (not ocean sand). If the soil is very dense, it is also a good idea to add crushed rock that will pass through a ⅜-inch screen (the equivalent of the "bluestone" that is often used to surface driveways). The amount of sand and/or rock required depends, of course, on the original consistency of the soil. As a starter, try a 2-inch layer of sand/rock to each 12-inch depth of soil, and add or subtract as necessary.

Humus also helps to lighten heavy soil and is beneficial for it. But use it in combination with sand, not alone.

Improving soil drainage. Lightening soil makes it drain better, of course. But the improvement extends only to the depth to which you have added sand and rock. If in order to keep plant roots from drowning it is necessary to provide drainage to greater depth, you should either install perforated drainpipes at the desired depth (see page 13) or you should pour 3 to 6 inches of coarse rock or gravel into each planting hole.

Making soil more moisture-retentive. Some soils are so sandy that water and soluble plant nutrients trickle down through them and out of the reach of plant roots at express-train speed. In Michigan, where this is a fairly common problem, agricultural engineers at Michigan State University developed an ingenious, low-cost method for spreading a layer of asphalt 2 feet below the surface of the soil. This acts like a layer of rock in preventing water from sinking deeper. As a result, plants have a chance to soak up the moisture; and during dry spells, farmers need not irrigate their crops as often as they used to.

This solution, however, is an unusual answer to an extreme situation. Most soils with poor moisture-retaining qualities can be improved simply by the addition of humus.

Humus is decayed vegetable and animal matter that not only soaks up and holds moisture but also lightens soil and provides nourishment for beneficial soil organisms. It is the most valuable of all soil constituents, and there are few soils in the United States that are not greatly improved by it.

The most common sources of humus are: (1) compost —a mixture of garbage, leaves, grass clippings, manure, and the like, all of which are tossed into a pile and allowed to decompose; (2) leafmold—decomposed leaves and hay; (3) well-rotted manure; (4) mushroom soil; (5) decomposed sawdust; (6) peat; (7) cover crops that have been plowed under the soil.

Compost and leafmold are the cheapest sources of humus because they are derived from waste materials that are found everywhere. The latter is very easy to make, because you need only rake leaves into a pile and leave them there. Compost, on the other hand, takes a lot of doing.

Manure is too difficult to find and too costly to be considered ideal humus today (even though it is much richer in plant nutrients than other sources of humus).

Dehydrated manure is an excellent substitute, but even it is rather scarce and costly.

Mushroom soil falls into the same category as manure, except that it is even scarcer.

Sawdust is plentiful enough is some parts of the country, but sawmills and furniture factories generally do not let it stand around until it decomposes. This means that you must buy it fresh and let it decompose in your own backyard.

Peat is the best modern humus simply because it is available in any desired quantity and at fairly reasonably cost. It has less nutritional value than compost and leaf-mold; but it contains fewer weed seeds and requires no effort to make. Since this is a book about easy gardening, that last fact alone is enough to make peat your number one choice not only when you are starting a new garden but also when you are rebuilding or replenishing an old one.

Peats of various kinds are on the market. Some are dark and fine-grained—like very soft soil. Others are light-colored and somewhat fibrous. I have a feeling that the latter types—the so-called sphagnum peats—are the best, especially for lightening soil; but this may be prejudice.

The amount of peat (and other humuses) needed to improve the moisture-retentiveness of soil is a guesswork matter. In its excellent booklet on lawn-building, the United States Department of Agriculture suggests that for the *average* soil, you should use 2 to 4 cubic yards of humus (the department does not specify peat) per 1,000 square feet of soil dug to a depth of about 6 inches. This figures out to between 54 and 108 cubic feet of humus for each 500 cubic feet of soil. Or putting it another way, for each 6-inch depth of average soil, you should mix in between ⅝ to 1¼ inches of humus. In *sandy* soil you would need much more.

Plowing under cover crops is another way of adding humus to soil. It is cheaper than using peat and is therefore recommended when soil requires the addition of a great deal of humus. On the other hand, the job usually takes months to complete and entails plenty of work.

Cover-cropping (as the process is called) is a simple operation: First broadcast the seeds of your selected crop on the ground to be enriched. (The ground does not have to be previously plowed; the seed will take hold even though there is existing vegetation.) Then, several months later, plow under the crop so that it will decompose. Then you may go over the ground with a disk harrow or rotary tiller preparatory to planting a lawn or garden; or you may sow a second cover crop, and even a third and fourth.

Any green annual or perennial plant can be used as a cover crop. Ryegrass, which is sown in the spring, and winter rye, which is sown in the fall, are among the best because they grow fast and tall and add considerable humus to the soil. If your soil is deficient in nitrogen, however, soybeans and hairy vetch are better because they add nitrogen to the soil as well as humus. Soybeans are planted in the spring and plowed under in the early fall; vetch is planted in the early fall and plowed under in early spring.

When plowing under any cover crop, it is good practice to apply a commercial fertilizer. This hastens decomposition of the cover-crop residue while adding to the soil's nutrient supply.

Soil tests. Although almost anyone can form a pretty accurate opinion of the moisture-holding qualities of a soil simply by looking at it and feeling it, a chemical test must be made to determine the soil's nutritional value and whether it is acid, alkaline, or neutral.

Your state Agricultural Experiment Station or Agricultural Extension Service are the organizations best equipped to make this test. In most states the service is free. Special containers for sending in soil samples are available from many of the stations or services.

The best time to make a test is in the spring, after the soil has had several months' "rest."

The test is made from a mixture of soil samples gathered from 10 to 20 different parts of your property. All samples must be collected in exactly the same way: With a shovel that has been washed and dried, dig a small, cylindrical hole 6 inches deep. Then take a thin slice of soil from the side of the hole with the shovel, and place it in a clean pail. The soil slices from all holes should be of the same thickness. Allow them to dry for a while if very wet. Mix them together thoroughly in the pail. Remove large stones and vegetation. Then trowel about a pint of the mixture into the test container or a clean coffee can or plastic ice cream carton, and send it to the Experiment Station or the Extension Service with your name, address, and the following information: (1) a concise description of the plants you intend to grow—for example, conifers, grass, annual flowers, flowering deciduous shrubs; (2) plants now growing on the property; (3) soil treatment with lime, fertilizer, and so on, in previous years—if you know it; (4) whether the land is hilly, rolling, or level; (5) whether drainage is natural or by drains or ditches; (6) underlying formation—whether it is rock, hardpan, sand, or gravel; (7) special soil features—whether very stony, very shallow, and so on; and (8) approximate size of the area represented by the sample.

The report that you receive from the station will contain recommendations for improving the soil.

Fertilizing. What your soil needs in the way of fertilizer is one of the things you will learn from a soil test. But aside from making simple note of this fact, there is nothing more for me to say at this point about fertilizing. The reason is that whatever fertilizer you apply at the time you start your garden will have little long-range effect on the garden or your gardening work. Even the slowest-acting fertilizers, such as bonemeal and urea, give up their nutrients within a year at the most and should be replaced soon afterward with a new supply of fertilizer.

In other words, fertilizing is one of those gardening chores you cannot avoid as long as you have a garden. There are, however, several ways the chore can be simplified. These are covered in Chapter XIX.

Changing pH. The second thing a soil test tells you is whether your soil is neutral, acid, or alkaline. This is expressed in pH. Soil with pH of 6.5 to 7.5 is neutral. Above 7.5 it is alkaline. Below 6.5 it is acid.

Although some plants (notably rhododendrons, azaleas, and camellias) require an acid soil, and a handful do well in alkaline soil, the great majority prefer neutral soil.

Once you know what the pH of your soil is, you can come to a decision about what you are going to plant. And if saving work is uppermost in your mind, the smart decision is to put in the kinds of plants that do best in soil of that approximate pH.

For example, if your soil is acid, put in the plants that prefer acid soil. If your soil is alkaline, put in alkalitolerant plants. If your soil is neutral, put in plants that prefer neutral soil. (Lists of plants that do best in acid and alkaline soils are given in Chapter VI.) By so doing, you eliminate the need for changing the pH of the soil when you start your garden and every few years thereafter.

Admittedly, there is one drawback to working in this way: If you have anything other than neutral soil, your selection of plants is limited. And of course if you have neutral soil, you cannot expect to be too successful with some of the acid-soil and alkaline-soil plants that you like. As a consequence, you may well say to yourself: "To heck with saving work here. I'm going to change the pH of my soil so I can grow what I want."

This is not difficult to do.

To lower the pH of soil over a large area by 1 point, you should apply sulfur at the rate of 1 pound per 100 square feet. Mix the sulfur in the soil or sprinkle it on the surface, and water in well. If you need to lower pH more than 1 point, make a second application of sulfur two to four weeks after the first. Another way to lower soil pH around individual plants is to mulch them with oak leaves or pine needles.

To raise the pH of soil, you should mix in or sprinkle the surface with ground limestone. (Hydrated lime works just as well but is effective over a briefer period.) The table shows how much is needed.

POUNDS OF GROUND LIMESTONE NEEDED TO RAISE THE pH
OF 100 SQUARE FEET OF SOIL TO 6

Original pH	In Light, Sandy Soil	In Average Soil	In Clay Loam
4.0	9.0	17.2	21.7
4.5	8.2	15.7	20.2
5.0	6.7	12.7	15.0
5.5	5.2	9.7	12.0

NOTE: Do not apply more than 5 pounds of limestone to 100 square feet of soil at one time. If more is needed, make several 5-pound applications at six-week intervals.

After three or four years, soil that has been limed or treated with sulfur usually reverts to its original pH and must be treated again. The only way to be positive about the need for treatment, however, is to make another soil test.

Preparing soil for planting. Most of the work involved in improving soil has been covered in the preceding pages. But what are the actual steps in the process? The following descriptions assume either that you are not plagued by problems of foreign matter in the soil, rock underlayment, and poor drainage, or that you have already solved them.

Planting trees, shrubs, or vines. Step 1. Determine the size of the planting hole. In all cases, it should be 8 to 12 inches deeper than the rootball. In width, make a 24-inch hole for a plant with a rootball under 12 inches in diameter; make a 42-inch hole for a plant with a rootball up to 24 inches in diameter; and for a plant with a still larger rootball, make the hole at least 24 inches wider than the ball.

Step 2. Dig up the topsoil and sod (if any) and pile to one side.

Step 3. Remove the subsoil and place it in another pile. (If the subsoil is not of fairly uniform consistency, place the better subsoil in one pile, the poorer subsoil in a second.)

Step 4. When the hole is dug, toss the topsoil and sods into the bottom, and mix in peat and sand as necessary.

Step 5. After the plant is set in the hole, mix even more peat and sand into the pile of subsoil. Then fill in the hole the rest of the way.

Step 6. Apply lime or sulfur and water it in.

Planting flowers, vegetables, or berries. Step 1. If peat, sand, lime, or sulfur are needed, spread them evenly over the surface of the soil.

Step 2. Turn the soil over to a depth of at least 8 inches with a power-driven rotary tiller. This will chop the sod into small pieces and mix it, along with the peat, and the like, into the soil.

Step 3. Plant the garden.

Alternate Step 1. If you dig the garden by hand with a fork or spade, turn over the soil to a depth of 10 to 12 inches. (The main advantage of hand-digging over rotary-tilling is that you can turn the soil to a greater depth, which is advisable, though not absolutely necessary, when preparing virgin soil for a garden. Deep tilling is not necessary, however, in established gardens.) Place the sods upside down at the bottom of the spaded soil.

Alternate Step 2. Mix peat, sand, lime, or sulfur as necessary into the soil above the sods. Then plant the garden.

Starting a lawn. Step 1. If grading is necessary, remove the topsoil and set it to one side. Then bring the subsoil to the desired grade.

Step 2. Spread peat, sand, lime, or sulfur, as necessary, on the subsoil and mix it in well with a rotary tiller.

Step 3. Spread the topsoil in a uniform layer over the subsoil.

Step 4. Spread peat, sand, lime, or sulfur as necessary on the topsoil and work it in thoroughly and evenly with a rake or rotary tiller.

Step 5. Sow grass seed.

Landscaping Your Lot

The main reason for landscaping a residential property today is to make it functionally useful to the owners. The secondary reason is to make it attractive.

Making a lot attractive, of course, involves the selection and placement of plants; and both of these things have a direct bearing on garden maintenance. But this chapter does not seem to be the place to discuss such matters. You will find plenty on the subject in later chapters.

The functional development of a lot, however, is one of the first things a family must consider when it builds or buys a new home. It has a bearing on where the house is placed, how it is designed, and even on how it is painted. And more to the point of this book—it has a decided bearing on the future maintenance of the garden.

What is a garden? By my definition (which I admit is rather peculiarly my own), a garden is "all of the developed parts of a residential property." It includes the flower beds, shrubbery borders, tree plantings, lawn areas, vegetable garden, orchard, terraces, driveway, walks and paths, pools, and so on. In other words, a garden is a variety of developed outdoor spaces within the boundaries of a single residential property (which for the sake of simplicity I shall call a lot).

Each of these spaces, of course, has one or more purposes. A flower bed, for instance, is to brighten the scene outdoors and in. A swimming pool is for fun and exercise. A lawn is to admit the sun, provide a setting for the house, open up a view from the house, and so on. A driveway is for cars and perhaps for basketball. And so on.

Some of these different spaces have rather closely related purposes and may therefore be grouped rather closely together. Other spaces have totally different purposes and are therefore likely to be separated by space or some kind of barrier.

It is the way in which garden spaces are fitted together inside a lot that determines whether a landscaping plan is successful functionally and whether the garden makes or minimizes work for the gardener.

Locating garden spaces. Planning so that one space does not adversely affect another is the ideal to strive for. But I'll be the first to admit that the ideal is rarely achieved. There are many other important factors to be considered in landscaping a garden, and some of these are bound to take precedence.

Remember, however, that if you are set on cutting down on your garden work, some spaces must be separated from others. For example, the children's play space should be well separated from the flower-filled terrace and lawn area where the grown-ups relax. Why? Because tricycles make ruts in soft turf. Balls mow down flowers. Sand from sandboxes messes up terraces. And so forth.

Here are a few other examples of spaces that should be separated:

Pools from orchards or shade areas—because it is a lot of work to fish leaves and dead flowers out of the water.

Vegetable gardens from main lawn areas—because for the sake of appearances you have to keep the gardens neater than they really need to be.

Flower beds from a windswept open space that lets in a view—because the wind either batters the flowers to bits or necessitates staking of the flowers.

Providing good circulation among spaces. Almost everyone who drives an automobile has at one time run into a detour sign that forced him to take a roundabout way to wherever he wanted to go. It is an exasperating experience. But when you stop to think of it, it is not half so exasperating as being forced constantly to take a circuitous route from one part of the garden to another.

That is one reason for making sure that the circulation in your garden is good. The other reason is that good circulation—easy, direct movement from space to space—conserves your energy. You don't have to walk so far, push a lawn mower so far, carry trash and tools so far, and so forth.

Providing good circulation is partly a matter of arranging garden spaces so that progression from one to another is natural or logical. It is also a matter of linking the spaces together with paths, walks, gates, ramps, steps, and the like. Neither of these things is particularly difficult to do if you take the time to study your property, your needs, your habits, and other such factors before developing your landscape plan.

III  For Easier Lawn Care

I have often wished there were a way to measure exactly how much work different gardening tasks and different parts of the garden entail. Such a study would not only be enlightening but would also—I suspect—put to rest the idea that lawns are the gardener's main source of trouble.

Twenty years ago they were. They had to be mowed by muscle power alone. They were large. And grass seed mixtures, fertilizers, and weed killers were limited in variety.

Today there is only one thing that makes lawn upkeep more troublesome than in 1950. That is the nationwide tendency to think of lawns as some kind of status symbol. This drives people to worry and work over them to an excessive degree. But I do not think that this new problem overbalances or even comes close to counterbalancing the advent of the power mower, improved varieties of grass, more potent fertilizers and more effective weed killers, fungicides, and insecticides. And you should add to our list of advantages today the fact that lawns are probably somewhat smaller than they used to be; there are new ideas for reducing trimming; and there are many other proven ideas for designing grass areas so that, in one way or another, mowing is simplified.

No, I do not think that lawn maintenance is the terrible burden it is generally considered to be. And I find that most landscape architects and expert gardeners agree. The reason they do is that there are so many things you can do —short of paving the lawn—to help yourself. Most of these come under the heading of advance planning.

Slopes that are difficult to mow. Eliminate them or cover them with something other than grass. The problems of slopes, banks, and walls are also discussed in Chapter XI, but deserve attention here.

It is obvious that some slopes are difficult to mow and some are not. But where the dividing line is I cannot say for sure because what I think is an easy slope you may call a hard one. Furthermore, our individual feelings toward any given slope are bound to vary according to how well we feel, how tired we are, how hot we are, and so on. Despite these variables, however, it is possible to make some general statements about slopes that have reasonable validity.

Consider the diagonal lines below. They represent slopes of different degree. The line marked number one is a 45-degree slope. It rises 1 foot vertically for every 1 foot horizontally. This is expressed 1:1.

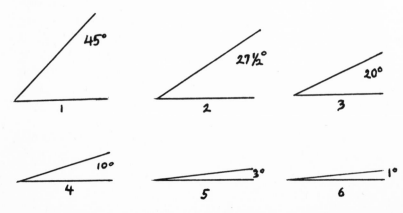

Line number two is a 27½-degree slope. It rises 1 foot in every 2 feet, or 1:2. Line number three is a 20-degree slope. It rises 1 foot in every 3 feet, or 1:3. Line number four is a 10-degree slope. It rises 1 foot in every 6 feet, or 1:6. Line number five is a 3-degree slope. It rises 1 foot in every 20 feet, or 1:20. Line number six is a 1-degree slope. It rises 1 foot in every 60 feet, or 1:60.

Looking at these lines, you can see instantly that a lawn sloping 1 foot in every 60 is no problem to mow. Neither is a lawn sloping 1 foot in 20, because even though you might eventually get tired mowing uphill and downhill, you could very easily mow across the hill. (In other words, there is no strain in emulating a sidehill gouger on such a slight slope.)

You could probably also mow a lawn on a 1:6 slope without too much trouble if it were small enough to be cut in, say, 15 minutes. (If your mower cut a precise 18-inch swath and you walked 1 mile per hour, which is extremely slow, you could cut 1,980 square feet of lawn in a quarter of an hour. That is the equivalent of a lawn measuring 40 by 50 feet.)

A 1:3 slope, however, is another matter. You could mow it, yes, but only if it were a very small patch or a long, low bank that you could mow by standing at the top and letting the mower coast downhill.

It is conceivable that you could also mow a bank with a 1:2 slope if it were not too long and had a rise of only 18 to 24 inches. But this is about as steep a slope as anyone can cope with. Certainly a 1:1 slope would be unbearable—and probably impossible.

Now even though this is a largely hypothetical discussion, it does lead to some useful conclusions:

1. You gain nothing by terracing a lawn area that slopes less than 1 foot in 20 or maybe even 1 foot in 15.

2. When land has a slope of no less than 1 foot in 20 and no more than 1 foot in 6, the lawn areas should be defin-

itely restricted in size. Figure how much you can mow in 15 to 30 minutes, and make the lawn no larger than this.

3. Land sloping more than 1 foot in 6 should definitely be terraced.

4. If a bank is to be grass-covered, it should have a slope of no more than 1 foot in 3. Ideally, it should be low enough so that you could mow it entirely from the top.

5. Banks sloping more than 1 foot in 3 should not be mowed at all but should be covered with a ground cover or replaced with walls.

(To determine how much your land slopes, fasten a carpenter's spirit level at right angles to the end of a pole 5 feet long. Stand at the bottom of the hill, set the other end of the pole on the ground in front of you, and adjust it back and forth until the bubble is centered in the spirit level. Then sight along the top of the level and mark the point on the slope that is level with your eye. Measure from this point to where you set your spirit level. If the distance is, say, 50 feet, it means that your land at this point slopes 5 feet in 50 or 1:10.)

Land sloping in several directions. This situation can make terracing difficult; so confine the lawn as much as possible to the most nearly flat area. This is not offered as a hard-and-fast rule but simply as an idea worth thinking about. I say this because there are aesthetic matters to be considered in developing a lawn, and these may well be more important in some situations than work-saving matters. On the other hand, if you can fit a lawn into a level area and still have it attractive and flattering to your entire property, then you should try to do so.

Consider the drawing on page 35. It represents the square area in front of a house. A fairly high ridge of land extends from corner A part way across the square toward corner C. If you were to put the entire square in grass—as many people would—mowing would be difficult and

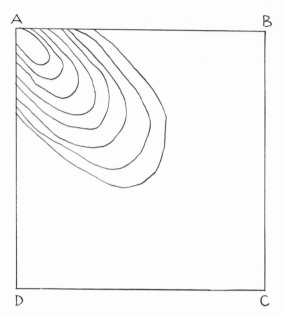

If ridge is planted to ground cover, shrubs, or trees, and only the flat area around it is planted to grass, lawn mowing is much easier.

perhaps even arduous. If you mowed around and around the square, you would have to mow uphill either from **D** to **A** or **B** to **A**. If you mowed in straight lines back and forth, you would have to go uphill at some point. And if you mowed the square in two sections—first the flat area looping around the ridge and then the ridge itself—you would still have to mow uphill.

Obviously, you would save a lot of difficult mowing if you made the lawn in a U-shape around the ridge, and planted the ridge to a ground cover or shrubs and trees.

There are many properties—especially large properties —with similar problems that can be solved in more or less similar fashion. The key to success is in remembering that lawns do not have to follow property lines. Sometimes they look just as well—and save a lot of work—if they follow the contours of the land instead.

Shaping land for continuous, easy mowing. Elimination of unnecessary uphill or crosshill mowing would be your first consideration in designing a lawn. Your next thought should be to shape the lawn to eliminate other tedious mowing operations. These include the following:

Mowing in anything except a straight line. A straight line is easier to follow than a wavy or curved line. And you do not have to exert any effort to steer the mower.

Stop-and-go mowing. This is the worst kind of mowing, because every time you stop, you must exert extra effort to get the mower moving again.

Turning the mower. Making a 180-degree turn takes the most time and effort; but any turn is bad not only because it forces you to come to a more or less complete stop but also because it requires you to swing the mower itself around.

Mowing over ground that is already cut in order to get at an unmowed area.

Mowing several small areas instead of one large one. Small areas are tedious because they necessitate too much stop-and-go mowing.

How far you can go to avoid these problems by careful design of your lawn depends on various things, such as the size of your property, whether the land slopes and in what way, the location of rocks and trees, the aesthetic effect you hope to achieve, and so on. But the following are goals worth striving for if labor-saving is of real importance:

1. Make your lawn square or rectangular, and round the corners. This gives you the advantage of straight-line mowing; and up to a certain point, you can go around and around the lawn in a continuous, non-stop movement. There comes a time, however, when the radius of the rounded corners becomes so short that you must stop and jerk the mower around them.

2. If a lawn is long and narrow, make the ends semi-

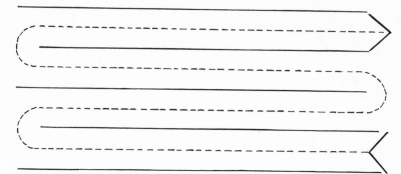

If you start and finish mowing a narrow strip of grass at the same end, as here, the strip should be made two, four, six, eight, and so on cutting swaths wide. But if you start mowing at one end and finish at the other, the strip should be three, five, seven, nine, and so on cutting swaths wide.

circular so that you can swing around them without stopping.

3. If for some reason your lawn must be of irregular shape, make the edges as straight as possible. Avoid sharp curves, scallops, acute angles, and so on.

4. Make your lawn at least as wide in the middle as at the ends. Then you can mow around and around, gradually working in toward the center; and you will never have to mow over an area that has already been cut. (By contrast, if a lawn is shaped like an hourglass, you must either mow it in two or maybe three small sections or you must keep going over the narrow section at the waist.)

Sizing grass areas to eliminate "leftovers." One of my landscape architect friends in the Southwest told me once that he takes pains not only to design lawn areas in easy-to-mow shapes but also to size them to a "mower-width module" so that each swath is the full width of the mower blade (less a slight overlap) and there is no narrow strip left over at the end. At first this struck me as an excellent notion because I have often had a silly little 2- or 3-inch strip of uncut grass left down the center of a lawn after an hour of mowing. On further thought, however, I am inclined to think that the idea has only limited applicability because most men will not take the trouble to overlap swaths so precisely that they always end up as planned—without a leftover strip.

But don't take this as a blanket condemnation. Actually, if a lawn is small, flat, smooth, and well turfed, it makes good sense to size it to your mower, because there is little difficulty in mowing such a lawn with precision.

The idea also makes very good sense in grass-covered walkways and narrow alleys. These should always be two, three, four, or more times as wide as your mower blade.

(Whether a walkway or other carefully sized area should be the width of the mower times an *even* number, or the width of the mower times an *odd* number, depends on where it is situated. For example, if there is no area at the far end of a walkway that needs to be mowed, then the walkway should be an even-number width so that you can finish your mowing at the place where you started. On the other hand, if the walkway is one in a chain of lawn areas, then it should be an odd-number width so that you will finish mowing at the end opposite your starting point.)

Heavily traveled areas. Avoid planting grass in them. You have undoubtedly heard this advice many times before. Yet how many lawns have you seen that are crossed by clearly defined paths that are not supposed to be paths?

If you were to make an observation tour of my property, you would be bound to notice a narrow, well-beaten, slightly erratic path that runs from the front door across the front lawn and around the corner of the house to the garage. And you would also notice a similar path that runs from my back door across a short stretch of back lawn, between several viburnums, to the terrace. Who made these paths? My pair of golden retrievers. And why did they make the paths? Because dogs believe that a straight line is the shortest distance between two points. They are also creatures of habit. Consequently, if there does not happen to be a paved path or walk where they like to go, they make their own path.

People do the same thing.

The result, in both cases, is the same: Wherever a path cuts across a lawn, the soil becomes packed so hard that the grass (which is also worn down by abrasion) cannot grow. And there you have another maintenance problem. A never-ending one—for no matter how often you aerate, fertilize, and reseed along the path, the path will keep reappearing under the insistent tread of dog and human feet.

But the situation really is not quite so hopeless as all that. There are some things you can do to prevent path building by both dogs and people.

First, figure out where traffic will flow. In many cases, this is obvious. For instance, you know for a fact that there will be heavy traffic from your front door to the garage; from the terrace door to the swimming pool; from the back door to the garbage cans; and from the back yard around one end of the house to the front yard. But many other traffic patterns are less obvious but no less predictible. For example, (1) If the lady of the house is a very neighborly person, she will beat a path from her back door to a low point in the side hedge so that she can talk with her friend next door. (2) If you have children and live in a neighborhood full of children of the same age, they will beat a path from your back door to the most enticing gap in the back hedge. (3) If you have a dog, you can be certain that it will beat a path all the way around your house within a foot or two of the walls or foundation planting.

Second, build walks along the most heavily traveled routes. And be sure they are placed where both grown-ups and children (and you hope, dogs) will really walk.

You should also make them as direct as possible. Walks that follow a devious route across open ground, say, from the front door to the street, fail to serve their purpose. Adults will use them because they are civilized; but children and dogs, being of a more untrammeled and practical nature, will make beeline paths of their own.

Third, do something about the secondary routes through your property. Several courses of action are possible:

You can pave the routes at least in those areas which are subject to the heaviest wear. For example, grass on slopes wears out faster than that on flat land because people must dig in their feet for traction; consequently, you should perhaps consider paving any well-used paths that cross a slope.

You can divert traffic from lawn areas by planting plants or erecting other kinds of barriers across the routes of travel. For example, I stopped my dogs from trotting across the back yard and through the viburnums by putting up a low wire fence in among the viburnums. This forced the dogs to take such a circuitous route from the back door to the terrace that they changed their travel pattern entirely.

You can eliminate the attractive nuisance which was responsible for the establishment of the travel route in the first place. For example, you can close up the opening in a hedge that stimulates children and dogs to cut across your yard to go visiting next door. Or you can persuade your neighbor that she would really be happier if she kept a top on her garbage can so that your dog would stop raiding it.

Eliminating obstacles you must mow around. Whether they are trees, rocks, flower beds, sundials, sliding boards, or whatever, they are a nuisance because they interfere with straight-ahead mowing and also because you must hand trim around them.

Man-made obstacles are the easiest to cope with. If you cannot simply move them out of the lawn area (or move the lawn area away from them), you can often figure out some way to recess them in the lawn. For example, a well cap should either be set flush with the soil or buried; the pole for a clothesline should not be embedded in concrete from which it cannot be removed but should be dropped into a pipe in the ground.

If a tree or shrub in a lawn serves no useful aesthetic or shade-producing purpose, it should be transplanted or chopped down. Stumps of trees that are felled can be quickly removed with a power-driven chipping machine.

Loose boulders that protrude above the lawn surface should be dug or bulldozed out when possible. Small sections of ledge rock can be removed with a jackhammer and/or dynamite; and sometimes you can dispose of them with a sledge. But remember that unless you remove rock down to a depth of 10 inches, you might as well leave it alone. The reason: If the soil covering a rock is much shallower than this, grass growing in it will probably burn out during dry weather.

Using flush paving around permanent obstacles. Trimming is the most exasperating and tedious lawn-maintenance chore; and in most gardens there is plenty of it. Yet it is easily eliminated.

For example, if a telephone pole is set in a lawn, it is soon fringed by grass that cannot be mowed but must be trimmed by hand. But is this really necessary? Of course not. All you have to do is surround the pole with a flat collar of concrete or brick set flush with the soil surface. The collar should extend at least 4 inches out from the pole on all sides so that you can roll one wheel of the mower

Paving around clothes poles and similar obstacles in a lawn eliminates necessity for hand-trimming around them. (Jacobsen Manufacturing Company)

over it without bumping the pole; and it should be in a square rather than a circle so that you can mow around the pole quickly, without leaving any little uncut triangles of grass.

Similar mowing platforms should be built around most other immovable lawn obstacles, such as gas and oil vent pipes, street signs, your own name sign, flagpoles, the legs of sliding boards and swings, boulders and ledge rock, and so on.

Trees and shrubs, however, should be handled in another way, since a rigid collar would interfere with their growth. Surround them with gravel or some type of mulching material, and surround this, in turn, with a mowing strip (see below).

Fences also require special treatment. The posts, in all

cases, should be surrounded with mowing platforms of concrete or brick. But if the stretcher sections between posts are hung so low that you cannot push your mower underneath, you should also lay a wide strip of concrete, brick, or gravel directly under these sections. The alternative—if it does not spoil the appearance of the fence—is to raise the pickets, rails, stretchers, or panels in these sections at least 7 inches off the ground (enough to allow clearance for a rotary mower).

Installing mowing strips. A mowing strip is a wide strip of solid material, such as concrete, that is designed to support one wheel of your mower so that you can cut the edges of your lawn and other grass areas during normal mowing operations and do not have to go back to trim them with shears, an edging knife, or a special edging machine. Such strips should be installed wherever a lawn area abuts a planting border, an area covered with gravel or mulch, a wall, fence, or curb.

Mowing strips should be at least 4 inches wide so that you can run one wheel of the mower along them without worrying too much about having it roll off; and they often are two or even three times this width. They must be set flush with the soil in the lawn area.

Construction is with redwood or cypress 2by4s, bricks, narrow flagstones, concrete patio blocks, or poured concrete. If you use bricks or other small blocks, set them

Brick mowing strip allows homeowner to trim lawn edges during regular mowing operation. (Jacobsen Manufacturing Company)

close together on a 4-inch-thick cushion of sand or crushed stone, and fill the points between bricks with a mixture of eight to 10 parts sand and one part Portland cement. This will help to prevent grass from growing up in the joints.

Concrete mowing strips can be poured in place between greased wood forms. The strips should be 4 to 6 inches deep. Slightly wedge-shaped mowing strips can also be precast in 2- to 4-foot lengths, and then set end to end in the ground.

(For another way to eliminate lawn edge trimming, see Chapter IX.)

Keeping paved areas flush with the lawn. When concrete, brick, and similar hard-surfaced paving is at the same height as the soil in the lawn, it serves as a mowing strip and allows you to reduce trimming operations. It also enables you to roll your mower effortlessly from one area to another.

Recessing gravel-covered areas. The problem here is to keep the gravel (and other loose paving materials, such as chopped tree bark) from being scattered onto adjacent lawn areas. The best solution is to recess the gravel surface 2 inches below the lawn surface, and to edge it with masonry curbs that serve as mowing strips (that is, the curbs should be at least 4 inches wide and set flush with the lawn).

In snow country, you should also install, between a gravel driveway and the curbs on both sides, 2- to 3-feet-wide gravel-catching strips made of brick, cobblestones, or other solid paving. These help to keep gravel picked up by snowplows from being pushed onto the lawn in large quantities. (But a better answer to this troublesome problem is not to use gravel on northern driveways at all.)

Solid walks, rather than stepping-stone paths. Although

Ramps connecting different levels of yard make it easy to move mower and the like from one area to another. (Jacobsen Manufacturing Company)

you can greatly reduce edge-trimming by building paved walks, terraces, and so on flush with the lawn, you usually cannot eliminate it entirely. The reason for this is that many grasses grow sideways over the top of adjacent paving and lie so flat that the mower blade passes harmlessly over them. Result: The edges of the paving occasionally become frazzled looking and need to be cleaned up with a sharp knife or shears.

This does not take much time if a walk is made of solid paving, such as concrete, because all you have to do is snip along the sides of the walk. But stepping-stones are completely surrounded by grass and therefore require a lot more trimming. Furtherfore, since each stone is fairly small, it looks as if it needs trimming more often than a walk simply because it appears to shrink in size so rapidly.

Free movement of your mower. You should be able to move it easily from one part of the garden to the other. Hoisting even a small mower over curbs and up and down steps and steep banks is a chore; and it is an impossible chore if you own a riding mower or tractor-drawn mower. The moral: Build ramps to help you over such obstacles. You will find they are also useful when pushing a wheelbarrow or loaded spreader.

Removing low branches over grass. Mowing is not only

difficult but hazardous when you have to duck under branches. So you should cut off all limbs from trees and shrubs that hang lower than the top of your head.

Grass under trees. If the ground is not too heavily shaded, it is possible to grow grass by doing the following things: (1) Plant red fescue or Chewings fescue in the North; Manilagrass in the mid-South; St. Augustine-grass in the deep South. (2) Fertilize heavily in the spring to give the grass a head start on the trees and fertilize often but lightly throughout the summer. (3) To reduce competition for the grass fertilizer, fertilize the trees every spring through holes punched 18 inches into the ground all the way around each tree and under it. (4) Remove low-hanging branches that shade the soil. (5) Cut out shallow roots that compete for fertilizer. (6) Lime the soil if it is acid.

"But that's more work than I want to do," you say?

Then forget grass and cover the shaded area with gravel, a mulch, or a shade-tolerant ground cover such as pachysandra, periwinkle, English ivy, or partridgeberry (see Chapter VII).

Bumpy turf. A lawn can be as flat as a billiard table and still be exhausting to mow if it is full of bumps. You should smooth these out, for not only do they make it extra hard to move the mower, but every time you hit one, your arm and back muscles are jarred.

Eliminating bumps in a new lawn requires only that you pick up stones, pulverize the soil well and rake it smooth, roll it lightly after seeding, and water gently until the grass is up far enough to break a harder spray of water.

In an established lawn, the best way to get rid of bumps is to rake screened topsoil into the grass to a depth of no more than ½ inch. If additional leveling is needed, apply more topsoil the following year.

Heavy rolling is a poor way to smooth a bumpy lawn because it is effective only when the ground is very soft and because it compacts the soil so much (especially when the ground is soft) that the grass roots may die for lack of oxygen.

Easy-to-maintain grass. Here are a number of varieties of grass that *generally* do well with relatively little maintenance; but whether they will be right for *you* is not certain. Even within a single community there may be enough differences in climate, soil, and so on, to make decided differences in the performance of the same variety of grass. For this reason, before starting a lawn, you should always ask a local nurseryman or seed dealer which single varieties of grass or mixtures of grass generally do best with least work in your community. Then you should have a soil test made to determine whether these grasses are likely to perform well in your garden.

Unless otherwise noted, the descriptions of the grasses below are taken from publications of the United States Department of Agriculture.

Bahiagrass. This is best grown in the southern coastal states. The Florida Agricultural Extension Service reports: "In locations where low-maintenance grass is desired and quality is unimportant, one of the finer-textured bahiagrasses (specifically Pensacola and Paraguay) would be an excellent choice. The bahias develop deep root systems on sandy soils that enable them to thrive well under dry conditions. Bahias also grow quite well on poorly drained soils. They form a coarse, open turf that looks good from a distance. Their worst disadvantage is the tall, heavy seed spikes that are produced prolifically during the summer."

Pensacola Bahia has the finest texture of this type of grass and maintains the best green color in winter. Paraguay forms the densest turf. Both must be cut with a rotary mower.

Bermudagrass. Bermudagrass grows as far north as Washington, D.C., in southern New Mexico and Arizona, and through much of California. The improved varieties are fine textured and velvety yet with unusually high resistance to traffic and wear. With high maintenance, they make an outstanding lawn. With moderate maintenance, they compare favorably with a good lawn of zoysia.

The Bermudas do poorly in shade, or if drainage is bad, or if the soil is very acid or infertile. They need heavy applications of nitrogen and moderate watering in dry weather (although they are quite drought-resistant). They should be clipped with a reel mower to form dense turf.

Of the improved varieties, Everglades Number One requires least maintenance. It is a putting-green type of grass, dark green, with good resistance to foliar diseases.

Tifdwarf, one of the newest Bermudas, is outstanding for lawns of putting-green quality. It grows slowly, and if it is not mowed, it should not exceed 4 inches in height in a season. It is more winter-hardy than some first-rank Bermudas and requires less top dressing. Though insects, such as the sod webworm, feed on it, they are readily controlled with modern insecticides.

Blue Gramagrass. This grass grows in the Great Plains region in a wide range of soil types. It forms a dense turf. Its principal advantage is that it is extremely resistant to drought, although it turns brown and becomes semi-dormant if not watered.

Buffalograss. An Oklahoma native, it is used in parts of the Great Plains region where water is limited. Highly drought-resistant, it survives hot, dry summers and close mowing. The fine-leaved grass is grayish-green but turns straw-colored when growth stops in the fall. The turf is dense, but not the equal of Bermudagrass or zoysia in this respect. It does best in fairly heavy, well-drained soils; is not adapted to sandy soil.

Carpetgrass. Another southern grass, it has good points and bad. A coarse-textured grass producing a dense turf, it must be mowed frequently with a rotary mower to look good. It requires considerable moisture and should therefore not be grown in dry soils or dry regions. And it is damaged by salt spray.

On the other hand, carpetgrass does well in poor soil without too much fertilizer. It is disease- and insect-resistant, and withstands heavy wear.

Centipedegrass. This variety is considered the best low-maintenance grass in the southern United States. It requires less mowing (with either a rotary or reel mower), less watering, and less fertilizing than other southern grasses; is seldom harmed by insects or disease; forms a vigorous turf that resists invasion by weeds; and does well in light shade such as is found under tall pines. However, it cannot withstand a great deal of wear, poor drainage, lack of iron, or salt spray.

Crested wheatgrass. It is recommended only for cool, dry areas in the Great Plains and intermountain regions, where irrigation water is not available. It turns brown in summer. Resistance to heavy wear is good if the grass is not cut too close.

Kentucky bluegrass. This one is the basic lawn grass in cool areas with adequate rainfall or irrigation water. It takes time to become established (and is therefore often mixed with faster growing grasses); but once it is established it is very resistant to drought and can go through hot summers in a semidormant condition. It prefers a heavy, well-drained, neutral soil and requires liberal feeding if the soil is infertile. It does not grow in shade and is damaged by mowing to less than 1½ inches.

Merion Kentucky bluegrass is superior to common bluegrass because it is more resistant to leaf spot disease, is more vigorous, can be cut closer, and is somewhat less affected by drought and heat. But you must give it more fertilizer and greater general care. On my tour of the nation's best gardens in 1966, I saw a considerable number of Merion lawns; but in several instances, the owners were beginning to have previously unsuspected troubles with them.

Manilagrass. A form of zoysia, this is rated the best shade grass in the mid-South. It forms a dense, carpetlike turf that has good resistance to wear, diseases, insects, and weeds. It is brown from the first killing frost well into the following spring.

Red fescue. This variety is the best shade grass in cool, humid regions and is also widely used in full sun. It is slow growing and does well in indifferent soil but must have good drainage. Its resistance to a low pH content and to wear is high. But it heals slowly when damaged by insects, diseases, or close cutting.

Chewings fescue is an excellent variety of red fescue and has the same characteristics.

Pennlawn produces better turf than red fescue and can be cut somewhat shorter. It tolerates leaf spot diseases and quickly recovers from them.

Illahee also produces excellent turf and is more resistant to cold than most varieties of fescue.

Redtop. It should be used in the North only for temporary lawns or in mixtures with slower-growing grasses, such as bluegrass. It normally lasts only two seasons. In the South it is used to overseed Bermudagrass to give year-round green.

St. Augustinegrass. This grass is a versatile one that

grows well in the shade in the Deep South. The Florida Agricultural Extension Service says: "Its worst disadvantage is its suceptibility to chinch bug damage. Chinch bugs can destroy a St. Augustine lawn rapidly unless adequate controls are applied. [Yet this] is still one of the best grasses for the average home because of its ability to adapt to a wide variety of growing conditions." It also withstands salt spray.

Bitter blue is an improved variety with shorter, narrower leaves than common St. Augustine and a closer, denser growing habit. Unfortunately, it is damaged by continuous wear and should therefore be used in lawns having little traffic.

Tall fescue. This variety is a vigorous, coarse, dense grass that grows under a wide variety of conditions over a good part of the United States. Two improved varieties— Alta and Kentucky 37—are recommended especially for playfields because they are very tough and resistant to wear. The latter usually remains green the year round in the Upper South. Alta stays green in summer even under near-drought conditions.

Zoysia. It has been badly oversold, especially in the North. It should be used only south of a line from Philadelphia to San Francisco.

Although it is slow to become established, zoysia eventually makes a dense turf with high resistance to wear and close clipping. It also does rather well in shade and near the beach. But it needs liberal applications of nitrogen and plenty of moisture; and contrary to what you may have heard, it is not disease and insect-free. It turns straw-colored at the first killing frost and does not recover until warm weather in the spring.

Meyer zoysia is the best-known variety, but Emerald, which is finer textured, is given a higher rating at the U.S.

Department of Agriculture's research stations at Beltsville, Maryland, and Tifton, Georgia.

Mowing at the right height. One of the surest ways to make extra work for yourself is to cut your lawn too short, especially in hot weather. This simply gives crabgrass and other weeds an extra chance to take over. Northern grasses should be mowed to a height of 1½ to 2 inches—no less. Bermudagrass is mowed to about ⅝ inch; other southern grasses to about 1 inch.

Mow often enough to keep the grass from growing so high that when you do mow you must take a great deal off the top. Cutting back too hard is a shock to the plants and also leaves clippings that must be removed. If clippings do not exceed ¾ inch in length, they can be left on the lawn. (See discussion of grass catchers in Chapter XVII.)

Other ways to reduce lawn maintenance are discussed in Chapters XV, XVIII, and XIX.

IV  Building a Green Garden

Several years ago I asked the leading garden supplies dealer in my town whether there had been any change in the public's flower-seed buying habits. Without a moment's hesitation he answered that, whereas his customers used to buy 30 or 40 different kinds of flowers, they now bought only about half a dozen.

One of the big national seed producers to whom I later talked refused to confirm this change. But neither did he flatly deny it. What he did say was that his total volume of flower-seed sales was greater than ever before, and that the public had a small number of favorites, such as petunias, zinnias, and marigolds.

In other words (if you read between the lines), my local seed dealer was right. And it stands to reason that he should be because relatively few flowers live on exactly the same schedule, and several of them require special care; consequently there is much more work to raising 30 different kinds of flowers than six. In fact, we might even go so far as to say that there is more work involved in raising only two plants of each of 30 species than in raising, say, 20 plants of each of six species.

Perhaps the most convincing evidence of our nationwide trend to limit the kinds of flowers we plant was my surprising (at least to me) discovery that of the 36 great gardens I visited in 1966, only one contained the really wide range of flowers that home gardeners used to favor. (This is not to say, however, that a number of others did not have a wide range of plants of other types.) *But six had no flowers at all.*

Here is a distressing thought. "Gardens without flowers?" I can hear my mother and grandmother exclaim.

Yes, I admit reluctantly, it is true.

But the effect need not be drab.

Limiting the Kinds of Flowers You Plant

This thought merits some amplification even though there is nothing very mysterious about it; and to start let me establish a few fundamental facts:

First, I don't think anyone will argue seriously that the class of plants generally referred to as flowers (meaning the annuals, biennials, perennials, roses, and bulbs) is not more trouble to grow than any other plant class of equivalent popularity. It is not that flowers are necessarily more fragile or demanding, but rather that during the course of a year you simply have to do more different things to keep them going. You have to sow seeds, thin seedlings, transplant, fertilize, water, disbud, stake, label, spray, divide, discard, and so on.

Second, as every gardener knows, even though most flowers require pretty much the same kind of care, there are differences between them. For instance, some live on from year to year; others do not. Some need staking; others do not. Some are rather susceptible to disease; others are not. But the main difference in flowers is their life cycle. Few if any of them do exactly the same thing at exactly the same time. For instance, if you sow zinnia and cosmos seeds on the same day, the zinnias will be up at least four days before the cosmos. Pansies are in bloom at the time you sow marigold seeds. Larkspur is ready to be torn up and thrown away when you plant chrysanthemums. And so forth.

Third, largely because of these differences in timing, the gardener never has a chance to get grooved into a set routine when he is caring for his flowers. He can't spend all of Monday staking flowers throughout the garden, all of Tuesday disbudding, all of Wednesday spraying. Rather, he spends Monday staking, disbudding, and spraying one scattered group of flowers; then Tuesday he stakes, disbuds, and sprays another scattered group of flowers, and so on. There is no continuity or rhythm to anything he does.

Here is the main reason why it helps to limit the number of flowers you grow: When you have fewer kinds, you are faced with fewer differences in timing, and therefore you have fewer different gardening jobs to do on any given day.

Another reason for limiting the kinds of flowers you grow is that this tends to allow you to limit the overall size of your flower garden. Why? Simply because you cannot make a pretty flower garden by planting one plant of each of 30 types. You need three, five or more plants of each type (as a rule). And that calls for a lot more space than if you grow only six types of flowers each with three, five or more plants.

Choosing flowers. When maintenance-conscious gardeners talk about limiting the kinds of flowers they plant, they are concerned mainly with limiting genera. Limiting species does less to reduce garden work because there are, by and large, smaller differences between species than between genera. And limiting varieties does even less good. This means that, even if you plant only six genera of flowers, you can still have a colorful and varied garden by planting several species and varieties within each genus.

Since I like variety in a garden, my personal choice of genera for the genera-limited flower garden would be those offering the widest array of colors, flower shapes, and sizes. The fact that some of these genera (dahlias, for example) are somewhat more difficult to grow than other flowers offering less variety does not seem particularly important *to me.* Just by limiting the kinds of flowers you plant, you make gardening work so much easier that you cannot gain a great deal more by planting the so-called easy-to-grow flowers.

Gertrude Kuh, Chicago landscape architect, makes this point most dramatically. When she has a client who wants to save work in the flower garden, she recommends roses. Why roses—a flower that is generally conceded to be one of the most difficult? First, because if you select roses carefully, they will give you magnificent bloom from spring through fall. Second, because once you get roses under way in the spring, they require only the same routine care week in and week out until you put them to bed in the late fall.

Making a Green Garden

The green garden goes a step beyond the garden with limited flowers. But it is not so frightening as the term suggests.

A green garden may in fact be an all-green garden. But the term is usually used to describe a garden without annuals, biennials, perennials, roses, and maybe bulbs— the plants that we immediately think of when we talk about color in the garden. Actually, a green garden may contain considerable color, but the color is derived from non-green foliage or from flowering trees, shrubs, and vines.

If this seems idiotic or confusing, I beg your indulgence. I didn't invent the term "green garden." But I know of none better.

It goes without saying that green gardens save work. That is, given two gardens that are identical except for the fact that one has small flowers and the other does not, the latter will be easier to maintain.

But what, you may ask, does it look like? Isn't it terribly dull?

The answer is that it can be, but need not be. There are various ways to make it attractive and exciting. Here are just three.

Planting flowering trees, shrubs, and vines. Few plants are more beautiful than these. In addition, some of them bring to the garden a glorious fragrance that is often lacking in smaller flowers.

Unfortunately, many of the plants require some maintenance or cause real maintenance problems; but the choice of plants is so wide that such difficulties are readily avoidable.

Here is a selected list of more or less trouble-free, easy-to-grow flowering trees, shrubs, and vines that will make your garden an extremely colorful one. The tropical plants are recommended by Frances Ely Zahm, a Buffalo landscape architect who spends half of the year at Delray Beach, Florida.

Abelia grandiflora. This 5-foot shrub is evergreen in the South but not in the North. It has shiny leaves and white or pink flowers and grows in the sun.

Allamanda cathartica hendersonii. A tropical evergreen growing to 30 feet, this has large, yellow, trumpet-shaped flowers. It needs full sun. By pruning, you can grow it as a shrub.

Azalea. Azaleas are our most popular flowering shrubs;

but unfortunately the bright red, coral, and magenta varieties that are most often used are far from the best. If you look around, you will be amazed at what truly beautiful evergreen or deciduous varieties you can find. They grow in sun or light shade in all but the most bitter climates. If you feed them a little cottonseed meal in the spring and pick off the dead flowers, they do not require much additional attention.

Callistemon lanceolatus. Here is a small evergreen shrub or tree with willowlike leaves and pendulous red flowers resembling bottle brushes (which is why the plant is called bottle brush). It is grown in warmest climates in a sunny spot that is sheltered from the wind.

Cape honeysuckle (Tecomaria capensis). This shrub is a half-climbing, evergreen, tropical variety with brilliant orange flowers. Its main trouble is that it grows fast and needs hard pruning once or perhaps twice a year. But it is easy otherwise. It needs sun.

Chionanthus virginicus. The fringe tree is deciduous and has bright yellow leaves in the fall. In June it is covered with panicles of feathery white flowers. It grows in the sun in mild and warm climates. Maximum height is about 30 feet.

Climbing hydrangea (Hydrangea petiolaris). This deciduous vine is covered with large white flower clusters in the summer. The vine can grow to 50 feet, but it does so fairly slowly and can be kept under control with ease. It grows in sun or partial shade in all but the most severe climates.

Confederate jasmine (Trachelospermum jasminoides). Mrs. Zahm calls this tropical vine "unexcelled; easily trained." It has dark, glossy, evergreen leaves and fragrant white flowers and thrives in sun or shade.

Crabapple (Malus). Here is one of the loveliest small (usually under 30 feet) spring-flowering trees. Use varieties that are recommended for your area by local nurserymen. Those with small flowers make less mess on the ground after petal-fall. Small-fruited varieties are preferable for the same reason. Those that hold their fruits through the winter are especially desirable because they give an extra season of color, and fruit-fall comes at the time when you must clean up the garden anyway. A few varieties have reddish foliage during the growing season.

Crape myrtle (Lagerstroemia indica). This deciduous tree has beautiful white, pink, or rose flower spikes in the summer. It grows in mild and warm climates in full sun but is subject to mildew if planted in a damp area. The trunk and branch structure is very attractive.

Daphne. Fine foliage and lovely, fragrant flowers characterize the daphnes. They are either evergreen or deciduous shrubs to 5 feet. They withstand temperatures as low as 10 degrees below zero. Grow them in sun or partial shade.

Dogwood (Cornus). A superb deciduous tree covered with white or pink bloom in the spring and gorgeous red foliage and red fruits in the fall. The Florida, or flowering, dogwood grows to about 30 feet; the Pacific dogwood is considerably taller. The kousa dogwood, which has more pointed white flowers in late June, grows to about 20 feet and is best of all. All dogwoods prefer sun but will grow in light shade.

Forsythia. Few plants make such a brilliant spot of yellow in the spring landscape. The shrubs are deciduous, to about 10 feet, and grow in full sun in temperate climates. Plant the newer upright varieties. Those that droop become a nuisance because the tips of the branches take root the instant they touch the ground.

Franklinia alatamaha. A deciduous tree to 30 feet, the franklinia has exquisite, fragrant, white flowers in the late summer and fall. The autumn leaves are a brilliant crimson. The tree grows in warm and mild climates and needs sun.

Goldenrain tree (Koelreuteria). A deciduous tree to 40 feet with large, yellow flower clusters in early summer and colorful seed pots, the goldenrain tree grows in all but the coldest climates. It is very adaptable but needs sun.

Leptospermum scoparium. This evergreen shrub to 20 feet has small leaves and in the spring is so covered with small flowers that it appears to be a solid pink. It grows in California in the sun. *L. laevigatum* is a somewhat larger shrub with white flowers.

Lilac (Syringa). The common lilac is gorgeous; the newer hybrids with their large, fragrant flower clusters in many colors are even more so. Lilacs are deciduous shrubs reaching 30 feet. They grow in the sun in temperate and cold climates. Just picking the flowers with long stems attached takes care of most pruning.

Magnolia. The tall (to 90 feet) evergreen species that grow in the South rank high in the list of the world's most beautiful trees. The large leaves are shiny and dark; the flowers are huge, white, and waxy. Although the seed pods litter the ground in the late fall and winter, and the leaves follow suit in late winter and early spring, they are easy to rake up. That is all the trouble the trees cause. The deciduous star magnolia, which grows in the North as well as the South, is also an attractive, easily maintained plant.

Mock orange (Philadelphus). A deciduous shrub growing to 12 feet and covered with fragrant white flowers in the spring, it grows in the sun in all but the most extreme climates.

Potentilla. Here is a maintenance-free deciduous shrub. It grows to 4 feet and is covered a good part of the summer with flowers that are usually yellow or cream-colored. Plant in sun or partial shade. It grows well even in very cold climates.

Pyracantha. An evergreen shrub than can be trained up a wall, the firethorn has nice but not sensational white flowers in late spring. But the large clusters of orange-red berries in the fall are gorgeous. The plant grows in all except the coldest climates and reaches a maximum height of about 20 feet. Give it sun or light shade.

Shrimp plant (Beloperone guttata). This evergreen shrub, under 5 feet, is popular in warm climates because it presents few problems and bears quantities of reddish-brown, shrimplike bracts the years round. It needs sun or shade.

Stigmaphyllon lingulatum. A choice, vigorous tropical vine, this one has clusters of small golden flowers in the late winter and spring. It may reach 20 feet, grows in partial shade, and prefers moist muck soil.

Styrax japonica. This is a wide-spreading, deciduous tree, to 30 feet, with dainty, pendulous white flowers in the spring. It grows in mild and warm climates in the sun.

Tabebuia pallida. This small tropical tree is covered with pale pink blossoms in the spring and usually again in the fall. It loses its leaves once a year, but briefly. There are several other fine related species.

Thryallis glauca. This low, fine-textured, evergreen tropical shrub has panicles of yellow flowers most of the year. Although young plants are weak and ungainly, they straighten themselves out and turn into the most un-demanding, cooperative plants possible.

Yellow elder (Stenolobium stans). An easy-to-grow, tropical evergreen tree or shrub to about 20 feet, it has clusters of tubular yellow flowers in fall and spring. It needs sun.

Shrubs and Trees with Colorful Foliage

Plants with handsome autumn coloring need no introduction. But have you considered how many have beautiful, nongreen leaves at other times of the year? These make it possible to put color into an easy-to-keep green garden without even contending with the problem of raking up the spent blossoms of flowering plants. Here are 15 good ones:

Aucuba japonica. The gold dust plant grows in warm and mild climates in partial shade to a height of perhaps 10 feet. The leaves are splattered with yellow. There are red fruits in the fall.

Beech (Fagus). The copper beech and purple beech are among the handsomest deciduous trees growing in cold and mild climates; but you need a large property to accommodate them.

Conocarpus erecta. A handsome evergreen for planting on tropical coasts, this one has leaves that are covered so densely with white hairs that the foliage appears to be silver-colored. It grows to 60 feet, and needs sun.

Croton (Codiaeum). This tropical shrub, to 6 feet, has beautiful leaves that are brilliantly marked with red, yellow, green, or white. It grows in partial shade.

Eucalyptus. Here is an enormous family of trees growing in California in sunny locations. Most are of picturesque habit, and some have off-green foliage. The latter include *E. caesia,* gray-green, growing up to 15 feet; *E. crucis,* blue-green, 20 feet; *E. leucoxylon,* gray-green, 60 feet; *E. pulverulenta,* silver-gray, 30 feet; *E. torquata,* gray, 20 feet.

Gleditsia triacanthos sunburst. This 30-foot deciduous honeylocust grows in cold and mild climates. Its fernlike branches are tipped with yellow. It grows in sun.

Japanese maple (Acer palmatum). It's hard to say whether these deciduous trees, under 20 feet, are most notable for their red coloring, for their delicate leaf shapes, or for their spreading, sometimes weeping habit. Whatever the answer, the Japanese maples are among the prettiest plants in any garden. They grow in sun or partial shade in temperate climates. In selecting a variety, remember that some stay red through the summer whereas others turn green.

Pissard plum (Prunus cerasifera). The several varieties of this deciduous tree have fine reddish-purple foliage that is most vivid when the trees are growing in full sun. The early spring flowers are pink but not of great importance. The tree grows in cold and mild climates. Its one drawback is that it needs to be pruned every year to keep the branches growing in the right direction.

Pittosporum tobira, variegated form. Pittosporum is an outstanding tropical evergreen shrub, to about 15 feet, with leathery leaves in whorls. The variegated form is gray and green.

Purple-leaved filbert (Corylus maxima atropurpurea). This is a 10-foot deciduous shrub with purplish or bronze leaves. It grows almost everywhere. Give it sun to bring out its best color.

Russian olive (Elaeagnus angustifolia). An exceedingly hardy tree that grows in extremely cold as well as much milder climates, this has narrow, gray leaves that shiver in the slightest breeze. The tree grows up to 20 feet and has a crooked trunk that adds to the overall effect. Plant in the sun.

Ti plant (Cordyline). A tropical shrub to 6 feet, the ti has red leaves that glint gorgeously in the sun.

Yeddo hawthorn (Raphiolepis umbellata). This is a sturdy, useful, tropical evergreen shrub to 10 feet. Its leaves are blackish green. There are also fragrant white flowers, but Mrs. Zahm considers these secondary to the foliage.

Conifers are not included in the above list, although various genera are popular for their colored foliage. They are not easy to use successfully. The bluish greens are the best, but they do not do well in city atmospheres and mild climates. Plants with yellowish or variegated foliage are weak and sickly and turn brown in cold weather. The purplish-hued trees also turn brown in winter.

Emphasizing Texture and Line

To create visual effects, artists use several different tools—not just color, but also line, texture, value, and chiaroscuro. In the garden even an unskilled person unconsciously tends to use most of these tools to create an effect; but his emphasis is almost always on color—especially bright color.

Well, it is possible to have an attractive garden without bright color—using only greens, browns, grays, blacks, and perhaps whites. The trick is to use some of the artist's other tools, particularly texture and line.

How do you master this trick? The best answer may be not to try. Hire a landscape architect instead.

But if you have confidence in your artistic talents, the alternative is to redesign and refine the small out-of-the-way corners of your garden until you are an expert in the use of texture and line yourself.

The first step is to become thoroughly familiar with the foliage plants that grow well in your area and that do not create unnecessary maintenance problems. Ask yourself the following questions about each plant:

What is its overall effect?

What parts do the general shape of the plant, the trunk and branch structure, the bark and the foliage play in the appearance of the plant?

What is the single standout feature of the plant?

How does the plant look in winter?

What does the foliage look like close up and from a distance?

How do the leaves react to a breeze?

How do the leaves compare in size, shape, color, texture, sheen, spacing, and position on the branch with the leaves of other plants?

This kind of examination of your area's foliage plants

will indicate which plants may be valuable in your garden for their lines and which may be most valuable for their texture. (Some may be valuable for both.) Knowing this, you are ready to start visualizing how the plants actually appear in the garden.

To help you here, look around your community to see how the same (or similar) plants appear in generally similar situations. Look in the available gardening and landscaping books, too.

If you are not sure how plants with different leaves would look together, place small cut branches side by side on a neutral gray or brown background. Or ask a local nurseryman to let you move a few plants together temporarily in the nursery.

When you are ready to make your initial planting, it will probably be advisable to consider it an experiment and to make it in a fairly unobtrusive spot. But use plants that you know you can use elsewhere if you should make a mistake.

There is no reason to think you will make a mistake, however. For one thing, green plants have an accommodating way of adapting themselves to awkward situations. Then, too, the ways to use such plants to best advantage are reasonably obvious if you pause to ponder the question. Here are several suggestions:

1. Use a few different kinds of plants and use them over and over again in different places. This gives the garden a greater sense of unity (which is important) than if you use one of this, one of that, and so on.

2. When arranging plants for their textural effect, make the gradation in leaf size gradual from plant to adjacent plant. When a plant with tiny leaves is set next to one with very large leaves, there is too much contrast.

3. Arrange plants with dense foliage in rather small, definite clumps with spaces between. The effect is deadly if they are stretched on and on in hedge fashion.

4. Do not shear plants used for texture; and when pruning, avoid cutting branches back to more or less even length. The more irregular a plant (within reason), the more interesting it is.

5. Plants with open, rather airy foliage (palms, honey-locusts, bamboos, and the like) gain enormously in beauty when displayed against the sky or a fairly smooth wall. Let them stand alone. One shrub or tree used effectively in this way can do more for the appearance of a garden than a dozen lumped together. And it saves work.

6. Silhouette plants with interesting, exposed trunk or branch structure against a wall. They are dramatic— and doubly so if the sun strikes them in such a way that strong shadow patterns are created on the wall.

7. Use trees with light-colored, straight trunks to introduce strong line to solid plantings of foliage plants. The paper birch is particularly useful but does well only in cold climates.

V  Planting a Wild Garden

I discovered the perfect way to minimize garden maintenance by accident. My wife and I fell in love with the meadow I have mentioned elsewhere and built our house in the center of it. Now my work is limited to taking care of the relatively small lawn and garden area right around the house. The only attention that the meadow beyond requires is a once-a-year mowing by a neighboring tractor-and-sickle-bar owner who charges $15 for his labor. This care keeps the field from growing up in brush, keeps the grass in good condition, and supplies me with all the mulching material I care to rake up.

Admittedly, meadows sweet with hay are not found everywhere. And I can tell by the looks on the faces of some of the people who drop by our home that meadow-dwelling is not for them. But the wild flowers and the wild strawberries and the waving grass (which stays a soft pinkish brown all winter) and the birds are a never-ending delight—the more so because they cost $15 and one day of raking a year.

A meadow is the most work-free type of wild garden. But all wild gardens rank high as labor savers except possibly jungle gardens. I know of a magnificent jungle garden on the wet side of the island of Kauai, in Hawaii, where plants grow so rapidly that the owner must keep ax and pruning shears in constant use just to keep the paths open. This growth, however, is more the fault of the climate than of the garden.

Kinds of wild garden. There are several kinds of wild garden that fall (from the maintenance standpoint) between the extremes of the meadow garden and the jungle garden. The woodland garden—which is often called "wild garden," as if it were the only wild garden—is the commonest. It is a shady garden of trees, shrubs, ferns, and shy, delicate flowers—a source of cool, calm comfort on a sunny day.

The bog garden may be either shady or sunny or both. It consists of swampy land filled with the smaller wildings that grow in the damp, acid soil found in such areas.

The water garden may be a bog garden, but it can also be a pond filled with water lilies and other aquatics.

The alpine garden is a rock garden with plants found at higher altitudes. It can be a labor saver if it is constructed and planted properly in an area conducive to the growth of mountain plants; but most people seem to prefer to make a to-do over it.

The desert garden is a western favorite that rarely works out well for reasons to be mentioned later. Cacti and succulents make up the major part of the plant list.

Size of garden. With the exception of alpine gardens, most wild gardens are rather large. I suppose this is because the word "wild" carries a connotation of size and means "untamed"—which automatically seems to denote something that is unkempt and not suited to small properties.

Actually, there is no particular reason why a small wild

area should not be incorporated into any garden. Even a plot of 10 feet by 10 feet can represent a work-saving. And it can be a hundred times more attractive than the ratty shrubbery borders that many homeowners tolerate.

Starting a wild garden. There are two rules to follow when you set out to develop a wild garden:

1. Put in the type of garden that suits your property and your climate. In other words, don't put in a bog garden unless you have a bog; don't build a northern woodland garden if you live in the South.

I know this seems too obvious to need stating; but as pointed out in Chapter VI, too many people think that plants, soil, and even climate can be readily tailored to the gardener's liking—and this simply is not so. For instance, you cannot grow white birches in the South or evergreen magnolias in the North unless you are willing to devote your life to them. Neither can you create a bog in sandy soil or a desert in clay soil.

If you really want to enjoy the work-saving benefits of a wild garden, take your cues from nature. If your property happens to include a natural wild area—a woodland or meadow or bog—tidy it up a little and then leave it alone. It is doubtful that you can improve on it very much. If you are not blessed with such a wild area, look around the neighborhood to see what kinds of natural areas have grown up, and copy these.

2. Once you decide on the kind of wild garden you will develop, take plenty of time to study how nature makes similar "gardens." Note which plants grow where and under what conditions. Note which plants grow together and which ones never grow together. Note how the plants are spaced. And so on.

I don't know how nature arrives at the scheme for the many wild gardens she builds; but I do know that there is a reason for everything she does and that she has proved the soundness of these reasons over countless generations. So it behooves you to emulate her success. To do otherwise is to make what should be an easy-to-maintain garden area into a burden.

Plants for the wild garden. Undoubtedly the thought of building a wild garden intrigues some people because they imagine themselves collecting charming little plants from here and there around the countryside. It is possible to do this—assuming, of course, that you do not run into irate property owners. Remember, however, that plants collected from the wild are often finicky and difficult to transplant. This is especially true of the woody specimens, because in nature they usually develop rather straggly root systems.

Dealers who specialize in raising and selling wild flowers and other wildings are a better source of supply because their plants have established, compact root systems. These generally withstand the shock of transplanting as readily as the cultivated species we more commonly use in gardens.

Developing a woodland garden. For out-and-out charm the woodland garden is hard to beat. No other type of wild garden captivates people to such an extent. But the work that a woodland garden demands of its owner is considerable. True, it does not compare with the work required by cultivated gardens. But neither does it compare with the very easy work required by meadow gardens.

The major drawback of a woodland garden is that branches shut off from the sun die and fall to the ground and periodically need to be picked up and disposed of if the garden is to be enjoyable. And if grape, bittersweet, and other vines ever get loose in the garden, watch out: They can make a snarl of the treetops in no time, and then you have even more trouble with falling branches. I speak from experience because my property

Delightful woodland garden outside Minneapolis is filled with undemanding ferns.

also includes a couple of acres of woods. But I don't mean to be too negative about woodland gardens: Picking up branches is a small price to pay for the delights they offer.

The woodland garden is characterized by three things: shade; soil with a high humus content (the product of falling leaves and twigs); and a fair amount of dampness.

If your idea of a woodland garden is of a beautiful grove of trees with relatively little growth at ground level, plant large forest trees. These will in time shut out the sun to such an extent that the ground beneath will be carpeted with leaves and little else. If, however, you want a woodland garden with small shrubs and flowers, you should plant smaller trees, such as dogwoods and witch hazels, which will provide dappled shade. Another reason for using these smaller specimens is that their roots do not compete so vigorously with the still smaller shrubs and flowers for soil moisture and nutrients.

Soil in a natural woodland usually contains all the humus that shade-loving plants require. But if you are creating a woodland from scratch, you should mix large quantities of peat or other humus into the soil before you do any planting. The addition of sand is also advisable if

the soil is dense. And you should also apply sulfur if you
need a high acid content.

Shade plus humus in the soil usually combine to keep
the moisture level of a woodland garden rather high (as
compared to the moisture level of a more open garden).
But it is good not to take any chances on this score, because many of the wild plants you will use have above-
average moisture needs. In other words, running a water
line into the area is advisable.

An even better way to provide water—at least from the
visual standpoint—is to make a little pond or recirculating
brook, and to set your small plants close to its edges. But
mosquitoes will almost certainly become a problem.

Plants suitable for woodland gardens vary from one
part of the country to another; and for that reason, no
attempt is made to list them here. To repeat my earlier
advice, just use whatever plants you find growing in local
woodlands. And don't overlook ferns. They are the woods'
most beautiful plants and also among the least demanding.

Developing an alpine garden. Not many people live at
altitudes where alpine plants grow naturally. But even at
lower altitudes, it is possible to raise these charming
little plants successfully if you take extraspecial pains to
start them off correctly.

Take your lead from Mrs. Pendleton Miller, of Seattle.
Mrs. Miller is a remarkable gardener who has created one
of the country's outstanding rock and woodland gardens.
This spreads over a couple of acres and is filled with an
array of plants (mainly western natives) that even arbore-
tums envy. Yet Mrs. Miller and her part-time gardener
probably spend no more than a day a week taking care
of the garden. "If I had to be a slave to it, I wouldn't
bother with it," she told me once.

Mrs. Miller has avoided slavery for one reason: She
makes a careful study of how plants grow in nature and

then tries to duplicate nature's ways. Here are several of her suggestions for making an easy-to-maintain alpine garden even at low altitudes. Most of them apply equally well to other types of wild garden.

1. Be sure to provide excellent drainage by mixing crushed rock and peat into the soil. (Probably more rock garden plants die for lack of adequate drainage than for any other reason.)

2. To keep the soil cool, bury the rocks so that only the very tops are exposed. Then the sun's heat is less likely to penetrate through the rocks into the soil beneath. Chunks of wood scattered on the soil surface and mixed into it also help to keep the soil cool. In addition, they hold in moisture and eventually provide humus.

A tiny area in Mrs. Pendleton Miller's Seattle garden, showing how she uses stones and chunks of wood to keep soil cool and moist.

3. Space plants close together so that they cover the ground completely. This not only helps to protect the plants from frost but also keeps the soil shaded and cool in hot weather. (Note, however, that close-growing plants require more water than those that are spaced farther apart.)

4. Even though many mountain plants grow naturally in a soil with a high pH, use of lime in the rock garden is generally not advisable. (By comparing similar plants growing with and without lime, Mrs. Miller has concluded that those without adjust more easily to rock-garden conditions.)

5. Do not fertilize newly planted plants, because it forces rapid growth and shortens their lives. Wait until they are well established.

6. Do not provide shade for alpines planted at low altitudes. "Such protection usually promotes overly lush growth, which weakens the plants. Plants seem to have a better chance if grown in the open, fully exposed, with protection provided by numbers of surrounding plants."

Mrs. Miller also has several highly unorthodox ideas. For one thing, she believes that moles in the rock garden improve drainage and do her cultivating for her. (The secret is to use plants that develop such a thick mat of roots that the moles are forced to burrow deeper than they usually do.) Mrs. Miller also likes to hoard fallen branches (she even lets them stay where they fall if they are not too unsightly) until they disintegrate enough to be used as a mulch and mixed into the soil.

"When setting out new plants, I believe that if you take pains to give them the exposure, soil, drainage, ground covers and so forth they need—*and then leave them alone*—they will soon learn to take care of themselves and do well," Mrs. Miller said in a speech several years ago. "You'll also find that your maintenance problems from then on will be greatly minimized."

Developing a meadow garden. There is nothing to this. Just plant the type of rough, perennial meadow grass that grows best in your area; and for added pleasure, toss in some wild-flower seeds. (In an existing meadow, flower seeds are scattered through the grass in the late fall. For even distribution, mix them with sand.)

Mowing the grass at least once during the summer helps to keep it in shape. If trees and shrubs are growing in the area, mowing also keeps brush out of the field. Whether you rake the grass is a matter of choice. I do it because I want the hay as a mulch and because a field containing fallen grass is more of a fire hazard than one without. But my neighbor with an identical field shuns raking, and I cannot see that his new grass is any worse for it.

Developing a desert garden. Very few desert gardens are artistic, work-saving successes; and the reason that they are not is that desert-garden builders generally seem unable to see or perhaps to comprehend how desert plants grow. Briefly put, desert plants tend to grow in groups of one or two kinds, and the individual plants are spaced far apart. By contrast, most homeowners jam a much wider assortment of plants into a small space, thus multiplying their own maintenance problems while creating an untidy jumble.

"If you're going to build a desert garden," F. J. Mac-Donald, a Phoenix landscape architect, told me, "either arrange the plants in some kind of studied design and don't pretend to be building a wild garden at all, or arrange the plants the way you see them out on the real desert."

In areas where cacti, succulents, and other desert plants grow naturally, little soil preparation, watering, and fertilizing are necessary to start the plants and keep them going. In marginal areas, soil preparation consists of providing a 3- to 6-inch layer of gravel 18 inches below the soil surface and covering this with 12 inches of loam, humus, and sand in equal parts. Water the plants only when they are making growth in the spring and summer, and give them a little bone meal when growth starts in the spring. Desert gardens should not be attempted in areas where desert plants are never found.

Developing a bog garden. Given a genuine bog or depression with a small but continuous supply of water, a bog garden is an excellent labor saver if only because it is impossible to grow anything except bog plants in such an area. That is the negative value of a bog garden. On the positive side, it is different, picturesque, beguiling, and undemanding.

The soil in a naturally swampy area should need little conditioning before you plant in it. But be sure to test its acidity, since most bog plants require a very low pH. Add sulfur or oak-leaf compost if necessary.

Provide firm paths into and around the bog either by building plank walks on low trestles or by excavating the soil to a depth of 6 inches or more and filling in with large rocks and gravel topped with chopped bark for appearance.

Developing a water garden. My southern cousin's way of doing this is simply to throw a water lily root into a pond in the early spring. A slightly better approach is to press the root 1 inch into the pond bottom at a point below the frost line. Add a few plants around the margins of the pond, and you have as pretty a garden as anyone could ask for. It is easy to care for, too.

VI 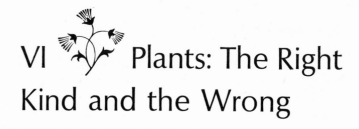 Plants: The Right Kind and the Wrong

Every once in a while, when I visit another part of the country, I am tempted to bring back to Connecticut some of the plants I see. I'd like to bring live oaks and *Magnolia grandiflora* up from Mississippi; paper birches down from Maine; Monterey pines from California. But so far I have had sense enough to resist. I could probably keep some of these plants alive—but only by slaving over them.

Plants have definite climate requirements and soil requirements; and when you ignore these, you simply make work for yourself. That is why the cardinal rule of gardening is to plant only those plants that are definitely known to thrive without constant attention in your particular corner of the world.

A second rule—by no means so important, but not to be forgotten if you are concerned with reducing garden maintenance—is to plant only those species and varieties that do *not* make work because of some inherent weakness, such as susceptibility to disease, or an undesirable trait, such as the female ginkgo tree's bad habit of littering the ground with malodorous fruits.

How do you go about determining which plants are suited to your garden and are relatively free of work-causing problems?

The lists that appear a little later should help—especially with the second part of the question. To find out which plants are suited to your garden, consult the best local gardening authorities you can find.

1. Hire a landscape architect. The home-grown gentlemen are, of course, most likely to have the answers at their fingertips; but a qualified out-of-towner will take it upon himself to seek out and produce reliable information. (For example, whenever Thomas D. Church, San Francisco's famous landscape architect, undertakes an assignment in a part of the country which he does not know well, he asks a nurseryman in that area to advise him on plant selection.)

2. Talk to your community's best nurseryman. Since he is in the business of raising plants, and since easy maintenance means even more to him than to you (it represents a good part of his profit margin), he is—or should be—acutely aware of which plants are most easily grown in your area.

3. Visit the most beautiful local cemetery and make a list of the plants it contains (the grounds superintendent will give you the names, if you do not know them yourself). The big, well-landscaped cemeteries must employ experts on planting and plant material if they hope to maintain their customer appeal.

4. Visit your local botanical garden, or ask the advice of the local garden center (not the kind of garden center that sells plants and garden supplies, but the nonprofit type that exists solely for the purpose of helping gardeners by presenting lectures and demonstrations and perhaps by maintaining a horticultural library).

5. Write your state Agricultural Extension Service for a list of plants that are known to do well in *your part* of the

state. (Note the emphasis. Even in a small state like my own, conditions vary so much from one section to another that no single list of plants is useful all over.)

Your own analysis. One trouble with relying solely on someone else's opinion about which plants are easy to grow is that no two people have had the same experience with and the same reaction to any given list of plants. I am perhaps unusually conscious of this lack of unanimity because recently I was trying to compile a list of perennials that professional plantsmen agree are easy to grow. I got nowhere: I can count on the fingers of one hand the species that received more than one vote.

In other words, in selecting plants for easy maintenance, you must also use your own judgment. And the best way to do this is to ask a series of embarrassing questions about each plant you consider.

Such a series of questions is given below for each type of widely used plant. Bear in mind that the questions are concerned only with the growing and maintaining of plants—not with the beauty, appeal, appropriateness, or produce of plants. Obviously, these four things must be given full consideration when you are deciding whether to use a plant in your garden; but if you are going to cut down on your garden work, you should not allow these factors to sway you in favor of a plant that fails miserably on the upkeep scoreboard.

Questions To Ask About All Types of Plants

Will the plant thrive in *your garden*'s climate? (Your particular climate may not be the same as your area's climate.)

If the rainfall in your area is inadequate and you know

you must depend on water from another source, does that
source supply enough water of the *right quality* to satisfy
the plant?

Is there anything in the atmosphere (salt spray, sulfur
fumes, ozone and the like) to which the plant will react
badly?

Does your garden afford enough sun or shade?

Is your altitude right? (This can be a problem with a
great many plants if you are building a cabin on top of
Pike's Peak; but it is also a problem with some plants at
lower altitudes.)

Is the plant a native of the region? (Native plants do not
necessarily grow better than those from elsewhere. And
they are not necessarily easy to grow. But the fact that a
plant is a native indicates that it is pretty well adapted to
the local climate and other conditions.)

Is the soil structure suitable? (This is not a question
of whether your soil is any good, but whether your garden
is underlaid with rock, hardpan, sand, or anything that
would interfere with plant growth.)

Is the planting soil suitable? If not, can it be easily
made suitable and can it be easily maintained in that condition?

Is the plant unusually susceptible to disease and insect
attacks?

Is the plant a favorite target of deer, rabbits, mice, or
whatever animal pests happen to run rampant in your
area?

Questions To Ask About Trees

Is the tree long-lived?

Does it litter the surrounding area to an excessive
degree with leaves? With twigs? With bark? With sap?
With flowers? With fruit, nuts, or seedpods?

Is the litter objectionable even though not excessive?

(Falling coconuts can kill a man or dent a car. Purple plums stain concrete.)

Is the litter hard to clean up? (Tiny leaves, for example, are much harder to rake up than big ones.)

Is the wood weak? Do branches split or come down frequently?

Does the tree blow over easily in hard storms (if you live in an area which has many hard storms)?

Does it need support against heavy snow and ice?

Does it require frequent pruning?

Does the tree sucker badly (as the black locust does)?

Does it self-seed badly (as Norway maples do)?

Do the roots clog sewer lines and septic fields?

Are the roots invasive (meaning, do they spread all over the place and interfere with the growth of other plants)?

Do the roots lie so close to the surface that grass is difficut to grow over them?

Is the tree canopy so large and dense that next to nothing will grow underneath?

Does the tree have vicious thorns? (In certain locations, such plants create a maintenance problem of one sort or another. They also create a major pruning problem.)

Does the tree grow to a size or in a shape that might interfere with another feature of your property and thus necessitate pruning? (For example, a tall tree planted under the power lines leading into your house from the street would have to be pruned almost every year to keep it clear of the wires.)

Questions To Ask About Shrubs

Is the shrub long-lived?

Does it litter the surrounding area excessively with leaves? With twigs? With flowers? With fruit, nuts, or seedpods?

Is the litter objectionable even though not excessive?

Is the litter hard to clean up?

Is the wood weak? Are the branches so arranged that they break readily?

Does the plant need special protection against snow and ice?

Does it need special protection against wind?

Does it sucker badly?

Does it self-seed badly?

Is it a drooping plant that roots at the stem tips?

Are the roots invasive?

Do the roots clog sewer lines and septic fields?

Does the shrub require frequent pruning?

Is it unusually difficult to grow smaller plants beneath the shrub because of its roots or dense canopy?

Does it have vicious thorns?

Do the flowers or foliage have an objectionable odor? (This kind could cause work either by forcing you to remove the flowers or to move yard furniture to another part of the garden.)

Questions To Ask About Vines

Is the vine long-lived?

Does it litter the area excessively with leaves? With twigs? With sap? With flowers? With fruit or seedpods?

Is the litter objectionable even though not excessive?

Is the litter hard to clean up?

Does the vine need special protection against the elements?

Does it self-seed badly?

Does it take root too easily along the stems?

Does it run rampant? (Kudzu, for example, can get out of hand and become a serious pest in no time.)

Are the roots invasive?

Does the vine require frequent hard pruning?

Does it grow in a way that makes it unusually difficult to prune?

Does it need to be trained by hand?

Does it make a mess of itself unless it is trained?

Does it grow up trees when you are not looking? (Getting vines out of trees is difficult. And some vines can kill the trees on which they grow, making an even worse problem.)

Does the vine work its way under shingles and into cracks in building siding? (Wisteria is a problem in this way.)

Can the clinging holdfasts that some vines have damage building siding? Or do they leave marks on the siding?

Does the vine grow so dense that it creates moisture problems in the lumber, plaster, or other material that it covers?

Can the vine be grown on a lightweight metal trellis that requires little maintenance? If not, can it be fairly readily pushed aside or taken down so that the trellis (or house siding) can be repainted and rebuilt as necessary?

Does the vine have vicious thorns?

Do the flowers have an objectionable odor?

Questions To Ask About Ground Covers

See Chapter VII. The things to think about in selecting a ground cover are well covered there.

Questions To Ask About Annuals

Is the annual difficult to raise from seed? (Of course you do not have to raise flowers from seed; buying ready-grown plants saves a great deal of time and effort. But if money is tight, this is a point to consider.)

Does it develop good flowers and a desirable shape without a lot of disbudding?
Does it need staking?
Does it self-seed badly?

Questions To Ask About Perennials

Is the perennial long-lived?
Does it require more than average fertilizer and water?
Does it require an excessive amount of disbudding?
Does it need staking?
Does it form a mat in which hard-to-eradicate weeds and grasses flourish?
Is it an invasive plant that can become a pest?
Does it self-seed badly?
How often need you divide it?
Does it require winter protection?

Questions To Ask About Bulbs

Can the bulbs stay in the ground the year round? (Summer bulbs that you must plant and lift every year are more work than hardy bulbs.)
How often do hardy bulbs have to be lifted and divided or replaced to keep them in top condition?
Does the plant require very heavy watering and feeding?
Does it need staking?
Are the bulbs difficult to store?

Lists of Plants

Here, for better or for worse, are lists of plants that make work and save work. Some lists represent the opinion of a single person; others represent a consensus. None should be taken as gospel because personal reactions and experiences are the basis of all judgments. But I hope that they help at least to stimulate some useful questioning about what you might plant to make your gardening work a little easier.

ORNAMENTAL PLANTS THAT REQUIRE ACID SOIL

Acer pennsylvanicum
Aletris farinosa
Andromeda polifolia
Arenaria greenlandica
Arethusa bulbosa
Azalea
Blueberry
Bunchberry
Caladium
California pitcher plant
Calla lily
Calla palustris
Calliandra
Calopogon pulchellus
Camellia
Chain fern
Cinquefoil, three-toothed
Clethra
Cyrilla racemiflora
Daboecia
Drosera
Empetrum
Enkianthus
Eurya emarginata
Fir
Fringed orchis
Gardenia
Gaultheria
Hare's-foot fern

Hartford fern
Heath
Heather
Holly
Ixora
Kalmia
Ladyslipper, pink and ram's head
Ledum
Leucothoe
Linnaea
Lyonia mariana
Magnolia virginiana
Mountain ash, American
Ochna multiflora
Osmanthus
Pitcher plant
Pogonia ophioglossoides
Rhexia
Rhododendron
Sand myrtle
Sarcocca
Trailing arbutus
Trillium
Venus flytrap
White cedar, southern
Yesterday-today-and-tomorrow

ORNAMENTAL PLANTS THAT ARE SOMEWHAT TOLERANT OF
ALKALINE SOILS

Alkali in soil and water is particularly troublesome in the West. Around Phoenix, for example, the pH is so high that only a very limited list of plants will survive without constant attention. The following list was prepared in the College of Agriculture of the University of Arizona.

Ailanthus altissima
Allenrolfea occidentalis
Antigonon leptopus
Arundo donax
Ash, Arizona
Asparagus plumosus
Atriplex species
Baccharis amoryi and
  glutinosa
Bignonia tweediana
Bird-of-paradise
Boussingaultia baselloides
Broom, desert and Spanish
Buddleia pringlei
Cape honeysuckle
Carob
Casuarina cunninghamiana
  and *equisetifolia*
Century plant
Clematis drummondii
Convolvulus japonicus
Cottonwood, Arizona,
  Fremont's, MacDougal's
Currant, Crendall and golden
Elderberry, Arizona
Elm, Chinese
Eucalyptus polyanthemos, ro-
  busta, rostrata, tereticornis

Euonymus japonicus
Fig, climbing, common, hotten-
  tot, seaside
Firmiana plantanifolia
Gourd, white-flowered
Grabowskia boerhaaviaefolia
Honeylocust
Honeysuckle, Japanese
Ipomoea dissecta
Ivy, Boston and English
Jasmine, Chinese, Italian,
  Spanish
Jujube
Kudzu
Lantana camara
Lilac, Chinese
Locust, black
Lycium species
Melia azedarach
Mesquite
Moonflower
Morning glory, evergreen,
  heavenly blue, purple
Myrtle, common
Natal plum
Nicotiana glauca
Oleander, common and yellow

Osage orange
Palm, California fan, Chinese windmill, date, Washington
Palmetto, Carolina and Texas
Pampas grass
Parkinsonia aculeata
Passion flower, blue
Pecan
Pepper tree, Brazilian and California
Pomegranate
Privet, Chinese and tall Japanese
Prosopis pubescens

Rosemary
Russian olive
Salpichroa rhomdoidea
Schinus dependens
Senecio longilobus, riddellii, salignus
Silk vine
Solanum wendlandii
Sweet potato vine
Tamarisk species
Virginia creeper
Willow, desert, valley, Wright's
Wisteria, Chinese
Yucca species

SALT-RESISTANT PLANTS

The trees, shrubs, vines, and ground covers listed here are those best able to withstand wind-driven salt spray and sand at the ocean's edge. Other plants can also be grown near the shore, but they must be either planted farther back or protected from the ocean blasts by screens of some sort.

Acacia armata and *verticillata*
Alder, black
Ambrosia hispida
Atriplex breweri
Aucuba japonica
Azalea indica
Baccharis halimifolia
Banksia ericifolia
Beach plum
Bearberry
Berberis thunbergii
Boussingaultia leptostachys
Broom

Buddleia madagascariensis
Callistemon rigidus
Cape honeysuckle
Carissa grandiflora
Carob
Casuarina equisetifolia
Chinaberry
Clianthus puniceus
Clusia rosea
Coco plum
Codiaeum punctatum
Colutea arborescens
Conocarpus erecta

Coprosma baueri
Corokia
Cotoneaster (several species)
Cryptostegia grandiflora
Cypress, Gowen and Monterey
Elaeagnus pungens
Ephedra distachya
Ernodea littoralis
Eucalyptus (several species)
Eugenia myrtoides
Flowering currant
Geobalanus pallidus
Germander
Goat willow
Griselinia littoralis
Heather
Hebe
Hedera canariensis
Holly oak
Kafir plum
Lantana montevidensis
Lathyrus littoralis
Lavatera
Leptospermum laevigatum
Leucadendron argenteum
Maidenhair vine
Manzanita
Metrosideros tomentosa

Muehlenbeckia complexa
Myrica
Night-blooming cereus
Norfolk Island pine
Ochrosia elliptica
Olearia
Palm, coconut, princess, Washington
Palmetto
Pine, Aleppo, Japanese black, pitch
Pittosporum tobira
Rhus laurina
Rosemary
Rosa rugosa
Russian olive
Santolina chamaecyparissus
Seagrape
Sea lavender
Shepherdia argentea
Snowberry
Spanish broom
Star jasmine
Swainsona galegifolia
Tamarisk (several species)
Virginia creeper
Yeddo hawthorn

ANNUALS THAT ARE RELATIVELY UNDEMANDING AND EASY TO GROW

"Easy-to-grow" is a term that every gardener interprets in his own way. In an attempt to arrive at a consensus about annual flowers, I asked five of the country's largest seed producers to give me their opinions. The list here is the result. Each of the flowers named received at least two votes. Those marked with an asterisk received three or more.

African daisy
Ageratum
*Alyssum
Anchusa
Balsam
Bells of Ireland
*Calendula
Candytuft
Cleome
*Cockscomb
Coreopsis
*Cosmos
*Dahlia (dwarf types)
Four o'clock
Gaillardia
*Globe amaranth
*Gloriosa daisy
*Larkspur

*Marigold (dwarf types especially)
Nasturtium
Nicotiana
Phlox
Portulaca (Author's comment: This is indeed easy to grow; but it self-seeds with such abandon that it is a dreadful nuisance the following year.)
Scabiosa
Shirley poppy
*Sweet pea (dwarf types that do not require staking)
Verbena
*Zinnia (especially varieties that are mildew-resistant)

PERENNIALS THAT ARE RELATIVELY UNDEMANDING AND EASY TO GROW

It is commonly assumed that perennial flowers are less work to grow than annuals. By and large, they are: (1) because established plants require less nursing to get them going in the spring than week-old seedlings, and (2) because the majority of perennials need to be divided and replanted only every third year whereas annuals must be planted every year. It is not, however, true that all perennials are easier than all annuals. Some perennials are very demanding; and they seem the more so if you plant a mixed assortment—each species with its own requirements and schedule (see Chapter IV).

The perennials listed below are relatively easy to grow

as individual plants. This does not, of course, mean that they necessarily produce the most or best bloom.

Achillea

Baby's breath

Bee-balm

Campanula (not biennial types)

Candytuft

Cinquefoil

Columbine

Coral bells

Coreopsis

Daylily

Flax

Gaillardia

Geum

Hosta

Inula

Lily-of-the-valley

Loosestrife

Lychnis

Oriental poppy

Pinks

Platycodon

Shasta daisy

Sedum

Stokes aster

Yucca filamentosa

PERENNIALS THAT SHOULD NOT BE DISTURBED ONCE THEY ARE ESTABLISHED

Most perennial flowers have to be divided every two, three, or four years. Those listed below, like roses, can be and often should be left alone once they are growing happily. This represents a work-saving as far as the gardener is concerned.

Anemone

Anthericum

Baby's breath

Bird-of-paradise

Daylily

Dictamnus

Hellebore

Hosta

Iberis sempervirens

Lily-of-the-valley

Monkshood

Oriental poppy

Oxalis

Peony

Platycodon

Purple coneflower

Red-hot poker

Scabiosa

Sidalcea

Yucca filamentosa

TREES THAT MAKE WORK FOR THE GARDENER

From the standpoint of beauty, many of the trees listed here are highly desirable; but they cause trouble because of one or more bad habits. Some are litterbugs; some sucker or self-seed badly; some have weak wood; some are subject to severe attacks by insects or diseases; some require almost constant pruning; and so forth.

Ailanthus

Amelanchier

Banyan

Birch (except paper birch)

Bottle tree

California pepper tree

Camphor tree

Catalpa

Chinaberry

Coconut palm

Elm

Erythrina indica

Eucalyptus globulus

Evodia

False cypress, sawara

Ginkgo (female tree only)

Hawthorn

Horse chestnut

Kentucky coffee tree

Locust, black

Madrone, Pacific

Magnolia, saucer

Maple, Norway and red

Mimosa

Mountain ash

Mulberry

Oak (in areas where oak wilt
   is prevalent)

Paulownia tomentosa

Pear

Poplar

Prunus species

Rubber tree

Shadbush

Sycamore

Tung

Walnut

Willow

TREES AND SHRUBS FOR A COLD, WINDY, AND DRY CLIMATE

These are species which have done well in tests made by the U.S. Department of Agriculture to find trees and shrubs which would provide shelter from wind, storm, and blizzard in the Central Great Plains area. The plants were rated for their ability to survive and to grow tall and plump. Those marked with an asterisk are considered superior and are recommended for use throughout this area. Others are recommended only for some parts of the area, or are considered worth a trial. I include the list not simply for the benefit of gardeners in the Central Great Plains area but because it would seem that if these plants can survive in such a severe climate, they are worthy of consideration for other areas with more or less similar climates.

*American plum	Manchu cherry
Boxelder	*Ponderosa pine
*Chokecherry, common	*Rocky Mountain cedar
*Eastern red cedar	*Russian olive
Hackberry, common	*Siberian elm
*Honeylocust	Siberian pea shrub
Honeysuckle	Skunkbush sumac
Lilac	Tamarisk

SMALL DECIDUOUS TREES RECOMMENDED FOR THE NORTHERN HALF
OF THE UNITED STATES

Small trees are not only more in scale with our small modern homes but, of greater importance, they require less care than large trees. They need less watering, less feeding, less pruning, less spraying, and, because their roots and tops are smaller, they interfere less with grass and other plants.

In recent years, because of the many advantages of small trees, municipal park and tree commissioners have started to use them almost exclusively along city streets. This, in turn, has encouraged a number of arborists to start looking for and developing new or improved varieties of small trees. Edward H. Scanlon, of Olmsted Falls, Ohio, is one of these men. Formerly the commissioner of shade trees for the city of Cleveland, he has since 1954 had his own large nursery, which supplies trees primarily to cities. He is an outstanding authority in his field. Following are northern deciduous trees that he recommends both for their appearance and because they present relatively few maintenance problems—a point of even greater importance to city tree men than to home owners. The great majority of the trees do not exceed 35 feet in height. The few that grow taller are slow growers, which Mr. Scanlon recommends because of their general excellence.

Ash, Dr. Pirone, Flowering, Globeheaded European, Golden Desert, Modesto, Rancho Roundhead, Spath's, Tailored Bunges, Weeping European

Beech, Dawyck Upright, European, Golden, Green-leaved Weeping, River's Purple, Tricolor

Birch, Columnar White, Cutleaf Weeping, Elm-leaved, European, Purpleleaf, Swedish Cutleaf, Young's Weeping

Caragana, Weeping Siberian

Catalpa, Golden-leaved and Purpleleaf

Cherry, Amanogawa, Chrysanthemum Weeping, Daikoku, Daybreak, Double-flowered French Mazzard, Florepleno, Hillier Spire, Hokusai, Juddi, Kofugen, Kwanzan, Mt. Fuji, Okame, Pandora, Pink Perfection, Rancho Sargent, Red Bark, Sargent's, Scanlon, Shirofugen, Shogetsu, Spring Glory, Tai Haku, Takasago, Taoyoma, Weeping Kwanzan, Weeping Yoshino, Wild Spring, Yedo, Yoshino

Chokecherry, Amur

Crabapple, Aldenham, Almey, Arnold, Beauty, Chinese Pearleaf, Columnar Siberian, Eley, Frau Louise Dittman, Katherine, Liset, Profusion, Redbud, Red Jade Weeping, Shakespeare, Strathmore, Sundog, Tailored Pink Bud Sargent, Van Eseltine, Wintergold

Elm, Camperdown

Flowering Peach, Peppermint Stick

Ginkgo, Lakeview, Mayfield, Palo Alto

Goldenchain tree and weeping form

Goldenrain tree

Hawthorn, Blue, Chinese Big-leaf, Columnar, Double White

English, Globe, Grignonensis, Lavalle, Paul's Scarlet, Toba, Washington

Hornbeam, European, Oakleaf European, Purple European, Pyramidal European

Horse chestnut, Bauman's, Pink, Ruby Red

Kentucky coffee tree

Lilac, Japanese tree

Linden, Crimean, Littleleaf XP 110, Mongolian, Pyramidal Cutleaf, Rancho Littleleaf, Royal, Silver, Silver Pendent

Locust, Fastigiate Black, Flowering Globe, Globe, Idaho, Mimosa-leaved, Monument

Maackia, Amur

Magnolia, Anise and Kobus

Maple, Almira Norway, Armstrong II, Charles F. Irish Norway, Cleveland II Norway, English Hedge, Faassens Black Norway, Gerling Red, Globe-head Norway, Golden-leaved Sycamore, Leopold Sycamore, Olmsted Columnar Norway, Pyramidal Sycamore, Red Coliseum, Scanlon Red, Schlesinger Red, Schwedlers Norway, Seneca Sugar, Sycamore, Tilford Red, Tricolor Sycamore, Trident, Upright Norway, Variegated Norway

Mountain ash, Columbia Queen, Korean, Paucicrenata, Pyramidal Oakleaf, Springer, Wilson Columnar

Mulberry, fruitless

Oak, sawtooth

Pear, Chanticleer, Rancho Callery, Snow

Plane, Pyramidal London

Plum, Blireana

Sophora, Pyramidal

Sweet gum, Golden

Yellow-wood

VINES THAT DEMAND UNUSUAL ATTENTION

Vines are among the most beautiful and useful plants that grow; but because of their habit of growth, size, and vigor, almost all require more than their share of maintenance. These listed are especially demanding, although several of them bring rare beauty to the garden.

Akebia, five-leaf	Honeysuckle, Hall's
Araujia sericofera	*Kudzu*
Bignonia capreolata	*Lycium*
Bittersweet	Moonseed
Dioscorea batatas	*Pandorea jasminoides*
Doxantha unguis-catii	*Passiflora*
Euonymus fortunei	Wild cucumber
Grape	*Wisteria*

ORNAMENTAL PLANTS THAT DEER DO NOT EAT

When deer attack gardens—as they do in many parts of the country—the usual way that gardeners protect themselves is to build fences. Unfortunately, these must be high, ugly, and expensive. A much more practical method of protection is to put in plants that deer generally will not eat so long as their usual feeding grounds contain an adequate supply of natural browse.

The following list was prepared by the California Agricultural Extension Service and Experiment Station. Species marked with an asterisk are particularly deer-resistant, though not completely so when the animals' natural food supply is low.

Abutilon species	*Angophora lanceolata*
Acacia species	*Arabis* species
*Adolphia californica	*Aralia spinosa
*Agapanthus africanus	*Araucaria* species
Agave species	Arborvitae species
Ageratum species	*Arbutus unedo*
Agonis flexuosa	*Arctotis tridentata*
Ajuga species	*Artemisia tridentata
Albizzia species	Artichoke
Aloe species	*Arundo donax

*Ash, Arizona
Barberry species
*Beaucarnea recurvata
Bidens ferulaefolia
Bleeding heart
Box elder
*Boxwood species
Brachychiton populneum
Breath-of-heaven
Broom, bridal-veil
*Broom, Scotch
*Broom, Spanish
*Buddleia davidii
*Cactus species
Cajeput tree
Calla lily
Calliandra tweedii
*Calycanthus occidentalis
Cape honeysuckle
Caragana species
Carob
Carpenteria californica
Cassia species
*Casuarina stricta
Catalpa, common
Cedar species
Centaurea species
Cherry-laurel, Carolina
Chinaberry tree
*Choisya ternata
Cinquefoil, shrubby
Cissus rhombifolia
Clarkia species
*Clematis species
Clianthus puniceus
Coleonema pulchrum

Columbine species
*Coprosma repens
*Cordyline australis
Coronilla glauca
*Correa species
Cotoneaster species
Cycas species
Cypress species
*Daphne species
*Datura species
*Delphinium species
Dendromecon species
Dodonaea viscosa
*Dogwood, Himalayan
Dovyalis caffra
Duchesnea indica
*Echinocystis lobata
*Echium fastucsum
*Elderberry, red
Eriocephalus africanus
Escallonia species
Eucalyptus species
Fabiana imbricata
False cypress species
Fir species
*Flax, New Zealand
Forget-me-not species
Forsythia ovata
Foxglove species
Furcraea species
Gaillardia species
Gaultheria shallon
Gerbera species
*Germander
Ginkgo biloba
Hackberry, European

Hakea suaveolens
Hawthorn species
Hellebore species
Hippophae rhamnoides
Holly species
Hollyhock
*Ivy, English
Incense cedar
Iris species
Jasmine species
Jasmine, Carolina
Juniper species
Kentucky coffee tree
Kerria japonica
*Kudzu
Lantana, trailing
Larch, European
Lavender species
Leptodactylon californicum
Lilac, common
Lithocarpus densiflora
Lobelia
*Locust, black
*Lupine species
Lyonothamnus floribundus
Magnolia species
Mahonia species
Maidenhair vine
Maple, big leaf
Marguerite
Marigold
Mayten tree
Melianthus major
Mesembryanthemum species
Metrosideros excelsa
Mimulus species

Moneywort
Monkshood species
Myoporum laetum
Myrica californica
Myrtle, common
Nandina
Narcissus species
*Nightshade species
Nolina parryi
*Oleander
Olive
Osage orange
Osteospermum fruticosum
Oxalis oregana
*Palm, date, European Fan, Mexican Blue, Washington species, Windmill
Palm, guadalupe and syrup
*Palmetto hispaniolan
Pandorea pandorana
Parkinsonia aculeata
Paulownia tomentosa
Penstemon species
Peony, tree
*Pepper tree, California
*Persimmon
Phaedranthus buccinatorius
Pine species
Pittosporum species
Poppy, California and oriental
Quillaja saponaria
Redbud
*Red-hot poker
Rhododendron species
Rhubarb

Rhus ovata
Rockrose species
Romneya coulteri
*Rosemary
Scabiosa species
Shasta daisy
*Smoke tree
Snowberry
*Snowflake
Spruce species
Strawflower species
Sunflower species

Sycamore, Western
Syzygium paniculatum
Tradescantia species
*Tree pepper
Trillium species
*Tulip species
Valerian
Vinca species
Yew species (Author's note:
    Easterners do not agree.)
Yucca species
Zauschneria species

VEGETABLE VARIETIES THAT ARE RESISTANT TO OR TOLERANT OF CERTAIN DISEASES

Diseases cause just one of the maintenance problems that vegetable gardeners must cope with. But if you can make your gardening work a bit easier by using disease-resistant varieties, then it obviously pays to consider them. Here are the vegetable varieties sold by several leading seed firms that are resistant to or tolerant of various common specific diseases.

W. ATLEE BURPEE COMPANY

Bean—Burpee's Richgreen, Executive, Improved Tendergreen, Kentucky Wonder WS, Pearlgreen, Rustproof Golden Wax, Tendercrop, Topcrop, Wade

Cabbage—Badger Market, Early Jersey Wakefield YR, Golden Acre YR, Marion Market, Wisconsin Hollander

Cucumber—Ashley, Burpee hybrid, Burpee's M & M hybrid, Ohio MR 17, Triumph hybrid

Muskmelon—Delicious 51 and Samson hybrid

Pepper—Bell Boy hybrid and Yolo Wonder

Peas—Alderman, Alaska, Burpee's Sweet Pod, Freezonian, Mammoth Melting Sugar, Progress Number 9

Spinach—Hybrid Number 7 and Virginia Blight Resistant

Tomato—Heinz 1350, Manalucie, Spring Giant hybrid, Sunray
Watermelon—Charleston Gray, Congo, Crimson Sweet, Dixie
Queen WR

FERRY-MORSE SEED COMPANY

Bean—Bush Blue Lake 274, Contender, Cornell 14, Dade, Earli-
wax, Early Harvest, GV 50, Harvester, Kentucky Wonder
Rust Resistant, Morse's Pole Number 191, Processor, Pure
Gold wax, Resistant Asgrow Valentine, Resistant Cherokee
wax, Slenderwhite, Slimgreen, Stringless Blue Lake FM-1K,
Stringless Blue Lake FM-1L, Stringless Blue Lake Prime
Pak, Tenderbest, Tendercrop, Tenderette, Tendergreen Im-
proved, Tenderwhite, Topcrop, White-Seeded Tendercrop
Beet—Detroit Dark Red Morse's Strain
Cabbage—Badger Ballhead, Badger Market, Early Jersey Wake-
field, Globe, Globe TBR, Globelle TBR, Greenback, Marion
Market, Resistant Glory, Resistant Glory TBR, Resistant
Golden Acre, Roundup, Wisconsin All Seasons, Wisconsin
Ballhead Improved
Celery—Florimart, FM-D5, Tall Utah 52-70, Tall Utah 52-70H,
Tall Utah 52-75
Corn—Carmelcross, Country Gentleman, F-M Cross, Goldcrest,
Golden Cross Bantam, Golden Cross Bantam T51, Iobelle,
Marcross, Preview, Stowell's Evergreen, Stowell's Ever-
green hybrid, Target, Treasure Gold 103
Cucumber—Ashley, Briney hybrid, Crispy hybrid, Hybrid Ash-
ley, Ohio MR 17, P 51 DMR, Palomar DMR, Piccadilly hy-
brid, Pico hybrid, Pixie, Poinsett, Polaris, SMR 58, Table
Treat, Wisconsin SMR 15, Wisconsin SMR 18
Lettuce—Calmaine, Calmar, Valverde
Muskmelon—Edisto 47, Honey Rock Fusarium Resistant, Perl-
ita, Resistant Number 45
Onion—Eclipse
Peas—Alaska wilt resistant, Giant Stride, Thomas Laxton
Pepper—Resistant Florida Giant, Yolo Wonder 43, Yolo Wonder
Improved B

Radish—Red Prince

Spinach—Califlay, Chesapeake, Dixie Market, Early Hybrid Number 7, Hybrid 424, Hybrid 425, Hybrid 612, Savoy Supreme, Viroflay 99, Wisconsin Bloomsdale

Tomato—CPC 2, Chico, Floradel, Heinz 1409, Heinz 1548, Homestead Elite, Homestead 24, Homestead FM 61, Indian River, Manalucie, Manapel, Marglobe Supreme Improved, Marion, Marzano P-4, Mechanical Harvester, Pearson A-1, Pearson A-1 Improved, Pearson S, Roma, Rutgers-FM Select, Supermarket, V. Early Pak 7, VF 14, VF 36, VF 428 F2, VF 686 F2, VF 689 F2, VF 1402, VF Roma, V. Red Top Number 9

Turnip—Crawford and Shogoin

Watermelon—Charleston Gray 133, Congo, Dixie Queen, Garrisonian, Graybelle, Klondike Striped Blue Ribbon

JOSEPH HARRIS COMPANY

Bean—Resistant Cherokee Wax and Tendercrop Green

Cabbage—Early Jersey Wakefield, Golden Acre, Harris' Danish Resistant Red, King Cole, Market Prize, Market Topper

Cucumber—Ashley, China, Crusader, Marketmore, Princess, Ohio MR 17, Saticoy, Tablegreen 65, Triple Purpose, Triumph, Wisconsin SMR 18

Eggplant—Black Magic hybrid

Lettuce—Dark Green Boston, Fulton, Great Lakes, Parris Island cos, Pennlake

Muskmelon—Delicious 51, Gold Star, Harper hybrid, Harvest Queen, Iroquois, Saticoy, Supermarket

Peas—Freezonian and Perfected Freezer 60

Pepper—Keystone Resistant Giant, Staddon's Select, Yolo Wonder B

Squash—Butternut

Tomato—Campbell 1327, Galaxy, Heinz 1350, Heinz 1439, Michigan-Ohio hybrid, New Yorker, Roma VF, September Dawn, Sunray, Superman, Tom-Tom

Watermelon—Charleston Gray, Crimson Sweet, Seedless 313

NORTHRUP, KING AND COMPANY

Bean—Blue Lake Stringless Line 7, Cherokee Wax MR, Contender, Dade, Harvester, Improved Tendergreen, Michelite, Pearlgreen, Resistant Asgrow Valentine, Sprite, Tendercrop, Topcrop, White Kentucky 191

Cabbage—Badger Ballhead, Badger Market, Globelle, Greenback, Improved Globe, Jersey Queen, Marion Market, Red Hollander, Wisconsin All Season, Wisconsin Copenhagen, Wisconsin Golden Acre, Wisconsin Hollander Number 8

Celery—Cornell Number 619 and Utah Pascal 15

Corn—Country Squire, Golden Hybrid Blend, NK 87

Cucumber—Ashley, Early Surecrop, Hybrid NK 805, Ohio MR 17, Pic-nik, Pixie, Poinsett, Polaris, SMR 58, Spartan Dawn, Wisconsin SMR 15, Wisconsin SMR 18

Eggplant—Florida Market

Lettuce—Parris Island cos

Lima Bean—Thaxter

Muskmelon—Cornell Delicious Number 51, Edisto 47, Harvest Queen, Iroquois, Perlita, PMR-45, Spartan Rock

Peas—Alaska 28-57, Code 1, Early Perfection, Freezonian, Giant Stride, Little Gem, Pacemaker, Perfection Dark Seeded, Pride, Thomas Laxton

Pepper—Delaware Belle and Yolo Wonder L

Radish—Red Prince and Scarlet Knight

Spinach—Hybrid No. 612, New Zealand, Savoy Supreme, Virginia Blight Resistant, Wisconsin Bloomsdale

Tomato—Floradel, Homestead 24, Indian River, Manalucie, Manapal, Marion

Watermelon—Blackstone, Charleston Gray, Congo, Garrisonian, Kleckley's Sweets, Klondike R-7, Klondike Striped, Rio Gray

GEORGE W. PARK SEED COMPANY

Asparagus—Paradise

Bean—Gardengreen, Golden Wax Improved, Tendercrop, Topcrop

Cabbage—Savoy King
Celery—Summer Pascal
Corn—Golden Beauty
Cucumber—Burpee hybrid, F1 Hybrid Surecrop, Triumph,
    Woodruff's hybrid
Eggplant—Burpee hybrid
Muskmelon—Edisto and F1 Hybrid Supermarket
Peas—Freezonian
Pepper—Parkwonder
Tomato—Climbing Triple Crop, Hawaii, Manalucie, Super Mas-
    ter Marglobe
Watermelon—Dixie Queen F1 hybrid

VII  Ground Covers for Problem-solving

Ground covers are planted where grass is hard to maintain and where paving materials, which might be used instead of grass, either do not look well or do not serve a useful purpose.

This is not to say that ground covers are strictly substitute materials—to be used only as a last resort. The fact is that well-established, well-nurtured ground covers are very attractive and often deserve to be used for this reason alone. For instance, my landscape architect called for a big bed of pachysandra across the front of my house, not because grass would not grow there (it actually would do better than the pachysandra), but because he and I figured that the pachysandra would look better than anything else.

This, however, is beside the point of this book. Ground covers are being discussed here simply because they are good looking plant materials that can save you work under certain circumstances.

What are these circumstances? Here are four:

1. Use a ground cover when grass is difficult to grow and maintain. Grass-growing can be a problem for various reasons, but in most parts of the country the problem is

Since grass would not grow under the heavy shade of this horse chestnut, a Connecticut gardener planted the area with pachysandra, one of the best ground covers.

usually attributable to too much shade. Few grasses grow well in light shade; and none grows in heavy shade. But many ground covers not only like shade but require it. Consequently, it is standard practice the country over to use them instead of grass in the shade of dense trees and shrubs, buildings, and so on.

Grass-growing and maintenance are also problems when the soil is extremely acid or alkaline, when soil is so rocky that it either cannot support grass or cannot be mowed, or when water is in short supply. In all these circumstances, you can often save work by planting a ground cover.

2. Use a ground cover on banks that are too steep or too high to mow. As noted elsewhere, banks with a pitch of more than 1 foot vertically in 3 feet horizontally are too steep to be mowed easily and safely. And the work can be tedious even on less steep slopes if they happen to be very high. It follows that these should never be planted to grass. Use a low-growing ground cover instead. It needs no mowing; looks neat; and once established, it should give full protection against erosion by water and wind.

3. Use ground covers to keep spring flower beds and rock gardens looking neat the rest of the year. Many gardeners limit their flower-growing activities to a few bulbs, rock garden plants, and shrubs that bloom in the spring. Their purpose in doing this, of course, is to free themselves of the work of caring for flowers in the hot summer months. But obviously their efforts in this direction would be fruitless if, after their spring flowers died away, they were left with empty beds and borders that had to be cultivated frequently to eliminate weeds and to keep the soil attractively stirred up.

To avoid this dilemma, they fill beds and borders with a ground cover that conceals the bare soil and discourages weeds yet does not interfere with the growth of spring flowers. (Various ground covers, such as periwinkle and ajuga, allow flowers to come up through them in the spring, when their foliage is relatively sparse, but keep down weeds the rest of the year.)

4. Use ground covers under litterbug trees to conceal fallen fruit, nuts, and leaves, and thus to simplify what would be a repetitious cleanup job if the trees were standing in a lawn area. Unfortunately, this idea sounds better than it really is. Here's why: In the first place, while almost all ground cover plants swallow up heavy fruits and nuts, none of them absorbs leaves—especially large leaves. However, they do trap the leaves sufficiently to prevent them from being blown away by the wind, which means either that you must allow the ground cover to build up an unsightly blanket of leaves or that you must get out your rake. And raking a ground cover is not as easy as raking grass.

In the second place, as fruits that fall into the ground cover rot, they attract wasps which make life in the vicinity unpleasant.

But perhaps I am overstressing the drawbacks. Certainly if good gardeners have found this idea helpful—and some have—it must have more merit than my own experience would indicate.

Growing a ground cover. Whether the ground cover you select is a perennial, shrub, or vine, you will find that, compared with grass, it demands little attention once it is established. The following points should be noted, however:

1. Until a ground cover becomes thick enough to crowd them out, weeds are likely to be a nuisance and hard to eradicate. Before planting an area with a ground cover, therefore, it is advisable to treat the soil with a herbicide such as DMTT or SMDC (see Chapter X). This should help to control weeds during the first year. Thereafter, if the ground cover is still not thick enough to keep out weeds, you can scatter a 2-inch mulch of chopped bark, peat, and so on, in among the plants. Some ground covers can also be treated with new weed killers (see Chapter X).

2. Just because ground covers seem undemanding in comparison with grass and flowers does not mean that you can grow them successfully without preparing the soil properly. The majority simply do not tolerate such cavalier treatment. In other words, dig the soil in which you grow a ground cover to a depth of about a foot and mix in plenty of sand and humus to give it good consistency. Then add fertilizer and lime or sulfur.

3. Like grass, many of the smaller ground cover plants are trampled down by dogs and soon display unsightly paths that are difficult to erase. The best solution is to use only tough, woody ground cover plants—such as spreading junipers, lantana, trailing roses, and cotoneasters—in those areas where large dogs are most likely to travel. Other solutions are to erect barriers that force the dogs to detour around the planting, or to eliminate whatever it is that encouraged them to run through the planting in the first place.

4. Although there is no truly easy way to clean leaves and twigs out of a ground cover, you can sometimes simplify operations by using a leaf blower or by giving the leaves a hard hosing down.

5. To keep a ground cover from growing outward into a lawn or other area where it is not wanted, encircle it with metal curbing that is 4 to 5 inches deep. A brick mowing strip set on a thick cushion of sand, or a concrete strip 4 to 6 inches deep, serves the same purpose and facilitates mowing of adjacent lawn areas.

6. Ground covers compete vigorously for food and moisture with trees, shrubs, and vines under which they are planted. You should therefore increase the amount of fertilizer given the trees (or the ground cover) by about 50 percent. You should also step up the frequency of watering.

Selected ground cover plants. No matter where you live and no matter what your reason for planting a ground cover, you can almost always find one or two good species to choose from. The following are among the best:

Ajuga. A favorite evergreen ground cover in all but the coldest climates, ajuga, or bugle, has glossy foliage and spikes of bright blue flowers in the spring. It grows in shade or sun to a height of 4 to 8 inches and makes a dense carpet. Spring bulbs are often planted in among it. There are several varieties of ajuga, including one with bronze foliage.

Bearberry (Arctostaphylos uva-ursii). A splendid evergreen ground cover growing almost everywhere, it requires acid soil and full sun but is difficult to transplant, so you should start with potted plants. The stems are several feet long and root at the joints, but the plants rarely grow more than 8 inches high.

Candytuft (Iberis sempervirens). This evergreen perennial can be grown almost anywhere in sun or light shade.

It is about 6 inches tall, grows in ordinary soil, and is covered in the spring with a sheet of lovely white flowers.

Ceanothus grisens horizontalis. A low evergreen shrub that grows best in warm parts of California, ceanothus is covered with dense clusters of blue flowers in the spring. You can grow it in sun or light shade.

Ceratostigma plumbaginoides. Plumbago, as it is often called, is a hardy perennial for mild and warm climates. It grows 8 inches tall, has rich green leaves and clusters of bright blue flowers in late summer and fall. It grows in the shade.

Christmas fern (Polystichum acrostichoides). Here is an attractive evergreen fern with dense clusters of fronds up to 2 feet long. It grows in moist, shaded areas in humusy soil in the East. Do not use it in areas where dogs or people will walk, because the fronds are easily broken.

Cotoneaster horizontalis. This 2-foot shrub is deciduous but hangs on to its small, boxwood-like leaves for a long time. In the fall it is covered with red berries. You can grow it in sun or light shade. It is fine for covering banks.

Other cotoneasters that are good ground covers include *C. adpressa, C. dammeri* and *C. microphylla.*

Dichondra. This evergreen perennial is fairly popular as a lawn plant in California and is also used occasionally in the South. It has kidney-shaped leaves; forms a dense, low-growing mat that requires only occasional mowing. It grows in sun or light shade; prefers a heavy soil but does not need a very fertile one; requires plenty of water. It withstands moderate traffic.

English ivy (Hedera helix). This handsome, dark, evergreen vine grows in all except very cold regions. It has a slight preference for shaded areas, but does well in the full sun. It needs to be thinned slightly every spring, and it may have to be headed back once or twice a year— especially if the soil is fertile. As a low-growing (up to 8 inches) bank cover, it has few rivals because it is rarely unattractive and it roots at frequent intervals, thus helping to anchor the soil. It is also often planted under trees, but be warned that you must keep after it constantly to keep it from taking off up the trunks.

Many attractive varieties of ivy are on the market. Some are considerably hardier than others, so be sure to ask which is recommended for your area.

Epimedium. This woody perennial grows in mild and warm climates. It is semievergreen, has heart-shaped, leathery leaves that are often bronze-colored in the spring. It also produces a profusion of red, white, or yellow flowers in the spring. The plants are about 9 inches tall and grow best in light shade, though they tolerate full sun.

Euonymus fortunei. The only real problem with this tough woody vine that grows in mild and warm climates is that it is often attacked by scale insects. Otherwise, it is an excellent ground cover for sunny or shady places. The foliage is evergreen, and there are clusters of orange berries in the fall.

Heather (Calluna vulgaris) and heath (Erica). These beautiful evergreens, from 6 to 18 inches tall, grow in mild and warm climates. The leaves are dense and small and turn bronze-colored in the autumn. The profuse spikes of flowers are white, red, pink, or purple. Heather blooms in the summer; heath in winter and spring. They require full sun and a well-drained, acid soil containing plenty of peat.

Honeysuckle. Lonicera henryi is an evergreen honeysuckle vine with rather insignificant but fragant flowers and fine blue-black berries in the fall. The plant grows almost everywhere, in sun or shade, to a height of 18 inches. It is a very good bank covering.

Iceplant (Mesembryanthemum). Iceplants are evergreen succulents growing only in dry, frost-free climates. The foliage is flat, glistening, and attractive; the daisylike flowers, which open only when the sun is high, are incredible. They come in many brilliant colors and completely blanket the plants. Maximum height is about 8 inches.

Ivy geranium (Pelargonium peltatum). This grows in

California in sunny locations. It reaches a height of 12 to 18 inches and produces many flowers in white to dark red.

Japanese snakebeard (Ophiopogon japonicus). Also called lilyturf or mondo grass, this is a slow-growing southern plant with evergreen, grasslike leaves and pale lilac flowers. It is 8 to 12 inches tall. It is favored for shady spots but grows in the sun; is resistant to salt spray; and supports light traffic.

Juniper (Juniperus). Included in this vast clan of evergreens are a number of spreading varieties ranging in height from 6 inches to a couple of feet. They grow almost everywhere in the United States in full sun and ordinary soil. They are extremely tough and make outstanding bank covers. One of their useful virtues is their ability to hide leaves and trash that blow across the landscape.

Lantana sellowiana. This vinelike shrub is used to cover banks and hillsides in very warm climates. It grows about 3 feet tall; is evergreen; and has yellow, pink, or red flowers in clusters. Grow it in the sun.

Lily-of-the-valley (Convallaria). Here is a beautiful, 6- to 8-inch ground cover in warm weather, but it disappears in winter. The fragrant white flowers are everybody's favorite. The plants grow in mild and warm climates and in shade or sun. They are not particular about soil, but perform best when fertilized liberally. Unfortunately, they need to be divided every few years to keep them from becoming too crowded and from dying out.

Lingonberry (Vaccinium vitis-idaea). This evergreen shrub grows up to 1 foot high with red berries in the autumn. It grows in cold climates; in sun or shade; in acid, well-drained, moist soil.

Lippia. A grass substitute used in warm parts of the Southwest, it is a low, creeping, fast-growing plant with dark green, oblong leaves. It can be mowed regularly. Nematodes are a serious enemy.

Mahonia repens. This 1-foot evergreen shrub is grown

mainly on the West Coast. It has leathery leaves, yellow flower clusters, and black berries.

Mother-of-thyme (Thymus serpyllum). An evergreen perennial only about 4 inches high, it is fine for filling in between rocks and also for covering larger areas. The foliage is gray-green; the masses of flowers, rose-red. Thyme grows in most parts of the country in the sun and is fairly resistant to traffic.

Pachistima canbyi. This plant has small, shiny, square-tipped evergreen leaves. It grows to 1 foot and requires very little care. You can raise it in sun or light shade wherever winters are not severe.

Pachysandra. Here is an outstanding evergreen ground cover in most parts of the country. It grows 8 to 12 inches high and has dense whorls of wedge-shaped leaves and inconspicuous white flowers. Best grown in light or heavy shade, where it forms a thick mat, it can also be grown in the sun if watered and fed enough. There is a variety with leaves edged in silvery white.

Partridgeberry (Mitchella repens). A lovely evergreen, partridgeberry forms flat mats in moist, fertile, shaded soil in warm and cold climates. It is a familiar sight in eastern forests. The leaves are small, round, and shiny. Flowers produced in spring are pinkish-white and are followed by scarlet berries.

Periwinkle (Vinca minor). In the spring, periwinkle (also called myrtle) is covered with charming blue flowers. The rest of the time it is dark green, glossy, and most attractive. It is an excellent ground cover, about 8 inches high, for use in cold and warm climates. Although it prefers shade, either light or heavy, it grows fairly well in the sun.

Polygonum reynowtria. An extremely vigorous plant in all but the coldest climates, this deciduous perennial can become a pest if you don't watch out. But it is one of the best ground covers for sunny spots. It grows to 12 to 18 inches, has fine foliage, and in the fall is covered with dense clusters of small red buds and then airy pink flowers. The leaves also turn copper-red.

Rose. Two trailing roses—*Rosa wichuraiana*, which has single white flowers, and Max Graf, which has single pink flowers—are among the best ground covers for banks. They grow about 18 inches high and are tough and dense, though they lose their leaves in winter. You can grow them anywhere. Wichuraiana has a tendency to take root wherever the stems touch the ground.

St. Johnswort (Hypericum calycinum). An evergreen shrub 12 to 18 inches high, this one spreads rapidly and is well covered in the summer with golden flowers. It grows in soil of average quality; prefers sun but does well in partial shade. Plant it in regions where temperatures do not fall below zero.

Salal (Gaultheria shallon). For warm climates, it grows to about 18 inches in partial shade. A sandy, acid soil is required. The flowers that appear in June are pinkish-white and feathery.

Sarcocca hookeriana humilis. An excellent evergreen shrub with rich, shiny leaves, sarcocca grows only in the shade in climates where the temperature does not fall much below zero. It is an upright plant about 1 foot high.

Saxifrage. Several plants in this large family can be used for ground covers in all but the coldest parts of the country. One is the familiar house plant called strawberry geranium (*Saxifraga sarmentosa*). Another even tougher plant is *Bergenia cordifolia*. Both grow to 12 to 18 inches and have handsome rounded leaves and small white or pink flowers. They grow in sun or shade.

Sedum. Many of these sun-loving, perennial succulents can be used as ground cover plants in mild and warm climates; but among the best are *S. acre*, with yellow flowers, *S. album*, with white flowers, and *S. reflexum* also with yellow flowers. All are creeping evergreens only a few inches high—very attractive in warm weather but inclined to become thin and wispy when the temperature drops. They are excellent for covering rocky soil or out-croppings because they take root and grow in very little soil (provided it is well drained).

Stephanandra incisa crispa nana. A deciduous shrub not much over 2 feet tall, stephanandra is recommended mainly for its small, bright green, fernlike leaves. It also has small clusters of white flowers. It grows in most climates in the shade.

Wandering Jew (Zebrina pendula). Grown only in the warmest areas, this vine spreads so rapidly in shady locations that it can become a pest. It grows up to 6 inches tall. The leaves are purple and white.

Wedelia trilobata. If the temperature drops below 30 degrees wedelia will lose its leaves; and it is killed at 20 degrees. So use it only in the warmest climates. It grows fast in sun or shade and in any soil. It is not damaged by salt spray. The height is 8 inches. There are yellow flowers in summer.

Wild ginger (Asarum). Here are several evergreen perennials up to 7 inches high, with aromatic roots and beautiful heart-shaped or kidney-shaped leaves. They can be grown only in moist shade under woodland conditions. Use in mild and warm climates only.

Wild strawberry (Fragaria). Here is an evergreen for warm climates. The plants are bushy, not much over 8 inches high. The leaves are very attractive and the fruit (if you can get it before the birds do) is delicious. Grow it in full sun.

Zoysia tenuifolia. This zoysia grass, called by various names, has very fine leaves giving an overall velvety texture. It grows only in warm climates and has the peculiar habit of forming bumps or ridges something like the skin ridges on the back of an English bulldog. It can be mowed (if you do it regularly); otherwise it grows to a height of 8 to 12 inches. Sun is required. It is beautiful on a steep slope or in small patches anywhere.

VIII  Gardens Featuring Stones

Stones are among the most important elements of a Japanese garden. Not only do the Japanese spend years (and many yen) searching for stones of exquisite beauty, but once they find one, they invest it with a special meaning or purpose, and place it just so in the garden. Upright stones have male character; horizontal stones are female. There is a Guardian Stone, a Stone of Worship, a Stone of Two Deities, and so on.

What it is in stones that appeals to the Japanese is difficult to define. And it is just as well not to try, for I have it on the authority of top American landscape architects that even if we knew the answer, we still could not use stones quite as the Orientals do. Nor should we.

But this is not to say that we should not borrow some of the Japanese gardener's enthusiasm for stones. Because stones can be beautiful—especially in the green setting of the garden. And they require not one iota of maintenance.

My interest in stones goes back many years, but I never really thought of them as garden features until several years ago. That was when my cousin Harry decided to

Two uses of stone in a Chicago area garden.

plant a few azaleas and yews in front of a granite cliff outside his living room windows. The cliff was—and is—
magnificently rugged. It is gray in the sunlight, streaked
with white in the winter snow, glistening black in an
evening rain, glowing green where the light from the house
strikes the tiny lichens that mat the surface.

Of course, it must be said that whether Harry liked the
cliff or not, it was there. Too huge to be eliminated. Too
prominent to be ignored. But Harry had the good sense
not just to accept the cliff but to make it a feature of his
garden. In fact, it *is* his garden; and in its own way, it is
as pretty as any garden I know.

After Harry's cliff opened my eyes to the beauties and
practicality of stones as garden features, I began to notice
more of them.

On a handsomely shrubbed, treed, and landscaped estate
outside Boston, almost the first things that caught my
eye were the pudding stones. Pudding stones are large,
rounded boulders that are pocked with pebbles. They have
a vague resemblance to the moon as seen through a giant
telescope. In this garden a couple of the largest stones had
been deposited aeons ago by the glaciers. But the others—
not more than three or four—had been brought in and
placed among the trees and shrubs by Stanley Underhill,
the landscape architect. They looked natural—as much at
home as the plants around them; but they imparted the
feeling of fine sculpture.

In Chicago, I saw two other uses of stones as features
of a small garden. Both were Oriental in feeling, though
not so much so that they seemed out of place in a de-
cidedly American setting. In a hillside area large, rough
rocks were prominently placed in among azaleas, and a
few were scattered across the gravel terrace below. Next
to the wood-block terrace behind the house, six stones of
varying sizes, shapes, and textures were set on a small
patch of black and white gravel. Tucked in among shrubs

Sleeping boulders surround swimming pool in San Francisco area designed and landscaped by Thomas D. Church.

and trees, the arrangement—almost like a flower arrangement—served as a focal point for the terrace.

Another garden I saw that made deliberately extensive use of stones was a much photographed swimming pool area created by the great San Francisco landscape architect, Thomas D. Church. The purpose here was to meld a perfectly round pool into a natural woodland setting (Mr. Church often strives for sharp contrasts between manmade garden elements and nature). To this end, Mr. Church built a stream bed of large, flat rocks on the hillside between the house and the pool; and he placed a few additional rocks, seemingly at random, around the flat rim of the pool. The latter not only help to unify pool and hillside and change the lines of the pool rim, but several look like great sea animals that have come ashore to sun themselves. In a somnolent way, they add an element of excitement or of the unexpected to the scene.

Finally, on the island of Hawaii, I saw an entire garden —a large one—that pivots around a rock. It is not a beautiful rock when you examine it. It is composed of black lava that flowed down from the old volcano, Mauna Kea, into the Pacific many years ago and that has since been worn down by waves. But seen from a distance of a hundred feet or more, the craggy mass standing at the tip of a small point of land and silhouetted against the brilliant blue and white sea is nothing short of gorgeous. One might argue that, because the rock is separated from the lawn and planting around the house by a depressed strip of crumbled lava and water, it has nothing to do with the garden but belongs instead to the sea. Actually, however, the rock is no different from the grass and trees and brilliant tropical shrubs. It belongs to the garden—and dominates it.

Yes, rocks, stones, boulders, outcroppings—whatever you call a mass of hard, nonmetallic mineral matter—are definitely garden elements. Beautiful ones that grow more so with age. And as I said earlier, they do not require any maintenance. So why shouldn't you feature them here and there instead of plants or other demanding garden elements?

Handling outcroppings. Some years ago, when a friend of mine built a home in the New York suburbs, he was mildly disturbed by a huge, whale-backed hunk of granite that rose out of the middle of his lawn. Bob came from a part of the country that is not blessed with the granite outcroppings found in New York and New England (and elsewhere), so it was not surprising that he wanted to get rid of this ancient gray whale. But since that was patently impossible without making a sizable outlay for dynamite, he did his best to hide it. He planted sedums and other small plants in the soil that had accumulated in the rock fissures. And he piled more soil around the rock's skirts and planted it with grass and occasional flowers.

What happened? When summer came and a couple of

weeks went by without rain, most of Bob's carefully planted plants shriveled and died. So Bob replanted—not once, but three or four times. And then finally the truth dawned: Trying to make pretty plants grow in the wispy soil on top of a rock outcropping is frustrating, never-ending work.

Bob quit. And soon he made a second discovery: His barren gray whale was really a pretty handsome thing.

Bob's original attitude toward the rock was by no means peculiar. Plenty of other people who have outcroppings in their gardens have tried to get rid of them or to cover them up; and most of them have failed. Rocks that barely stick out of the ground you can cope with (though not always easily or successfully). But big rocks don't just go away. So instead of fighting them, you should make the best of them. And the best way to do this—if you want to reduce your garden work—is either to let nature take its course or to clean the rock as thoroughly as you can.

Nature's way is not, unfortunately, always tidy or attractive. Weeds and sometimes even trees and shrubs have an ability to establish a foothold in the thin soil in rock seams that cultivated plants lack. But occasionally—very occasionally—the results can be delightful.

By and large, however, you will do better to rid the rock of all its encrusting soil. My friend Bob did this finally by scraping the soil out of the seams and away from the edges of the rock with a trowel and knife. Another method used by a gentleman in Greenwich, Connecticut, is to drive out the soil with high-pressure hoses. The results of this treatment at first strike you as abnormal, because in Connecticut, where giant outcroppings are a dime a dozen, you expect to see all kinds of things growing in the rock seams. But the treatment actually enhances the beauty of the outcroppings by exposing all surfaces and allowing you to see each seam—not as a streak of dirt and moss—but as a clean line.

Handling "imported" stones. The main disadvantage of outcroppings is that they are not always located in gardens as well as they might be from an aesthetic standpoint; nor are they always perfectly formed. By contrast, stones that you introduce to the garden can be selected and placed just right.

Placement. This aspect generally should precede selection. But since Americans have no experience in using stones in the garden, there are no rules for placing them. Common sense suggests the following points, however:

1. Stones are made to order for those spots in the garden where lack of sun, poor soil, bad drainage, and so on, make it difficult to grow plants. Needless to say, however, you should not use them in such locations unless they improve the appearance of the areas and are, in turn, complimented by the areas.

2. Since stones weigh too much to permit you to experiment very much with their placement, one of the first things you should decide is whether to use a stone as a

Massive outcroppings in Connecticut garden were washed down with hoses to remove soil and bring out the full beauty of the granite.

prominent feature (like a statue) or as a subtle element designed to surprise and delight the visitor. Stones that fall into the first category need to have plenty of space around them, and should be set against a contrasting back drop. (They are especially effective when placed on an open paved or graveled surface. And they would be equally effective on grass—if you could figure out some way to avoid trimming the grass around them.)

Stones that play a subtle role in the garden can be tucked away almost anywhere, but should not be so hidden that visitors might trip over them.

3. Stones usually look attractive in front of walls made of brick, concrete block, vertical boards, and plywood but not in front of shingled or clapboard walls.

4. Because they are natural objects, stones should be placed where you would find them in nature—on the ground. This does not mean that they must always be at your feet, of course. They can be at eye level or even higher, if they are on a hillside. But they should not be raised by artificial means. They should neither sit atop tree stumps or pedestals, nor be placed in an obviously precarious position from which logic tells you that they would fall if someone had not indulged in a little trickery with mirrors.

5. It is important, too, that a stone be set in a vertical or horizontal position according to its placement in nature. For a slab of limestone to be set on end, for example, would not only be unnatural but would make it look like a tombstone. By the same token, it would be wrong to lay a spire of sandstone from a desert canyon flat.

6. The textured quality of a stone is enhanced when it is in sunlight or light shadow. It suffers when it is in mottled sun and shade. And in deep shade it looks like nothing at all.

7. Some types of stone are great collectors of lichens, which add immeasurably to their beauty. The conglomer-

ate rocks found in the Shawangunk Mountains of New York State, for example, are noted for their coverings of these strange little plants. If you can find handsome samples of similar lichen-covered stones, grab them quickly. If you can't, look for stones with a rather rough surface, and place them in an exposed part of the garden where they will be struck by the winds that carry lichens across the country.

8. Avoid using too many stones together unless you are imitating a natural scene (as Mr. Church did in the stream bed above the swimming pool). In an artificial scene, a collection of stones must be handled with great skill to keep it from looking like only a rock pile. I do not always think that the beauty of a flower is improved by its use in a flower arrangement; but the chances that it may be improved are good because so many women have practiced so long in making flower arrangements. But we know nothing about arranging stones; so it is better to eschew arrangements and let the inherent beauty of individual stones speak for itself.

Collecting stones. Finding suitable stones for garden ornament is often a problem. Not every lot is endowed with a natural supply. And there are large regions of the country that do not have a good supply either. As for Connecticut and similar areas where there is too much rock— surprisingly, you can run into problems here, too.

I discovered this when we moved into our present house and I set out to rebuild the 400-foot stone wall that separates our meadow from our woods. I needed a lot of stones, and I did not care what they looked like. But my own land is not rocky and yielded almost nothing. I refused to steal from other people's walls. And it offended me to think that in Connecticut, of all places, I had to buy stones. So I was left with picking up whatever I could find that would not represent a loss to the owner.

After three years, I still have a great many feet of wall to rebuild. And I doubt that I have come up with a single stone that would be worthy of use as a garden feature. (As a matter of fact, I doubt that in my entire standing wall—which contains about 100 cubic yards of Connecticut's best granite and gneiss—are there more than two or three stones that you might call passable.)

In other words, to find beautiful or interesting stones, you must hunt and hunt and hunt. There is no telling where you will come on them: in stream beds (especially at the foot of mountain brooks), on rocky coasts, in gravel pits, in the tailings dumps of quarries, in talus heaps at the foot of high ridges, in mountains and deserts, along a superhighway.

If you need assistance in tracking down a certain kind of stone, you might get in touch with the U.S. Geological Survey office in your state, with your own state geology commission, or with the geology departments of state universities. Be sure to give fairly specific details about the kinds of rock you are looking for.

If you want to go it alone, maps and other published materials are abundantly available in the largest city libraries and in the Geological Survey offices. Geologic maps are the best source of information because they show the actual distribution of rocks in an area, and they also bear a legend giving rock descriptions. Topographic maps show the location of quarries and mines, even abandoned ones.

Whether you feel free to pick up and walk off with the rocks you discover in countryside or city I leave up to you. They *are* somebody's property, and you really should ask if you may have them. The answer, in most cases, will be: "Of course."

The kind of stone you want for a garden depends on how you want to place or use it. But it is possible that you may come upon a stone for which you have no planned place but it is so beautiful you must take it anyway. Never fear, you will be able to use it.

By and large, the stones that make the best prospects for garden use are those that have been lying loose in the open or in the water where they have been subject to weathering. Stones that have been fairly recently broken out of large bodies of rock, as in a ledge or quarry, are likely to look a bit angular and raw. Yet I have seen chunks of ropelike lava, called pahoehoe, which cried out to be blasted from one of Hawaii's endless flows.

Some specific features to look for in rocks are the contorted layers that result from the writhings of the earth's crust; fine laminations of different colors; narrow or ribbonlike intrusions of stone of one color into a body of another color; fossil imprints; a frothy texture as in pumice; and large quartz crystals.

Here are a dozen kinds of rock that are likely to produce particularly handsome garden objects:

Basalt is a very heavy, fine-grained rock; dark gray, black, and without any luster to speak of. It is found almost everywhere, but the largest deposits are in the Northwest, the Hudson River Palisades, and the Connecticut River Valley.

Pahoehoe, so plentiful in Hawaii, is a black basalt.

Conglomerate consists of rounded or angular pebbles held together in a fine, cementlike matrix. The pebbles may be large or small, of uniform size or mixed. The color varies. Conglomerates are coarse rocks that break into ugly, irregular fragments; but when they have been worn down or eroded, they are often interesting in appearance.

Dolomite is frequently confused with limestone, which it resembles, but it is not dissolved by acid. It is fairly fine-grained, usually gray on fresh surfaces but weathering to buff. It frequently contains shells. It occurs in many parts of the country.

Gneiss resembles granite but has pronounced straight or wavy bands alternating light and dark. Most gneiss is predominantly gray. Large masses are found in New England, the Appalachians, and the Rockies.

Granite is hard and heavy and contains crystalline feldspar and quartz. It is usually gray, but often almost white, pale pink, or brownish red, and occasionally yellow or green. Granite is the most common rock in the earth's crust and is found just about everywhere. The largest supplies, however, are in New England, upper New York State, the Blue Ridge, Wisconsin, Minnesota, the Rockies, southern Arizona, California, and Washington.

Limestone is a fine-grained stone that occurs abundantly in the Middle West and South. It is usually white or gray but may be creamy, buff, yellow, red, brown, or black. The stone is often found in flat beds broken by strong vertical joints. It is readily dissolved by acids and acid atmosphere.

Florida's so-called "coral rock" is a very attractive variety of limestone pock-marked with irregular cavities. Other interesting limestones from the same state are coquina and oolite.

Pegmatite is a coarse type of granite containing very large, perfect crystals of feldspar, quartz, mica, tourmaline, topaz, and so on. The rock is found in association with ordinary granite in Maine, New Hampshire, Connecticut, North Carolina, the Black Hills of South Dakota, and many other places.

Sandstone is usually a fine-textured but porous, sandy rock in white, gray, yellow, brown, red, or green. It does not have the glitter of granite. The rock is found almost everywhere. It often contains fossils. If you're lucky, you may find some stones that show ripple marks like those in the sandy bottom of quiet bays along the shore.

Serpentine is a compact, soft, waxy-looking rock containing the mineral serpentine and other minerals. It is green, yellow, or brown and covered with a network of pale lines. You might think it was marble. It is found in California, Oregon, and various parts of the East.

Soapstone (Talc) is a soft, gray or greenish rock found mainly in Vermont, New York, Pennsylvania, New Jersey,

Maryland, North Carolina, Georgia, and California. When broken, it has a rough surface with a silvery sheen.

Handling stones. Although stones vary considerably in weight, a rough average for one measuring exactly 1 cubic foot is about 170 pounds. It is clear from this that, if you have to move a large stone, you should let some one with a strong back and the proper mechanical equipment do it for you. The stone should first be wrapped in quilts or some other covering to protect the surface from scratching and gouging by crowbars, chains, bulldozers, and the like.

If a stone is just light enough for you to lift, wear leather-palmed gloves and hard-toed shoes. Stand close behind the stone and squat down by bending your knees; grasp the stone firmly; and then stand straight up. Let your leg muscles do all the work. Keep your back straight.

If you lug stones in your car, cover the bottom of the trunk with an old rug and shove the stones as far forward as possible. It does not take many of them in the rear end of the trunk to make your tail pipe drag.

IX  Growth-Regulating Chemicals

Chemicals that in one way or another help to reduce work in the garden are an old story. They include fertilizers, insecticides, fungicides, animal poisons, and so on. Now a new group of work-saving chemicals is being developed. Called growth regulators, they are organic compounds that are harmless to men, animals, and birds but cause plants to perform in unusual ways. You will be hearing more about them in the future. Several are either ready for you to use right now or will be available within a fairly short time.

Inhibiting Plant Growth

Maleic hydrazide, also known as MH, is one of the oldest of the growth regulators. It was developed by UniRoyal, Inc., at Naugatuck, Connecticut, in 1947. Today it is widely used by highway departments, parks, airports, golf courses, electric utilities, and the like, to slow the growth of grass, trees, shrubs, and vines and thus to reduce the need for mowing and pruning. Although MH is not sold by garden supply stores at this writing, it is available to anyone through the manufacturer's chemical distributors.

Controlling grass growth. MH is a translocated chemical that halts cell division in treated grass blades but does not halt cell expansion. Thus while it slows leaf growth and prevents formation of seed heads, it does not stop grass from growing thick, lush, and green.

MH can be applied safely to any three-year-old or older turf except one containing St. Augustinegrass, which becomes badly changed in color. MH should be used only on grass areas that are not supposed to look in perfect trim—on meadows or roadside edges, for example. It is not recommended for fine lawns because the different kinds of grasses that are often used in lawns react in slightly different degrees to the chemical; consequently, the lawns sometimes develop a somewhat hummocky look.

Only one application is needed per season. This one retards grass growth to such an extent that by the end of the year it may not be more than 6 to 12 inches high. If this height is more than you want, you can cut it. Even then, only one or two mowings will be required.

MH is mixed in water at the rate of 7 tablespoons per 2 gallons of water and is applied by sprayer. To treat an acre requires 50 gallons of solution.

Application should be made only when grass is growing vigorously and can absorb the chemical at the maximum rate. The best time is in the spring when the grass is 2 to 4 inches tall. Seed heads will not form, and growth of the leaves will be inhibited for about six weeks on bluegrass and longer on fescues.

If spraying is delayed too long in the spring, the grass may have to be mowed to no less than 4 inches one week after the chemical is applied. Leaf growth will be retarded as usual, but seed heads may form.

The spray should never be applied soon after grass has been mowed, because the absorption surface is reduced, and the clippings shield the short grass from the spray. Similarly, all tree leaves should be raked up before spraying.

A dry period of 12 hours is essential after MH is applied to allow the grass to absorb the chemical. If rain should fall too soon, the MH would be washed away and a second application would be required.

To control weeds, 2, 4-D can be mixed with the MH when it is applied in the spring. A separate application of 2, 4-D can be made in June or July for weeds that may emerge later.

Grass that is treated in the spring may turn slightly yellow for a few weeks but will recover. Discoloration of Bermuda and bent grasses can be reduced by using only 3½ tablespoons of MH in each 2 gallons of water.

Autumn application of MH is also successful in reducing the growth of northern grasses, but should not be made on southern grasses. Spraying should be done while the grass is growing and before it becomes dormant and brown. It makes no difference if there has been a frost before you apply the chemical. UniRoyal points out that, as a rule, the closer the application is to the time when the grass goes dormant, the longer growth will be inhibited the following spring.

One problem with fall treatment is that the grass greens up one or two weeks later than usual in the spring. On the other hand, fall treatment gives better control of wild onion, garlic, dandelions, and plantains in the lawn.

Trimming grass edges. Although MH is not recommended for general use on lawns, it can be used to excellent advantage to keep all lawn edges looking neat without weekly trimming.

Dilute the chemical at the rate of 4 tablespoons to 3

quarts of water and spray a continuous 3-inch strip along the lawn edges when the grass is about 2 inches tall and growing vigorously. Application can be made in the spring or fall. When the edges do require trimming, do not cut the grass shorter than 2½ inches.

Controlling hedges, trees, shrubs, vines, and ground covers. When I was last in Florida it was spring pruning time and in front of almost every house was a mountainous pile of branches cut from the trees, shrubs, and vines that grow so luxuriantly in the subtropics. The sight reminded me once again that the job of keeping large plants in check is one of the most time-consuming and difficult gardening chores. It is bad in the North and absolutely horrendous in warm climates.

There is no reason why this should be so, however. Maleic hydrazide holds the answer. It retards the growth of woody plants in the same way that it works on grass.

All plants respond to the chemical, although not to the same degree. Conifers are generally the least responsive; nevertheless, results are good enough to warrant their treatment. But you definitely should not apply MH to flowering plants—not because it damages them, but because it inhibits their bloom. The chemicals described later should be used instead.

Because MH slows the growth of only those branches to which is is applied, you can use it to limit the growth of either part of a plant or the entire plant. For instance, if you want to prevent a plant from growing upward, you spray only the top of the plant down halfway into it. Or if you want to keep a plant from growing outward, you spray the side branches at least halfway into the plant. Or if you want to control an entire plant, you spray it all over, making sure that the chemical reaches well into the plant so that the interior branches will not grow out through the exterior ones.

The amount of spray needed depends on the size of the plant and on how much of the growth you aim to control. Four to 5 gallons of spray are enough to treat the top of a medium-size tree; 6 to 7 gallons are needed for the whole tree. Leaves should be sprayed just to the point where they start to drip. If you apply too much spray, the excess will drip onto the grass under the tree and cause it to grow slowly, too.

For use on trees, shrubs, and vines, mix MH with water at the rate of 4 tablespoons to the gallon (this is the equivalent of 1 pint plus 1 ounce of MH to 10 gallons of water). If you live on the West Coast, add 2 teaspoons of Multi-Film X-77 to each gallon of the MH mixture. This material is made by Colloidal Products Corporation of Sausalito, California.

Application of MH should be made only on vigorous new growth. Most plants make such growth only in the spring; but some (notably tropical species) make it in other seasons.

Before spraying a plant trim it to the proper shape and slightly less than the desired size. Apply the spray a week or two later when the new leaves have expanded and stems have put on 2 to 4 inches of new growth. The weather must be dry for 12 hours after the application.

To illustrate the procedure for treating a plant with MH, let us assume that you want to control the growth of a privet hedge. The first step is to trim the hedge while it is dormant to a slightly smaller size than you actually want it to be. When spring comes, let the hedge grow up and out 2 to 4 inches. Then spray it completely, outside and in, with MH. This treatment will slow the growth to such an extent that, except for clipping off a few isolated shoots that the spray did not reach, you probably can leave your hedge shears in the garage for the rest of the summer. The hedge will stay in perfect trim.

Plant at left was treated with UniRoyal's Alar, a growth-retarding chemical. Similar plant at right was not treated.

Retarding Growth of Flowering Plants

Here are four chemicals that not only reduce the need for pruning flowering broadleaf plants in order to keep them to manageable size but also produce more shapely, compact plants with superior bloom. They are known as growth retardants. Unlike MH, which suppresses the growth of stems, leaves, and flowers, these chemicals simply limit the elongation of the plant stems.

B-Nine and Alar are made by UniRoyal; Cycocel, by American Cyanamid Company, Princeton, New Jersey; and Phosfon, by Virginia-Carolina Chemical Corp., Richmond, Virginia.

Phosfon, which comes in powder form and is available in small packages at garden supply stores, is designed to help you raise better, shorter chrysanthemums that do not require staking. The manufacturer's instructions for using the chemical are as follows:

"Remove 1 quart of soil from the location where the rooted chrysanthemum plant is to be planted. (A hole 5 inches in diameter and 3 inches deep will give 1 quart.)

Place soil in a suitable container. Sprinkle ½ level tea-spoon of Phosfon over the soil. Using a trowel, thoroughly and uniformly mix the Phosfon with the soil. Replace soil in the hole and plant rooted cutting in the center of the treated area. Follow your normal schedule of watering, fertilizing, and plant care."

Cycocel is a liquid sold through Cyanamid distributors. It is used on poinsettias to produce shorter, more compact plants with better flowers and on azaleas to limit vegetative growth. On other ornamentals, such as rhodo-dendrons, camellias, chrysanthemums, lilies, and gerani-ums, it seems to have the same effect as it has on poinset-tias; but at this writing, it is still being tested on these plants.

For poinsettias, mix 1 quart Cycocel with 10 gallons of water and drench the soil in which the plants are growing. The exact amount of the chemical needed depends on the size of the pot in which the poinsettia is planted. Treat-ment is made when roots are growing actively in the late summer and fall.

To treat azaleas, the chemical is applied as a spray at the rate of 3 ounces to 1 gallon of water. The application is made in the spring or early summer when the azaleas have reached the desired size following prunning. The plants must be well watered and growing vigorously; the foliage must be dry; and rain must not fall for 24 hours after the spraying. A second application of the chemical is required one week after the first.

B-Nine and Alar are closely related chemicals. The former is used primarily by commercial growers of orna-mental plants, including shrubs and annuals; the latter is used by farmers. In addition to retarding plant growth and improving flowering, both chemicals help to increase the drought resistance of plants. Either product may be used in the garden. B-Nine is available in liquid form and Alar in powder form from UniRoyal distributors.

For growth control, the chemicals are sprayed on flowering trees and shrubs in the spring two to three weeks after final pruning or when new growth is about 3 inches long. Herbaceous perennials, such as chrysanthemums, should be sprayed one to two months after growth starts, and repeat applications may be made three and/or six weeks later provided the last application is made at least one month before the flowers are formed. In all cases, application should be made on a day when no rain is anticipated for 12 hours. The treated plants should be thoroughly watered at the roots, but the foliage must be dry.

B-Nine is mixed with water at the rate of 12 ounces to 1 gallon. Use 5 teaspoons of Alar per gallon of water. Leaves on treated plants should be wet to the dripping point; and for best results, most of them should be covered.

When used on annuals (such as petunias, marigolds, zinnias, cosmos, asters) to produce more compact, drought-resistant plans, B-Nine should be applied when the tops of the little plants are just beginning to stretch. Plants usually have four to six leaves at this time. Additional applications may be made every three to four weeks throughout the season.

Chemical Pruning

One of the jobs all gardeners must do in the spring to make young plants bushier is to remove the tips of the main stems. This is a pruning process known usually as disbudding or pinching. It is not difficult but it takes time.

Now U.S. Department of Agriculture scientists have discovered that the job can be done simply by spraying plants with certain common chemicals. The terminal buds are killed as effectively as if they were cut off with a knife; but the side buds are not harmed.

Tests so far indicate that about two out of three plants can be pruned in this way. They include such flowers as marigolds, snapdragons, chrysanthemums, and geraniums;

vegetables such as tomatoes and beans; semiwoody plants such as hydrangeas and poinsettias; and woody plants ranging from azaleas to weigela.

When the new pruning chemicals will be available to gardeners is uncertain at this writing. They need to be further refined before release. But if the number of people who are working on them means anything, you should not have to wait long.

Controlling Transpiration with Chemicals

It has long been known that if foliage is covered with a coating of wax or plastic (called an antitranspirant) it does not give off moisture by transpiration as rapidly as uncoated foliage. Thus a coated plant can survive longer on a given quantity of moisture than an uncoated plant, which, in turn, means that if anyone wants to make watering less work, all he has to do is spray his plants with an antitranspirant.

Few if any people have ever done this, however; and the reason is money: The plastic antitranspirants currently on the market are too expensive to use except on isolated plants of unusual value.

But this situation is due to change. Investigation that has been going on at the Connecticut Agricultural Experiment Station at New Haven demonstrates that certain chemicals can also be used to retard transpiration. Their principal advantage is that they give much more extensive coverage than any coatings. In consequence, you can look forward to the day when it will be economically feasible to spray plants in your garden with a chemical antitranspirant and thus reduce their water consumption during droughts and save you from dragging out the hose as often as you must today.

X  Still More Chemicals: The Amazing Weed Killers

Of all the chemicals that the gardener uses, the weed killers, or herbicides, do most to save you work. They have already revolutionized lawn-weed control; now they are beginning to make equally drastic changes in weed-control methods in other garden areas.

A number of basic terms are used to describe these wonderful materials. They include the following:

Selective herbicide. This chemical kills some plants but not others. Selective herbicides are the backbone of current weed-control operations because they make it possible to eradicate weeds growing in the midst of desirable plants without harming the desirable plants. However, it should be noted that no selective herbicide yet developed kills all weeds. Neither is there one that is safe to use around all desirable plants. A few selective herbicides are called "broad spectrum" materials because they control a rather long list of weeds; but most selective herbicides are effective on only a limited number of weeds. All must be handled with great care to prevent accidental damage to desirable plants that do not happen to be resistant to the chemicals.

Nonselective herbicide. This one kills almost everything in sight.

Preemergence herbicide. This is generally thought of as a chemical that is used to kill weed seeds in the soil before they germinate. Technically, there are other kinds of preemergence herbicides, but they do not figure in the home gardener's life.

Postemergence herbicide. Used to kill plants after they have sprouted and started to grow, the three types of herbicide mentioned next below are postemergence chemicals:

Translocated herbicide. It is a chemical which, in effect, enters the bloodstream of a plant and thus affects all parts of it. If applied in adequate amounts, it usually causes the death of the plant. *Contact herbicide.* This material kills primarily by contact with plant tissues rather than as a result of translocation. Tiny plants that are treated with a contact herbicide may die. In larger plants, however, only the leaves and stems struck by the herbicide are likely to die; consequently the plants may send up new growth. *Soil sterilant.* Here is a material that kills all vegetation—the good as well as the bad—and prevents new plants from growing for months thereafter. Although you may be tempted to use a sterilant to keep weeds and grass out of driveways, walks, and the like, don't: Water running across the ground may wash the chemical out of the treated area into adjacent areas where desirable plants are growing.

Fumigant. It is usually a volatile liquid that is injected into the soil to kill weed seeds and roots. Some fumigants also kill soil insects, fungi, and bacteria. Treated soil can be planted in as soon as the last traces of the chemical have disappeared.

How To Use Chemical Weed Killers

Specific directions for using several weed killers are given later, but the following points generally apply to the use of all weed killers.

1. Identify the weeds you need to control. At the same time make sure you know what the surrounding desirable plants are. If you do not do this, you may wind up using a weed killer that damages the good plants while having no effect on the weeds. Either a knowledgeable garden supplies dealer or your state Agricultural Extension Service will identify the plants in question if you cannot do it yourself.

2. Read the package label with care. All weed killers are in some way and to some degree hazardous to humans, animals, birds, and fish. They can also damage plants that you do not want to damage. So you should never use one without studying what the manufacturer has to say about it.

3. Use the weed killer only around desirable plants that are definitely known to be tolerant or resistant to it. And do not use it around edible plants unless the manufacturer specifically says it is safe to do so.

Before a weed killer is released to the public, it must be cleared by the federal government for use on different kinds of plants. The specific plants or classifications of plants around which it can be used safely are listed on the package label. If a plant is not listed, you should keep the weed killer far away from it.

The problems that you can run into if you ignore this rule are exemplified by a homeowner who got hold of a very potent weed killer that is used by farmers to keep weeds out of corn. The man was so delighted with the effect that the chemical had in his own corn patch that he decided to try it out on the weeds in his lawn. Two years later what had been his lawn was still bare earth. Nothing —weeds or grass—would grow in it.

4. Apply the weed killer in carefully measured doses. This rule does not apply to all herbicides; but in some cases, it is of critical importance because just the slightest overdosing may result in damage to many desirable plants.

Usually, to control dosage, you must measure out the weed killer in precise amounts; and you must also measure the square footage of the area to be treated. Then apply half of the chemical evenly over the entire area, and go back and apply the other half at right angles (if possible) to the first.

(To make application of certain kinds of weed killer simpler and more accurate, several manufacturers are at this writing working on the idea of impregnating cloth or plasticlike sheets with herbicide. The sheets are spread on the ground to be weeded and then wet with water. Within several weeks, the sheets disintegrate and disappear, leaving the herbicide in the soil underneath.)

5. Prevent the weed killer from drifting to desirable plants. Chemicals that are applied as a spray or in the form of a fine dust drift in the wind. For this reason, they can be applied safely only on quiet days.

Chemicals that are applied to the soil may be carried across the garden by surface water; and in porous soil, they may be carried down into the soil in such concentrations that they injure plant roots. To avoid these problems, do not use such herbicides on slopes, bare ground, pavements or very sandy or gravelly soils. And do not drain or flush the application equipment in places where runoff or leaching may occur.

6. Mulch weeded areas in flower and vegetable gardens, shrubbery borders, and the like. The value of mulches to keep down weeds is extolled repeatedly in this book. But there is one small fly in the ointment: Unless you have a home-grown supply of mulching material, it costs a lot to cover soil deeply enough—about 3 inches—to give complete weed control with a mulch alone. However, if you treat soil with a preemergence weed killer and then cover it with mulch, you can get just as good control, or better, with only 1 inch of mulch.

The effect that the mulch has on the weed killer is also

beneficial. For one thing, it helps to hold some of the more volatile weed killers in the soil, thus giving them more opportunity to act on weed seeds. It also helps to prevent runoff water from carrying the weed killer into adjacent areas.

7. Clean sprayers and dusters thoroughly after use. Modern weed killers are so potent that even minute amounts can damage or kill plants. It follows that you must go to extremes to make sure that sprayers or dusters that have been used to apply herbicides are clean before they are used for any other purpose.

Actually, the best idea is to have one sprayer (or duster) for weed-killing and another one for applying insecticides and fungicides. If you do not want to spend so much money, the sprayer (or duster) must be thoroughly cleaned inside and out after it has been used for weed-killing. First, wash it as well as possible with clear water and run water through it. Repeat this procedure with a strong solution (at least 2 teaspoons to a quart) of household ammonia. Soak the tank overnight in a second ammonia solution. Then rinse with clear water.

8. Neutralize a preemergence herbicide that kills grass or other desirable vegetation. For example, suppose that you mistakenly treat a lawn with a weed killer that also kills grass. Or suppose that a weed killer that is safe to use only around woody plants drifts into a flower bed. What can you do to make the soil plantable soon again?

Answer: Counteract the effect of the weed killer with powdered activated carbon. If you are setting out individual plants, such as flowers or strawberries, in poisoned soil, dip the roots of each plant in the carbon; or make a slurry of the carbon and pour it around each plant. To correct a large area, as in a lawn, apply 4 to 8 ounces of activated carbon per 100 square feet of soil, and mix it in well with a rotary tiller.

Selected Weed Killers

Many superlative weed killers are too tricky or dangerous for use by anyone except professionals. A number of others, however, are safe and easy enough for the home gardener to use without fear—but always with caution.

In the descriptions below, many of the plants listed as weeds or as undesirable are not commonly thought of in this way (the birch is an example). But under certain circumstances, you might want to get rid of them; and it is useful to know how to do so.

In selecting preemergence weed killers for use in your flower beds, shrubbery borders, ground covers, vegetable garden, and around trees, you will probably find that you need several types to take care of all needs. But note that because of the questionable compatibility of some weed killers, it is advisable not to use two different chemicals close together. This means that, in order to get maximum value out of this kind of weed killer, you may want to rearrange your garden so that, say, shrubs that are safe for treatment with one chemical are well removed from those that are safe for treatment with another. You may also want to tear out flowers that cannot safely be treated with any weed killer and replace them with others that can be treated.

Amiben. This selective preemergence herbicide is used to keep weeds out of flower and vegetable gardens and shrubbery borders. It controls the following weeds:

Carpetweed	Panicgrass, fall
Chickweed	Pigweed
Crabgrass	Purslane, common
Foxtail	Ragweed
Johnsongrass (seedling)	Smartweed
Lambsquarter	Velvet leaf

Amiben can be used safely around the following plants:

Arborvitae	Holly	Pumpkin
Ash	*Iris*	*Rhododendron*
Asparagus (seedling)	Ivy, English	Rose
Aster	Juniper	Snapdragon
Azalea	Lima bean	Spirea
Celosia	Marigold	Spruce
Chrysanthemum	Peony	Squash
Dahlia	Pepper	Tomato
Daylily	*Petunia*	Yew
Dogwood	Pine	*Zinnia*
	Privet	

Amiben is applied to bare soil after it has been weeded. If no rain falls within four days, the chemical should be watered in by hose. Do not disturb the soil for several weeks thereafter. One 1½-pound package treats 250 square feet. Weeds are kept under control for six to eight weeks.

Shrubs, trees, and perennial flowers should be treated in the spring; and a second application can be made during the summer to continue weed control.

In treating transplanted annuals, perennials, shrubs, tomatoes, and peppers, first set out the plants and give them two to three weeks to become established. Then remove weeds and apply amiben. Tomatoes and peppers should not be treated again during the growing season; the other plants may be.

When planting lima beans, pumpkins, squash, and seedling asparagus, prepare the garden in the usual way, plant the seeds and at the same time sprinkle amiben around them. Be sure to water it in if rain does not fall within a few days. Do not make another application of the chemical.

The manufacturer specifically cautions against the use of amiben around pansies and seeded flowers prior to their emergence.

Amitrole-T. This translocated herbicide is applied as a

spray. It controls the following weeds and undesirable plants—some of which are not touched by other common weed killers:

Ash	Horsetail rush	Quackgrass
Bermudagrass	Kudzu	Ripgut grass
Blackberry	Locust, black	Salmonberry
Cattail	Maple, big leaf	Spurge, leafy
Cherry, wild	Milkweed	Sumac
Dock	Nutgrass	Thistle, Canada and sow
Honeysuckle	Phragmites	Water hyacinth
Horsenettle	Poison ivy	Whitetop
	Poison oak	

Although Amitrole-T kills or damages many desirable plants, it can be used around them if care is taken to prevent drifting spray from reaching them. Make application in dry weather when weeds and other pest plants are growing vigorously. Wet the foliage thoroughly. Re-treatment may be necessary in several weeks to control plants that were not thoroughly covered the first time and others arising from seeds and old roots.

Amitrole-T should not be used after October 1 in the vegetable garden; and no crops can be grown in the garden for eight months following treatment.

AMS (Ammate) is a highly soluble, granular contact herbicide that kills most plants that it strikes. It also acts as a soil sterilant for about six months. It is particularly effective in the control of poison ivy, poison oak, poison sumac, brambles, and other woody plants and weeds in driveways, terraces, and the like.

Except when it is used to kill trees and to prevent stumps from sprouting, AMS is applied as a spray. The day should be quiet; and for best results humidity should be high. Plants can be treated at any time while they are in full leaf. Wet foliage thoroughly. Make a second application if necessary.

Bandane. A granular, preemergence crabgrass killer,

Bandane is applied in the spring before crabgrass seeds germinate. Formulations containing 15 percent Bandane are applied at the rate of 35 pounds per acre; but other formulations are applied at different rates. The chemical is used on established turf; and because it shows a mild selectivity between crabgrass seed and the seeds of desirable grasses, it can also be used on seedling grass. In addition to controlling crabgrass, Bandane kills ants, grubs, and other soil insects; and it reduces earthworm populations.

Bensulide (*Betasan*). This is a preemergence chemical that controls crabgrass, annual bluegrass, redroot pigweed, watergrass, lamb's-quarters, shepherd's purse, goosegrass and deadnettle. It is safe to use around the following plants:

Grasses

Bahiagrass
Bentgrass
Bermudagrass
Bluegrass
Centipedegrass
Fescue

Poa trivialis
Red top
Ryegrass, perennial
St. Augustinegrass
Zoysia

Flowers and Bulbs

Alyssum
Aster
Bachelor's button
Calendula
Candytuft
Coral bells
Dahlia
Daisy
Freesia
Gladiolus

Marigold
Narcissus
Pansy
Primrose
Ranunculus
Stock
Sweet pea
Tulip
Wallflower
Zinnia

Shrubs and Trees

Abelia
Azalea
Azara
Boxwood
Cypress, Monterey
Daphne
Holly
Juniper

Myrtle
Pine, Monterey
Pittosporum tobira
Privet
Pyracantha
Star jasmine
Viburnum sandankwa
Zylosma

Ground Covers

Ajuga
Campanula
Dichondra
Festuca
Gazania
Hypericum

Ivy, English
Mesembryanthemum
Pachysandra
Periwinkle
Sedum
Strawberry, wild

Bensulide can be used only on established lawns (those that have been mowed at least twice) and around established flowers and woody plants. Areas planted to dichondra, however, can be treated at the time of seeding or any time thereafter.

To control crabgrass, bensulide is applied in the late winter or early spring. One gallon of Betasan 4-E mixed in 40 to 50 gallons of water treats 17,400 square feet. To control other weeds, application is made before the weeds appear. The same solution treats 13,900 square feet. (In California, a stronger solution is used for all weeds.) After application sprinkle the treated area with water for 15 minutes to wash the chemical off the grass and into the soil. The area must not be reseeded for four months (allow six to eight months if there is a drought or if the soil is heavy clay).

Cacodylic acid. This translocated weed killer is used primarily for quick removal of virtually all plant growth from an area that is to be planted or replanted. It is especially useful when you are rebuilding a lawn completely, because you can sow grass seed only two days after the area is treated.

DCPA (Dacthal). This preemergence herbicide won attention first as a crabgrass killer; but it has also proved to give excellent, though rather short-lived control of other weeds in a variety of garden areas. It is effective against the following weeds:

Amaranth, palmer	Johnsongrass
Annual bluegrass	Lamb's-quarters
Barnyardgrass	Lovegrass
Carpetweed	Millet, Texas
Chickweed, common	Panicgrass, browntop and fall
Crabgrass, hairy and smooth	Purslane, common
Dodder	Pigweed, redroot and spiny
Filaree, red stem	Sesbania
Foxtail, green and yellow	Spurge, prostrate and spotted
Goosegrass	Stinkgrass
Groundcherry, Wright's	Witchgrass

DCPA is safe to use around the following plants:

Flowers and Other Herbacecus Plants

Ageratum	*Coreopsis*	Heath, pink
Alyssum	Coral bells	*Iris*
Anchusa	*Cosmos*	Larkspur, candle
Aster	*Cuphea*	Lavender cotton
Baby's breath	*Dahlia*	Lily
Bleeding heart	*Delphinium*	Lupine
Bloodleaf	Evening primrose	Marguerite
Campanula	Feverfew	Marigold
Candytuft	Forget-me-not	Morning glory
Chrysanthemum	Four-o'clock	Mother-of-thyme
Cinquefoil	Foxglove	Nasturtium
Columbine	*Gaillardia*	Orpine
Coleus	Geranium	Peony
Coneflower, purple	*Gladiolus*	*Petunia*

Pinks, mourning	Snapdragon	Sweet pea
Portulaca	Spiderwort, Virginia	*Verbena*
Red-hot poker	Stonecrop	Violet
Salvia	Strawflower	Wormwood
Scabiosa atropurpurea	Sundrops	Yarrow, fernleaf
Scarlet sage	Sunflower	*Zinnia*

Ground Covers

Ivy, English	Honeysuckle	*Pachysandra*

Shrubs and Trees

Abelia	*Euonymus*	Peony, tree
Andromeda	Fir	Pine
Arborvitae	*Forsythia*	*Pittosporum*
Ash	Gum	*Podocarpus*
Azalea	Hawthorn	Poplar
Barberry	Holly	Privet
Boxwood	*Hydrangea*	Redbud
Birch	Juniper	*Rhododendron*
Camellia	*Lantana*	Rose
Chestnut	Lilac	*Spirea*
Cotoneaster	Locust	Spruce
Cottonwood	*Magnolia*	Sycamore
Crabapple	Maple	Tulip tree
Cypress	Mock orange	*Viburnum*
Deutzia	Mountain laurel	Walnut
Dogwood	Oak	*Weigela*
Elaeagnus	*Pachistima*	Willow
Elm		Yew

When used on lawns to control crabgrass, Dacthal W-50 (there is also a 75 percent mixture) is applied in granular form at the rate of 10 pounds per acre. The treatment should be made in the spring shortly before the weeds appear. New grass seed should not be sown for four months following treatment.

Around other plants, Dacthal W-50 is applied before weeds appear in the spring or after the area has been rid of them. On light soil, use 1 pound per 2,900 square feet; on medium soil, 1 pound per 2,400 square feet; and on heavy soil, 1 pound per 2,000 square feet. An additional application later in the year may be necessary.

Dichlobenil (Casoron). A preemergence weed killer for use around shrubs and trees, this controls the following weeds:

Annual bluegrass	Henbit	Pigweed
Carpetweed	Horsetail	Pineapple-weed
Chickweed	Knotweed	Purslane, common
Crabgrass	Lamb's-quarters	Shepherd's purse
Foxtail	Mustard	Smartweed
Groundsel	Nutsedge	Spurge

Dichlobenil is safe to use around the following plants provided they have been planted for at least four months:

Arborvitae	*Euonymus*	*Podocarpus*
Ash	Fir	Privet
Boxelder	*Forsythia*	*Pyracantha*
Boxwood	Hackberry	*Rhododendron*
Caragana	Holly	Rose
Cedar	Honeylocust	Russian olive
Cotoneaster	Juniper	Spruce
Cypress, Elwood	Pine	*Viburnum*
Elm	*Pittosporum*	Yew

The chemical must not be used around edible plants. Treated areas cannot be seeded or planted with small plants.

Application is made at any time from early spring on. Areas to be treated must first be cleared of existing weeds, cultivated thoroughly, and smoothed. Dichlobenil is then applied at the rate of ¾ ounce per 10 square feet. After this, the soil is sprinkled to wet it to a depth of about ½ inch. For best results (since the chemical is somewhat volatile), cover the treated area with a light mulch.

To control perennial weeds, such as quackgrass, mugwort, and bindweed, apply dichlobenil between November 15 and April 1 by dusting on the surface. Do not plant in the area during the next growing season, but rotary till the soil occasionally to a depth of 1 inch.

DMA. Here is a postemergence crabgrass control for use on all lawns except those containing bentgrass and St. Augustinegrass. It should be applied when the crabgrass appears and the soil is damp. Two or three applications at seven to 10-day intervals are necessary.

DMPA (Zytron). This chemical is a granular preemergence crabgrass control for lawns. It is also effective against barnyardgrass, goosegrass, prostrate knotweed, nimblewill, panicgrass, and stinkgrass.

DMPA is applied in the early spring at the rate of 15 to 20 pounds per acre. Only established turf can be treated; do not use the chemical on new grass. Bentgrass may be injured slightly. Reseeding must be delayed at least four months, otherwise the new grass will be killed.

DMTT (Mylone). This one is a fumigant that kills seeds and plant parts in treated soil. It also controls soil fungi and nematodes. It is safe to use around all plants, including edibles, provided it is not applied within 3 feet of them or under the branches of trees and shrubs.

Soil to be treated should be thoroughly cultivated to a depth of 6 inches or more, and should be kept moist enough to encourage weed seeds to germinate for several days prior to the herbicide application. Treatment should be made three weeks prior to planting desirable plants— longer if the soil temperature is below 60 degrees.

Apply 85 percent formulation DMTT at the rate of 7 pounds per 1,000 square feet with a fertilizer spreader. Then work it into the soil with a rotary tiller, or water it in with 1 inch of water. If possible, cover small areas with large sheets of polyethylene film, which further delays reinfestation with weeds. If a crust forms on the soil (whether it is covered with film or not), cultivate it shallowly five days before replanting to help rid the soil of lingering amounts of the herbicide.

EPTC (Eptam). This selective, preemergence weed killer is for use in ornamental plantings. For home gardeners it is put up in granular form, but it is also available as a liquid. It controls the following annual weeds:

Annual bluegrass
Annual ryegrass
Chickweed, common
Corn spurry
Crabgrass
Florida pusley
Foxtail, giant, green, yellow
Goosefoot, nettleleaf
Goosegrass
Henbit
Lamb's-quarters
Nightshade, hairy
Purslane, common
Pigweed, redroot, prostrate, tumbling
Sandbur
Stinkgrass

EPTC can be used safely around the following:

Flowers

Alyssum
Ageratum
Amaranthus
Aster
Balsam
Begonia
Chrysanthemum
Dahlia
Daylily
Dianthus
Marigold
Nasturtium
Pansy
Petunia
Zinnia

Ground Covers

Ajuga
Gazania
Hypericum
Ivy, English
Mesembryanthemum
Pachysandra
Periwinkle
Sedum
Strawberry (ornamental types only)

Trees and Shrubs

Andromeda
Barberry

Boxwood

Camellia

Citrus

Dogwood

Euonymus

False cypress

Fir

Hemlock

Holly, American and Japanese

Juniper

Leucothoe

Lilac

Linden

Magnolia

Maple

Oak

Pine

Podocarpus

Rhododendron

Rose

Spruce

Viburnum

Yew

EPTC is applied to ground covers, trees, and shrubs after growth starts in the spring or two weeks after they are transplanted. Flowers are treated two weeks after transplanting or when new growth is 3 to 5 inches high. Weeds that are growing must first be removed, and the soil should be pulverized. Apply Eptam 2.3 Granular at the rate of 1 pound per 200 square feet. Immediately (within minutes) after application, rake or cultivate the granules into the soil to a depth of 2 to 3 inches. The alterative is to water them in until the soil is wet 2 inches down.

EPTC can also be used to control Bermudagrass, nutgrass, and quackgrass around *established* trees and shrubs. The grasses must be hoed out; then the chemical is applied at the rate of 1 pound per 160 square feet. Mix into the soil to 3-inch depth, and water lightly for five minutes.

This herbicide is less effective on soils rich in organic matter than on those primarily of mineral composition. The manufacturer specifically warns against its use around all flowering bulbs, ornamental pepper, phlox, salvia, and snapdragon.

PMA. A postemergence crabgrass killer, PMA is applied to lawns at weekly intervals after the weeds appear. It is particularly recommended for use on bentgrass. It is likely to damage Merion bluegrass.

Siduron (Tupersan). This preemergence crabgrass killer is mixed in water and sprayed on lawns. It also controls barnyardgrass and foxtail. It can be applied to most lawn grasses except Bermuda and some bents.

Siduron is unique in that it is safe to use on young grass and on newly seeded areas as well as on established turf. Application is made in the spring. At least ½ inch of water must be provided by rainfall or watering within three days after treatment. On established grass and new grass 1 inch tall, apply the chemical at the rate of 16 to 24 pounds per acre (use the lower rate on sandy soils; the higher, on clay). On newly seeded areas, make a first application at 4 to 6 pounds per acre; follow one month later with another application at the same rate.

Silvex. This translocated weed killer is similar to 2,4,5-T. It is often used in combination with 2,4-D. It kills the following weeds and woody plants:

Ailanthus	Buttercup, corn, creeping, and tall
Alder	
Amaranth	Cat's-ear, spotted
Ammannia	Chickweed, common, field, and mouse-ear
Arrowhead	
Bedstraw	Chicory
Beggarticks	Chittam
Birdrape	Cholla, jumping
Black-eyed Susan	Coffeebean
Bladderwort	Coffeeweed
Blue mustard	Coneflower, tall
Box elder	Coyotillo
Broomweed	Croton, Texas and woolly
Bullthistle	Dandelion
Burclover	Desert parsley
Burdock, common	Dock, broadleaf and smooth
Burhead	Dogfennel

Ducksalad
Evening primrose
Fanwort
Fiddleneck, coast
Fleabane, annual and rough
Galinsoga, hairy
Geranium, Carolina
Groundcherry, Wright's
Ground ivy
Groundsel, cressleaf
Hedge mustard
Henbit
Honeysuckle
Horseweed, mare's tail
Knapweed, spotted
Knawel, annual
Kochia
Lamb's-quarters, common
Locust, black
Loosestrife, purple
Lotus, American
Lupine, silvery
Maple
Marsh-elder
Medic, black
Mexican-tea
Mexican-weed
Milkvetch
Milkweed, showy
Morning glory
Mule-ears
Mustard, black, Indian, wild
Needlerush
Nightshade, purple
Norcalbean
Oak, post, shinnery, turkey

Palmetto, saw
Parrotfeather
Partridgepea
Passionflower
Pennycress, field
Pennywort, lawn
Peppergrass, clasping, Virginia, yellowflower
Persimmon, Texas
Pickerelweed
Pigwood
Plantain, blackseed, common, English
Poison hemlock
Poison ivy
Poison oak
Pokeweed
Ponyfoot
Primrose-willow
Purslane, common
Radish, wild
Ragweed
Redbud
Redstem
Rocket, London
Rose, Cherokee
Rush
Russian thistle
Sagebrush, sand
Salmonberry
Saltcedar
Shepherd's purse
Smartweed, Japanese and lady's thumb
Spanish-needles

Spatterdock

Speedwell, purslane

Sumac, Chinese

Sunflower, common

Swamp loosestrife

Tie-vine

Trumpet creeper

Vetch, wild

Water hemlock, spotted

Water hyacinth

Waterlily

Water milfoil

Water plantain, common

Water primrose

Watershield

Water stargrass

Water starwort

White clover

Wild celery

Willow

Willowweed

Woodsorrel, yellow

Wormseed-mustard

Yucca smalliana

Silvex is applied in the same way as 2,4-D (which see).

SMDC (Vapam). This one is a fumigant that kills seeds, plant parts, nematodes, fungi, and insects in treated soil. It is safe to use around all desirable plants, including edibles, provided it is not applied within 3 feet of them or under the branches of trees and shrubs.

Cultivate soil to a depth of 6 inches or more and keep it damp for several days before applying the fumigant. Treatment should be made two weeks prior to planting of desirable plants; four weeks, if soil temperature is below 60 degrees.

Use 33 percent formulation and apply 2 to 3 gallons per 1,000 square feet with a watering can or sprayer. Immediately work the herbicide into the soil with a rotary tiller and water the surface, or water it in with about 1 inch of water. Covering with polyethylene film is advisable but not necessary. One week after application cultivate the soil shallowly to allow gas to escape. Planting can be started a week later (if soil is not cold).

Trifluralin (Treflan). Here a preemergence weed killer used to kill the germinating seeds of broadleaf and grassy weeds and also grassy weeds up through the two-leaf stage. It is effective against the following:

Annual bluegrass
Barnyardgrass
Brachiaria
Bromegrass
Carlesweed
Carpetweed
Cheat
Chickweed
Crabgrass
Florida pussley
Foxtail
Goosefoot
Goosegrass
Johnsongrass
Jungle rice

Knotweed
Kochia
Lamb's-quarters
Nettle, stinging
Panicgrass, Texas
Pigweed, spiny and redroot
Puncturevine
Purslane, common
Russian thistle
Sandbur
Shepherd's purse
Smartweed
Sprangletop
Stinkgrass

Trifluralin is safe to use around the following plants provided they are established (flowers must be at least 2 inches, and preferably 3 inches, high):

Flowers

Achillea
Ageratum
Arctotis
Aster
Balsam
Calendula
California poppy
Calliopsis
Carnation
Centaurea
Cosmos
Dahlia
Dianthus

Dimorphotheca
Forget-me-not
Four-o'clock
Gaillardia
Gladiolus
Hollyhock
Lobelia
Lupine
Marigold
Morning glory
Nasturtium
Nicotiana
Periwinkle

Petunia
Portulaca
Rudbeckia
Scabiosa
Shasta daisy
Snapdragon
Snow-on-the-mountain
Stock
Sunflower
Sweet alyssum
Sweet pea
Sweet William
Zinnia

Trees and Shrubs

Apple
Arborvitae (*Thuja occidentalis, T. o. nigra,* and *T. o. pyramidalis*)

Ash, white
Azalea indicum formosa, obtusum hindoegiri, and *obtusum
    kaempferi*
Bald cypress
Barberry (*Berberis mentorensis*)
Birch, European white
Boxwood (*Buxus microphylla* and *sempervirens*)
Camellia japonica and *sasanqua*
Cherry-laurel (*Laurocerasus caroliniana*)
Chestnut, Chinese
Cleyera japonica
Cotoneaster apiculata and *zabellii*
Cottonwood
Dogwood, flowering and kousa
Douglas fir
Elaeagnus pungens
Euonymus alatus, fortunei and Newport
Feijoa sellowiana
Fir, balsam
Forsythia
Gum, sour
Hemlock, Canada
Holly (*Ilex crenata* and *hetzii*)
Honeylocust
Juniper, Pfitzer, Hetz's, shore
Larch, Japanese
Locust, black
Maple, Norway, red, silver, sugar
Mock orange
Oak, pin, red, scarlet
Pine, Austrian, Japanese black, red, Scotch, white
Pittosporum
Plane, London
Podocarpus
Privet (*Ligustrum erectum, japonicum, odoratissimum,
    ovalifolium, vicary*)

Prunus species
Pyracantha
Redbud
Red cedar
Rose
Spruce, Colorado blue, Norway, white
Sweet gum
Sycamore
Tulip-tree
Viburnum odoratissimum, plicatum, suspensum, wrightii
Walnut, black
Weigela
Yeddo hawthorn
Yew (*Taxus cuspidata* and *media*)

The manufacturer specifically cautions against the use of trifluralin on ground covers.

When applied in the early spring, trifluralin usually gives complete weed control throughout the growing season. The area to be treated should first be freed of weeds, cultivated, and smoothed. Work the powder lightly into the upper inch of soil. Watering is not necessary but increases the activity of the chemical.

One package of pure trifluralin—weighing 1 pound and 9 ounces—covers 250 square feet. (The chemical is also sold in packages containing special fertilizer mixtures. These weigh 2 pounds and 8 ounces and cover 400 square feet. Two applications are necessary for continued weed control.)

Although trifluralin is used by farmers in raising a number of edible crops, it is not recommended for use in the home vegetable garden. The manufacturer further warns that soil treated with the chemical should not be planted to vegetables for one year.

2,4-D. This familiar translocated chemical is used as a spray or dust to kill broadleaf weeds and various woody plants, including the following:

Absinthe
Alder
Amaranth
Ammannia
Arrowhead
Aspen, quaking
Aster ericoides
Bachelor's button
Baileya, desert
Ballmustard
Barberry, Colorado
Beggarticks
Bindweed, hedge
Birdrape
Bittercress
Bitterweed
Blackeyed Susan
Blessed thistle
Bloodweed
Box elder
Broomweed
Bullnettle
Bullthistle
Burdock
Burhead
Bur reed
Burroweed
Bush honeysuckle
Buttercup, corn, small-flower, tall
Buttonbush
Carpetweed
Catnip
Cat's-ear, spotted
Ceanothus, wedgeleaf
Chicory

Cinquefoil
Cocklebur, common
Coffeeweed
Coneflower, tall
Coontail, common
Coralberry
Cottonwood
Coyote bush
Croton, Lindheimer, Texas, woolly
Currant
Dandelion
Dayflower
Deathcamas
Deerbrush
Deerweed
Desert parsley
Devil's-claw
Dock
Dogbane, spreading
Dog fennel, yellow
Dogmustard
Ducksalad
Evening primrose
Falseflax
False hellebore, California
Fanwort
Fiddleneck, coast
Filaree, redstem
Fleabane
Florida pusley
Flower-of-an-hour
Four-o'clock, wild
Galinsoga, hairy
Geranium, Carolina
Goatsbeard

Gooseberry

Goosefoot, nettleleaf, oakleaf

Groundcherry, Wright's

Groundsel, cressleaf, riddell

Gumweed

Hare's-ear mustard

Hawkweed

Heal-all

Hedge mustard

Hemp, wild

Hogpeanut

Hydrangea, smooth

Ironweed, western

Jerusalem artichoke

Jewelweed

Jimson weed

Knapweed, black and diffuse

Knotweed, sakhalin

Kochia

Lamb's-quarters, common

Leatherwood

Lettuce, prickly

Locoweed

Lotebush

Lotus, American

Lupine

Marsh elder

Mexican tea

Milkvetch, astralagus and
   two-grooved

Milkweed, bloodflower

Moneywort

Morning glory

Mountain misery

Mule-ears

Mustard

Needlerush

Nettle

Orache

Parsnip, wild

Partridgepea

Pea, wild

Peavine

Pennycress, field

Pennywort

Peppergrass

Persimmon, Texas

Pickerelweed

Pigweed

Pincherry

Plantain

Poison hemlock

Ponyfoot

Poorjoe

Poplar, balsam

Poppy, Roemer

Povertyweed

Prickle poppy

Primrose-willow

Puncturevine

Radish, wild

Ragweed

Rape, wild

Redstem

Rocket, annual London

Rubberweed

Rush

Russian pigweed

Russian thistle

Sage

Sagebrush

Salsify, western

Sandwort, thymeleaf
Saskatoon
Sassafras
Scotch broom
Sea myrtle
Shadbush
Shepherd's purse
Skeletonweed
Skunkbrush
Skunk cabbage
Smartweed, Pennsylvania and water
Sorrel, heartwing, sour-dock
Sourwood
Sowthistle, annual and spiny
Spanish needles
Speedwell, purslane
Spicebush
Stickseed, European
Stinkwort
Sumac
Sumpweed, rough
Sunflower
Sweetclover, yellow annual
Swinecress
Sycamore
Tansymustard
Tansy-ragwort

Tarbush
Tickseed
Toyon
Tumblemustard
Velvetleaf
Vervain
Vetch
Viburnum, maple-leaf
Walnut, black
Waterchestnut
Watercress
Water hemlock, spotted
Water horehound
Water hyacinth
Waterlily
Water milfoil
Water primrose
White clover
Willow
Willowweed
Witchweed
Wolfwillow
Wormseed-mustard
Wormwood
Yellow-rattle
Yellow-rocket
Yerba-santa

Although innumerable plants—bad and good—are resistant to 2,4-D, you should not use it near any desirable plant except on very still days. Even then, you must use great care not to let the spray, dust or volatile fumes drift. When using 2,4-D on bentgrass, on a brand new lawn of any kind, or on a lawn containing clover that you want to save, apply it at one-quarter to one-half normal strength. The strength also should be reduced 50 percent for St. Augustinegrass.

2,4-D is more effective when applied on warm (but not over 85 degree), sunny days when no rain is expected for eight hours, when the soil is damp, and when weeds are growing actively. Do not use on a lawn immediately after mowing: Wait several days for the clippings to settle. Apply just enough of the chemical to moisten or dust the foliage lightly. Do not get any more on the soil than necessary. One application is usually enough, but if weeds are not dead within three weeks, make a second. Weeds usually take two to four weeks to die.

2,4,5-T. This translocated herbicide is related to 2,4-D and is often sold in combination with it. Although it kills many broadleaf weeds, it is used mainly to control woody plants not affected by 2,4-D. It is effective against the following:

Ailanthus	Bullthistle
Alder	Burcucumber
Alyssum, hoary	Burdock, common
Amaranth	Burhead
Ammannia	Burroweed
Arrowhead	Buttercup, corn, creeping, tall
Aspen	Buttonbush
Baileya, desert	Catnip
Barberry, Allegheny	Cat's-ear, spotted
Beggarticks	*Ceanothus*, varnishleaf and wedgeleaf
Bindweed, hedge	
Birch	Chickweed, common and field
Birdrape	Chicory
Biscuit root	Chittam
Bitterweed	Cinquefoil, sulfur
Blackberry	Cocklebur, common
Black-eyed Susan	Coffeebean
Bladderwort	Coneflower, tall
Blue mustard	Coontail, common
Box elder	Coyotillo
Broomweed	Croton, Texas and woolly
Bullnettle	Currant

Daisy, oxeye
Dandelion
Deerweed
Dock, broadleaf, curly, smooth
Dogfennel
Ducksalad
Elderberry
Evening primrose
Fiddleneck, coast
Fleabane, annual and rough
Flower-of-an-hour
Galinsoga, hairy
Geranium, Carolina
Gooseberry
Goosefoot, nettleleaf, oakleaf
Groundcherry, Wright's
Groundsel, cressleaf
Guava, common
Hackberry
Hedgemustard
Hemp, wild
Horseweed, mare's tail
Indigo, curly
Ironweed, western
Ivy, English
Jerusalem artichoke
Jimson weed
Kochia
Lamb's-quarters, common
Leptotaenia, carrotleaf
Lilac
Locust, black
Lotebush
Lotus, American
Lupine, rivularia and silvery
Magnolia

Marsh-elder
Mexican-tea
Mexican-weed
Milkweed, bloodleaf
Morning glory
Mountain misery
Mule-ears
Mustard
Norcalbean
Oak, post, shinnery, white
Orache
Osage orange
Parsnip, wild
Partridgepea
Pea tree
Peavine
Pellitoryweed
Pennycress, field
Pennywort, lawn
Pepperweed, clasing, field,
   Virginia, yellow-flower
Pickerelweed
Pigweed
Plantain, blackseed, common,
   English
Poison ivy
Poison oak
Poison sumac
Pokeweed
Ponyfoot
Poorjoe
Primrose-willow
Purslane, common
Radish, wild
Ragweed
Redbay

Redstem
Rocket, annual London
Rose, prairie
Russian thistle
Sage, creeping
Sagebrush, big, California,
 sand
Salmonberry
Sassafras
Scotch broom
Sea myrtle
Shepherd's purse
Skunk cabbage
Smartweed, lady's thumb and
 Pennsylvania
Snowbrush
Snow-on-the-mountain
Sorrel, sour dock
Sowthistle, annual and spiny
Spanish-needles
Speedwell, purslane
Spicebush
Spirea
Spurge, flowering
Sumac

Sunflower, common
Sweet gum
Sycamore
Thimbleberry
Tickseed
Tulip-tree
Tumblemustard
Velvetleaf
Vetch
Viburnum, maple-leaf
Water hemlock, spotted
Water hyacinth
Water milfoil
Water plantain, common
Water primrose
White clover
Wild buckwheat
Wild indigo
Willow
Willowweed
Witch hazel
Witchweed
Wormseed-mustard
Wormwood, annual
Yellow rocket

2,4,5-T is applied in the same way as 2,4-D (which see).

What Weed Killers to Use for Specific Purposes

Controlling crabgrass in lawns. In building a new lawn, fumigate the soil with DMTT or SMDC; or apply siduron at half strength at time of seeding. In established lawns, apply Bandane, bensulide, DCPA, DMPA, or siduron to prevent crabgrass seeds from germinating.

For established lawns, many gardeners use herbicides that come mixed with fertilizers (and sometimes with insecticides as well). These are work savers (because you apply both materials at the same time) provided they are effective. You should ask two questions before using them: (1) Is the herbicide in the package one of those listed in the paragraph above? It should be, because these are the best at this writing. (2) Are the season for applying fertilizer and the season for applying preemergence crabgrass killer the same? Your state Agricultural Extension Service can best answer this.

You may wonder also whether the combination herbicides-fertilizers contain enough of each material to do the best possible job. This is almost impossible to determine simply by looking at a package label; but as a rule they do.

One definite problem with the combinations, however, is that you can use them only on the lawn. The presence of the herbicide makes them unsafe to use in flower and vegetable gardens.

Controlling broadleaf weeds in lawns. When building a new lawn, fumigate the soil with DMTT or SMDC. In established lawns, spray or dust 2,4-D or a combination of 2,4-D and silvex on growing weeds; or to prevent all drift hazards, daub a solution of these chemicals on individual weeds. The timing of treatment depends on whether the lawn has been treated with a preemergence crabgrass killer. If it has been treated, the broadleaf weeds can be killed at any time. But if the lawn has not been treated for crabgrass control, delay action against the broadleaves until late summer (otherwise crabgrass is likely to come up in the spots vacated by the broadleaves).

For whether you should use "weed-and-feed" materials to control broadleaf weeds in established lawns, see the paragraphs above about controlling crabgrass.

Treating weeds and grasses in paved areas. Spray with

AMS. Be careful not to allow the spray to reach adjacent planted areas.

Handling weeds in flower beds. Treat soil with amiben, bensulide, DCPA, EPTC, or trifluralin.

Controlling weeds in rose gardens. Treat soil with amiben, DCPA, dichlobenil, EPTC or trifluralin.

Treating weeds around trees and shrubs. Treat soil with amiben, bensulide, DCPA, dichlobenil, EPTC, or trifluralin.

Handling weeds in ground covers. Before planting the ground cover, fumigate soil with DMTT or SMDC. In existing beds of some ground covers, apply bensulide or EPTC. DCPA may also be used on pachysandra.

Controlling weeds in vegetable gardens. Before planting, fumigate soil with DMTT or SMDC. Amiben can be used around lima beans, peppers, pumpkins, squash, tomatoes, and seedling asparagus.

Treating weeds in berry patches. Before planting, fumigate soil with DMTT or SMDC.

Controlling poison ivy, poison oak, and poison sumac. Spray with AMS, Amitrole-T, 2,4,5-T or so-called brush killers (mixtures of 2,4-D and 2,4,5-T).

Eliminating underbrush and weeds in woodlands. Spray when plants are in full leaf. Be careful to avoid spray drift. To kill large trees and shrubs, apply AMS to the trunks in the manner described below.

Herbicides used for woodland weed control are 2,4-D, 2,4,5-T, silvex, AMS, Amitrole-T, and combinations of 2,4-D and 2,4,5-T. Which one you use depends on what plants are to be killed, of course. But you should also consider what trees you want to save, and try to use chemicals that will do the least damage to them.

According to the *Herbicide Manual*, published by the U.S. Department of Agriculture, the following common trees are hard to kill with the chemicals listed:

Ash—silvex, 2,4-D, 2,4,5-T, and AMS (but combinations of 2,4-D and 2,4,5-T are dangerous)
Basswood—2,4-D, 2,4,5-T, AMS
Beech—2,4-D, 2,4,5-T
Birch—2,4-D
Chinquapin—2,4-D, 2,4,5-T
Cottonwood—2,4,5-T
Dogwood—2,4-D, 2,4,5-T, silvex
Elm—2,4-D, 2,4,5-T
Fir, balsam, red, white—2,4-D
Fir, balsam—AMS
Gum, sour—2,4-D, 2,4,5-T, silvex
Hemlock, Canada—2,4-D, 2,4,5-T
Hickory—2,4-D, 2,4,5-T, silvex
Honeylocust—2,4-D, 2,4,5-T, AMS
Hop hornbeam—2,4,5-T
Juniper—silvex, 2,4-D, 2,4,5-T, AMS
Kentucky coffee tree—2,4,5-T
Larch—2,4,5-T
Maple—2,4-D, 2,4,5-T
Oak, black, Oregon, post, shinnery, turkey, white—2,4-D
Oak, blackjack, bluejack, gambel, live, red, scrub—2,4,5-T
Persimmon—2,4,5-T, silvex
Pine, jack, red, white—2,4-D, 2,4,5-T
Pine, lodgepole—2,4,5-T
Red cedar, eastern—2,4-D, 2,4,5-T
Sweet gum—2,4-D
Tamarack—2,4-D, 2,4,5-T

Killing undesirable trees and large shrubs. Make a continuous cut or "frill" around the trunk near the base with an ax. The cuts should slant downward and go through the bark into the sapwood. Fill the frill with a continuous band of dry AMS crystals, or saturate it with a solution of 4 pounds AMS to 9½ pints water.

Keeping tree stumps from sprouting. Cover the freshly cut stump surface, especially around the edges, with dry AMS. Or spray or swab the stump surface liberally with a solution of 4 pounds AMS to 9½ pints water. This treatment is effective at any time of year.

Controlling aquatic weeds in ponds, lakes, and brooks. Do not do this. It is a tricky and hazardous operation—so much so that some states require that each project be licensed.

If you have water that needs to be weeded, ask your state department of fish and game or pesticide control board to recommend a professional to do the job for you.

XI  Terracing Sloping Land

The usual ways of dealing with a sloping residential lot are to leave it as is or to grade it into a series of more or less flat terraces (sometimes called benches or bench terraces). The reasons for terracing sloping land are many but only two are important here. One is to flatten the land in order to retard the runoff of water. The dual effect of this is to reduce or actually stop erosion and the work that it causes and thus to shorten the time you must spend using hoses and sprinklers.

The other reason for leveling land is simply to make all gardening work easier; for who can deny that it takes less time and energy to mow, dig, rake, and so forth, on flat land than on hilly land?

Terracing is discussed in several places in this book. Here I shall try to cover the subject thoroughly.

When to terrace? Unfortunately, I must start out by admitting that there is no pat answer to the question of when a lot slopes enough to justify terracing.

If your only concern were erosion, a soil and water conservation engineer could tell you in short order whether your lot would benefit by terracing. Erosion control is today a well-understood science.

But no one knows which slopes are hard for the gardener to work on and which are not. For one thing, no one has figured out how much energy a person exerts when gardening. For another thing—as I said in Chapter III—no two people react in exactly the same way to a given slope; and for that matter, no single person reacts in the same way every hour of the day and every day of the year.

How then can I or anyone else say to you (if you are the owner of a sloping lot): "You can make gardening work a great deal easier if you terrace your lot" or "Terracing won't help you a bit"?

I can't.

All I can tell you is what you already know: The difficulty of doing gardening work on a slope depends first of all on the kind of work you are doing. In other words, mowing is more arduous than raking; and raking is more arduous than kneeling on the ground and cultivating the soil with a three-pronged hand cultivator.

In addition, the difficulty of doing gardening work on a slope depends on the slope itself: (1) How steep is it? (2) How high is it, or if it is a gentle slope, how long is it? (3) What is the soil like? (4) How much traction does the soil-covering provide?

These questions are four good criteria for determining whether a sloping lot should be terraced. If you have been living on the lot for any length of time, the answers to each question are probably obvious. If you are looking at an undeveloped lot, however, you should quiz yourself carefully.

First, consider the steepness of the slope. Does it worry you in the slightest as you look at it? What is your reaction when you walk up and down it? Do you think it would bother you only when you mow the grass? (If that is the case, perhaps only the lawn area needs to be terraced.) Or do you think it would make all gardening work more difficult?

Second, consider the height or length of the slope. It should be obvious that the higher a steep slope is, the more quickly it will tire you. Similarly, the longer a gentle slope is, the more quickly it will tire you if you have to walk back and forth from one end to the other.

Third, consider the soil underlying the slope. The chances are it is ordinary stuff and therefore will not affect working conditions on the hillside in one way or another. But there are places in the United States where the soil is almost pure sand; and as anyone who has ever climbed a sand dune knows, this is miserable to walk on even when it is stabilized with dune grass.

Fourth, consider what covers the soil. Many soilcovering materials that are easy and pleasant to walk on on flat land are treacherously slippery on a hillside. Pine needles are one of these. Grass turned brown and dry by summer drought is another. Even the most luxuriant lawn grass can make your feet slide out from under you when it is damp.

Finally, consider the total results of your little study. True, you do not need more than one reason for terracing a sloping lot if it is a sufficiently compelling reason. But if there are two reasons, or even three, then there can be no question about the need for terracing.

Terracing a sloping lot. The sketches show just a few of the countless ways that slopes, viewed in cross section, are most commonly terraced. But it is doubtful that any of these is "just right" for a given lot.

The correct way of terracing depends on many things: the size of the lot; its contours; the way it is to be landscaped; the size of the house; whether there is to be a swimming pool; how much flat space is desired and for what purposes; whether a high bank is needed at the rear of the lot to provide protection against winds and/or neighboring houses; how neighboring lots are terraced; and so forth.

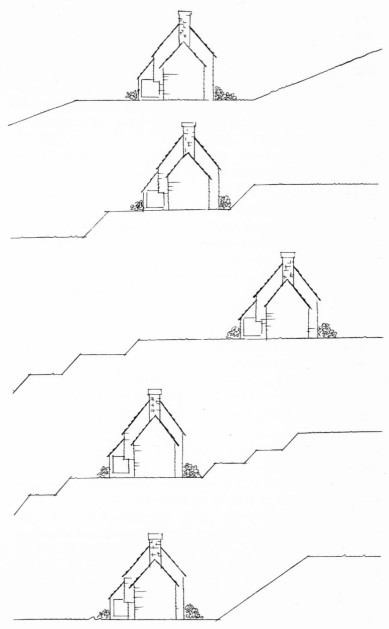

Here are several ways to terrace a sloping lot.

Terracing of a lot, in other words, needs to be studied carefully—perhaps with the help of a landscape architect and maybe even an expert on erosion. There are no rules that you must follow. Here, however, are several terracing practices that may be rated as generally sound:

1. Provide a flat area next to your house on the uphill side. This may help to let more daylight into the house, and it keeps water coming off the hill away from the foundations. However, it is also possible to solve the water problem by building diversion ditches on the side of the hill above the house.

2. Make level areas as large as possible. They greatly increase the usefulness of the lot and also help to make your gardening work easier.

3. Don't, however, make level areas so large that you are forced to make the banks or walls supporting the terraces extremely high. As a rule, the higher the vertical surfaces on a terraced lot, the less attractive they are. Furthermore, high banks are much harder to maintain than low ones; and high walls are much more difficult and expensive to build than low ones.

This is not to say that an unusually high bank or wall does not sometimes serve a purpose that warrants its construction. For example, it may help to shield the rest of the property from winds. Or it may serve as a privacy screen. Or it may be needed as a backdrop for the rest of the landscape plan.

4. In areas where foot traffic is heavy (the front yard, for example), limit the height of banks or walls to 5 feet. The purpose of this is to eliminate long flights of steps, which are tiring to walk up and dangerous to walk down.

The Federal Housing Administration's Minimum Property Standards stipulate that the maximum total rise of a single flight of exterior steps should be 5 feet and that the landing at the top of each flight should be at least 3 feet long. These dimensions need not rule your life, but they constitute a good guide.

In less heavily traveled areas, of course, long flights of steps are less objectionable. Even so, you should avoid them if possible.

5. Provide ramps between each terrace so that lawn mowers, wheelbarrows, bicycles, and the like, can move smoothly from one level to another. For safety's sake, they should slope no more than 2 inches per foot. Anything steeper would also be tiring to ascend.

6. Do not slope driveways more than 1¾ inches per foot.

Building banks. Banks are easier and cheaper to build than walls, and they become progressively easier and cheaper the higher they go. But from the standpoint of easy maintenance, banks do not hold a candle to walls. They are subject to erosion. If they are covered with grass, they need to be mowed; and if covered with any other kind of plant material, the plants must be given a certain amount of care to keep them healthy and attractive. Furthermore, banks planted with a ground cover tend to become cluttered with trash that has to be cleaned out occasionally. And to complete this list of problems—banks invite plant trampling traffic that walls discourage (for example, children sometimes use banks as sliding boards, and grown-ups may use them as shortcuts across the countryside). Be all this as it may, people do build banks; and perhaps you will, too. In that case, remember that a bank should not slope more than 1 foot vertically in 3 horizontal feet if it is to be covered with grass that you intend to keep cut. To simplify mowing, round off the ground at the top of the bank so that your mower does not "hang up" on what would otherwise be a sharply angled ridge; and round off the ground at the bottom of the bank so that the mower moves smoothly from the slope to the flat and vice versa.

On steeper banks, plant an evergreen perennial or woody ground cover that will hold the soil and will not require too much attention. Descriptions of a long list of excellent ground cover plants are given in Chapter VII. On very steep banks and in very rainy climates you should set the plants unusually close together to minimize erosion until the plants are large enough to cover the soil completely. Other ways to minimize erosion during this period are to cover the bare soil with burlap or a mesh material called Erosionet or to set boards on edge between the plants as miniature dams.

Extremely steep banks—those with a slope of 1 foot vertically to 1 foot horizontally or more—need to be supported with large stones or timbers in addition to woody ground covers. If you use stones, dig them in so that they are buried to at least half their depth. Set them at random about 1 foot apart—or less if you live in an area with heavy rainfall.

The best timbers for reinforcing banks are old railroad ties, but smaller timbers or tree trunks that have been thoroughly impregnated with wood preservative can be used. Lay the timbers up the bank in closely spaced steps. To hold them in place, dig them slightly into the soil and drive 18-inch stakes into the bank in front of them.

Timbered banks are not always planted but look better if they are. Banks reinforced with stones must be planted unless the stones are set edge to edge; otherwise the soil between them will soon be washed out.

Building retaining walls. To achieve maximum work savings on a sloping lot, terrace it with walls rather than banks. Walls do not need to be mowed or planted with a ground cover. They do not erode; nor are they damaged by people climbing over them (if anyone is foolish enough to try). If they have to be painted occasionally, it is your own fault for having painted them in the first place.

The only problems in building walls to support terraces are the difficulty and cost of construction. The reason: Because of the weight and pressure of the soil and

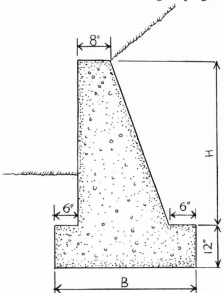

Concrete retaining wall has a wide base to keep it from tipping.

water behind the walls, there is always danger that the walls may be toppled over. Therefore, they must be more scientifically designed and carefully constructed than ordinary walls.

The illustration above shows one type of retaining wall recommended by the Portland Cement Association. It is made of poured concrete, and has both extra thickness at the base and a wide footing to prevent tipping. A wall with a height (H) of 6 feet should have a base (B) 4 feet wide.

It is pretty obvious that to build a high retaining wall like this is a major undertaking—especially for the home-owner. Low retaining walls—those no more than 3 feet high *above ground*—are relatively simple, however, because the pressure behind them is generally not too great.

Poured concrete, because of its weight and strength, makes the best retaining wall. The footing should be at least 8 inches deep and should extend 6 inches in front of the wall and 12 inches behind. The bottom of the footing should be at least 18 inches below ground level. The wall itself should be 8 to 12 inches thick and have straight sides, front and back. To relieve water pressure behind the wall, make weepholes 3 inches in diameter at 10-foot intervals through the wall just above the ground line.

A less sturdy retaining wall, but one that should be satisfactory in well-drained soil, is made with concrete blocks. Build a footing in the way described above. To reinforce the wall, insert ½-inch reinforcing rods down through the cavities in the blocks and well into the footing. The rods should be spaced 2 feet apart, and the cavities around them should be filled with concrete. Top the wall with concrete cap block.

If soil in a terrace is extremely sandy or gravelly, or if there is a great deal of bedrock under the terrace, dry walls made of rock or railroad ties can be built. In both cases, the walls should extend down below the frost line and rest on a thick base of crushed rock. Slant them backward 2 to 3 inches in each vertical foot.

In a rock wall you should, for the most part, use rocks that are so large that you are just able to handle them. Make the wall 18 to 24 inches thick.

In a wood wall, lay the ties horizontally, end to end, and stagger the joints from one tier to the next. Spike the ties together—but loosely, so that the water can flow out through the joints.

No matter how a retaining wall is constructed, if grass is planted at the foot, a mowing strip about 6 inches wide should be installed flush with the lawn. This will eliminate grass trimming (see Chapter III).

A shrubbery border, flower bed, or wide strip of ground cover should be planted at the top of the wall to keep the unwary from getting too close to the edge. To prevent the soil in such a border from washing down over the wall in heavy storms, level it off 1 to 2 inches below the top of the wall.

XII  Growing Plants in Raised Beds

The initial reaction of most gardeners to the suggestion that they elevate their flower beds above the lawn and other garden areas is a pleasantly surprised: "Why, isn't that a good idea! Then I won't have to lean over so much when I'm working. And I won't have to kneel. Why I can even sit down to work!"

I am of the opinion, however, that this advantage of raised beds is secondary to another: The walls surrounding the beds keep out encroaching grass and tree roots. And they protect the plants from passing bicycles, errant dogs, and people who simply don't look where they are going.

But why argue the point? The simple truth is that raised beds are topnotch labor savers in several ways. They can also add to the appearance of gardens by providing a change of elevation on flat land; by "scaling down" the high walls and fences against which they are often placed; by serving as colorful railings or parapets on porches and raised terraces; and by cutting garden spaces visually in two.

And for added measure—raised beds permit you easily to give pernickity plants the special soil mixtures they

Raised planting bed in a Boston garden is not only easier to tend but also protects plants from children playing in the area.

Raised beds add to the sculptured lines of this large Florida garden.

require. You can have beds with different degrees of pH, different amounts of sand, different amounts of humus, and so on. It is much simpler to change and maintain soil conditions in a definite, walled-in space than in the open garden.

Defining a raised bed. It is nothing more than a plot of cultivated soil raised above the surrounding garden and held in by low walls. It is very much like a well-filled children's sandbox except that it need not have a solid bottom.

Where to use. Unless you have back troubles that require you to elevate all plant beds, you should build raised beds, first, where plants need protection from passing traffic and, second, where the beds will serve a useful aesthetic purpose. I can think of plenty of situations in which raised beds built for aesthetic reasons do not have a practical, plant-protecting role. I can also think of situations where beds built to protect plants do not play an aesthetic role. But ideally, raised beds should serve both purposes.

It is no trick to determine which of your flower beds needs to be raised for the safety of the flowers (and to relieve you of the necessity of protecting and replacing them). But to decide which old beds should be raised or which new raised beds should be built for aesthetic reasons is something else again. This question is one of design; and as I have said before in this book landscape design is a problem that you should let the experts (meaning in this case, the landscape architects) solve.

This much is fairly obvious, however: As a general rule, the best place (aesthetically) to build a raised bed is against a high, blank wall, fence, or hedge. For one thing, the bed helps to relieve the blankness of the wall and to make it look lower. For another thing, the bed does not look so high itself because it is next to a wall that is even higher.

In short, the relationship of a raised bed and a blank wall is so logical, and the effect of one on the other is usually so good, that you can hardly make a mistake in juxtaposing them.

Another good way to use a raised bed is as a barrier or divider. Most such beds are long and narrow and—for reasons that are unknown to me—are called planters. If you have ever looked around a development of contemporary homes, you almost certainly have seen planters used to keep people from falling off front stoops; and in these locations they look completely natural because they are taking the place of railings. Less common are planters that are used to delineate where a parking area that sweeps right up to the front door ceases to be a parking area and becomes a front walk. Planters of this kind are

Beds of herbs at the John Blair Kitchen in Colonial Williamsburg are raised just a few inches, not to make them easier to maintain, but to keep dirt and mulch off the walks and thus to make them easier to keep clean.

akin to those used inside houses to separate the front hall from the living room, or the living room from the dining alcove. But they, too, appear quite natural—because they serve a definite purpose. Still another kind of raised bed that usually looks good is the one that is built in a circle around the base of a tree.

But large, low, raised beds that are, in effect, set out in the middle of nowhere are something else again. Unless a first-rate designer has a hand in creating these, they are likely to look completely out of place.

Dimensions. The degree to which a raised bed saves work depends on how high it is and how deep it is. (The length is immaterial.)

The minimum height is 6 inches. Anything lower is unlikely to stop a bicyclist and is difficult to sit down on and get up from. (Even 6 inches is difficult.)

If you are going to sit on the raised bed wall while you work, the maximum height is 24 inches plus or minus 2 or 3 inches, depending on the length of your legs. On the other hand, if you are content to work standing up, the height of the bed can range from about 30 to 42 inches.

If one of your purposes in raising a flower bed is to make it easier to work in, it should not exceed 30 inches in depth. This is about as far as you can comfortably reach whether you are sitting on the edge of the bed or standing and leaning over it.

On the other hand, if you want to climb right into the bed while you work, you can make it as deep as you want. In this case, however, it should not be much more than 15 inches high. That is about as high a step as most people can manage—especially when they are laden with rakes and cultivators.

Construction. If you build a raised bed against a hillside or a concrete or masonry wall, you need to construct retaining walls only in front and on the sides. If you build the bed against a wood wall or fence, however, you need retaining walls on all four sides. Otherwise, the wall or fence will soon rot out or be devoured by termites. (Free-standing raised beds obviously need walls on four sides, too.)

The walls are best constructed of masonry, but may be of heavy redwood or cypress lumber or of railroad ties. Masonry walls should be secured to poured concrete footings laid at least 18 inches deep. The width of the footing should be twice the thickness of the wall; the depth should equal the wall thickness. Wood walls do not require footings, but it is a good idea to stabilize them by bolting the pieces of lumber together and bracing them with heavy timbers slanted against the front wall, underground. Another way to stabilize them is to bury a heavy concrete block inside the raised bed and to tie the walls to it with iron rods.

If a wall is over 24 inches in height and the soil in the bed is not well drained, provide 1- to 2-inch weepholes at about 6-foot intervals in the wall just above the outside ground level.

Walls less than 8 inches thick are not wide enough to sit on comfortably and keep your slacks clean; so they should be capped with flagstones, heavy planks, bricks laid at right angles to the wall, or the like.

On the outside of all retaining walls, level with the lawn, build mowing strips (see Chapter III). These will eliminate the need for hand-trimming grass growing close to the walls.

Soil. The soil in a raised bed should be prepared to a depth of at least 2 feet. If the natural drainage is not good, pour in a 3- to 4-inch layer of crushed rock at this level. The actual planting soil should also be well drained but moisture-retentive; so add liberal quantities of sand and peat. (In other words, a raised bed is like a flower pot in that, if the drainage is not excellent, the soil may become waterlogged and sour.)

Whatever else you do to improve or change the character of the soil depends on the requirements of the plants you grow.

Fill the bed initially to the top of the retaining walls, and even slightly higher. Try to let the soil settle for a week or two before planting in it; then add enough new soil to bring the level to within ½ inch of the top of the walls. Thereafter, maintain it close to this level—especially if water other than falling rain and snow enters the bed. The reason for this is that, if the soil level is too low, the excess water has no chance of escaping over the walls but must, instead, percolate down through the soil. Even if this did not cause a waterlogged condition, it would carry the soil nutrients quickly out of reach of the plant rests.

Since soil in confined areas tends to lose its vitality, have the soil in each of your raised beds analyzed annually; and replenish the supply of nutrients and peat as the test results indicate. Some gardeners follow the practice of replacing at least the top 12 inches of soil entirely every two or three years; but whether you need to do this should be indicated by the soil analysis.

Planting. Although I have talked about using raised beds only for flowers, there is no reason why they should be limited to them. Anything except plants with extensive root systems will grow in them. But they are best for flowers, herbs, the smaller vegetables, roses, and other small shrubs that do not withstand the ravages of traffic very well and that need frequent cultivation, feeding, disbudding, and so on.

Care of such plants is the same as it would be if the plants were growing in a conventional bed or border.

XIII  Gardening in Containers

Whether or not gardening in containers requires less work than conventional gardening is a moot question. Many people think it does; some think it doesn't.

It saves work:

—because you can prepare the soil exactly to the needs of each plant (this is not so easily done in a garden). This means that the plants *should* grow better with less attention.

—because you can bring the plants close to where you spend most time outdoors. Consequently, a few plants appear to make as much of a show as you would get with a larger number of plants that must be planted farther away. (In other words, six plants in pots right on a terrace give about the same visual impression as, say, plants in the ground around the edge of the terrace.)

—because animal pests that burrow cannot damage the plants.

—because potted plants generally require less weeding than those in the open.

—because if a plant is suddenly struck by disease, it

can be isolated or disposed of before the disease spreads to neighboring potted plants.

—because plants are in no danger of being damaged by the unusual water conditions (flooding and the like) sometimes encountered in the garden.

—because you don't have to bend down so far or kneel to work on the plants. In fact, you can deliberately raise many potted plants high off the ground to make your work easier.

On the other hand, container gardening makes extra work:

—because potted plants need to be watered more frequently than those in the garden.

—because the soil in the containers needs to be completely replaced every once in a while.

—because potted plants must be repotted occasionally as they grow larger.

—because potted plants need to be fertilized more frequently.

—because plants in exposed positions are more prone to damage by extreme heat or cold or winds (of course they do not necessarily have to be placed in such positions). In cold climates, potted plants must be given special protection in the winter.

—because the containers themselves require occasional scrubbing.

—because plants set on a paved surface dirty the surface enough to require rather frequent sweeping or washing. Either operation may necessitate moving the pots.

Just how this list of pluses and minuses adds up, I am not certain. I am inclined to think that work-saving is a secondary virtue of container gardening and that its main value is that it permits you to change your garden around quickly and easily at moment's notice. On the other hand, the fact that container gardening is so popular in

California, where the minimum-maintenance movement started, must mean that it is much more of a work saver than I think it is.

What containers to use. A good container is large enough to give plant roots a chance to grow. Generally, when plants are planted singly, the container should be about as deep as it is wide. Annuals and perennials go into containers that are 6 to 8 inches in diameter. Large perennials and vines need 10- to 12-inch containers. Small shrubs, such as azaleas and lantana, need 12- to 18-inch containers. Medium-size shrubs, such as camellias, rhododendrons, viburnums, boxwood, and conifers, need 18- to 24-inch containers or larger.

The container must have the weight and/or proportions that will keep it upright when planted. This simply means that if you are planting tall-growing plants, you should put them either in squat, fairly wide pots or in heavy pots; otherwise, they may easily be blown or knocked over. Similarly, heavy, spreading plants need low pots.

The container must be durable if you want to use it for any length of time. And the container must provide bottom drainage so that the soil does not become water logged and sour. Such drainage is made possible by holes in the bottom of the container. Small containers that do not have such holes are often used but definitely are not desirable. Very large containers without bottom drainage are also undesirable; however, if they have enough depth to permit you to provide drainage by other means, they are acceptable.

The following are not essential traits to look for in a container but are highly desirable:

It should be easy to clean. Better still, it should not get dirty too rapidly in the first place.

It should not be so heavy that it adds to the difficulty of lifting and moving the potted plant. This is especially true of containers of 12-inch diameter and over. In larger containers, the soil alone is often too heavy to move.

It should not allow the soil to dry out quickly. Wire baskets lined with sphagnum moss are the worst offenders in this respect. Red-clay pots are also porous enough to allow moisture to escape through the sides.

Which containers come closest to meeting these requirements? There are a number of good ones, but none is perfect.

Clay pots. The familiar red-clay pot is excellent from the standpoint of cost; but from the standpoint of maintenance, it does not hold a candle to a glazed pot *that provides bottom drainage* (many do not). The latter is slow to soil and easy to clean. It is somewhat more durable than the red-clay pot. And it loses very little moisture through the sides.

An excellent substitute for the glazed pot is a plastic pot. This has the glazed pot's advantages and, in addition, is much lighter in weight. However, it is not attractive and does not seem to be available in such a range of sizes.

Wooden tubs and boxes. For the most part larger than clay pots, they are consequently used mainly for larger plants. They are not easy to clean; but they are lightweight and hold in moisture quite well. They also have enough insulating value to keep the soil from heating up excessively on very hot days.

All wooden containers must be made of decay-resistant wood, such as redwood or cypress. They must be secure at the joints. And the bottom should be raised off the ground to prevent rotting.

Unpainted containers are preferable. True, they becomed discolored. But painted containers almost always require repainting every year or two because the finish is peeled off by the moisture in the wood.

If you build plant boxes or other types of large wooden containers, you should make them of 1-inch-thick redwood or cypress and fasten the boards together with long brass screws. Provide five ½-inch drainage holes per square foot of bottom area.

Barrels. These containers are primarily for very large plants, such as small trees. Use only the kind that is made to hold liquid (old whiskey barrels, for example). The hoops are likely to rust out before the wood decays.

Concrete tubs. They are usually very large. Some are more or less shallow and saucer-shaped; others are deep and roomy. They meet none of the requirements outlined above; but for very large plants or for large plantings of small plants, they are almost indispensable.

Other containers. The list is endless. Some of the containers are excellent; some are bad. If you bear in mind the essential and desirable features of a container, you will not have much trouble in making a wise selection.

What soil to use. Every pot gardener has his favorite soil mixture (or mixtures). I recommend the oldest and simplest:

2 parts good garden loam
1 part coarse sand
1 part humus (probably peat unless you have a supply of something just as good)

This mixture can be used for the majority of plants; but it is easily changed to suit the special requirements of the minority by doubling the volume of sand or the volume of humus. Typical plants requiring a very sandy potting mixture are the cacti and succulents. Those requiring a very humusy mixture are begonias, ferns, bananas, and the like. To make soil acid for rhododendrons, azaleas, camellias, and so on, add 1 teaspoonful of powdered sulfur to each container under 12 inches in diameter.

The best way to mix soil for potting is to pour all the ingredients, when dry, into a pile on a flat surface and turn them over and over with a shovel. When the mixture is uniform, add water in small quantities and continue turning until the soil is just damp enough to hold together when you squeeze it in your hand. It is now ready for use.

Potting a plant. If the container has been used, your first step must be to scrub it well with soap and water to remove lurking microbes. Clay pots (new ones as well as old) should then be soaked for several hours in clear water in order to fill the pores. (If they are not soaked, they may suck moisture out of the soil to such an extent that you will never be able to water the plant properly thereafter.)

Cover the drainage holes on the inside of the container with one or two shards. Then pour in a layer of coarse drainage material, such as gravel or pebbles. In containers under 10 inches in diameter, a ½-inch layer is sufficient; in larger containers, use 1 inch or more. (In containers that do not have bottom drainage holes, you need about 1 inch of drainage material in containers under 6 inches in diameter; 2 inches in those under 12 inches in diameter; and 3 inches or more in larger containers.)

Fill the container about halfway with potting soil; set in the plant and spread out its roots; and fill in around it with additional soil. Firm the soil, but not so much that water will not penetrate. The crown of the plant should be at the soil level; and for ease in watering, the soil should be ½ to 1 inch below the rim of the container (less in small containers, more in large).

If the potting soil is damp to start with, little additional water is needed for newly planted plants. It is a good idea, however, to pour a little starter solution (dilute liquid fertilizer) around small plants.

Keep seedlings and other bare-root plants out of direct sunlight for a day or two after they are potted: they may not survive otherwise. Large plants that have a ball of earth around the roots do not need this protection.

Repotting. Plants need to be repotted when their roots fill the container. In some cases, the roots start growing out through the bottom drainage holes. In many other cases, the only way to determine the condition of the roots is to set a container on its side, rap the walls with your knuckles or a stick to loosen the rootball, and then slide out the rootball. If the ball is almost completely covered with fine white roots, the plant is probably "potbound" and should be repotted.

Still another way to tell when a plant needs repotting is to observe its performance. If it stops making growth in the spring or summer (when it usually should be growing vigorously), the chances are that it wants more root room.

When a plant does need repotting, shift it into a container that is only a little larger than the previous container. If you are using conventional pots, the rule is to move the plant into the *next-size-larger pot*. If you are using other types of container, the new container should be about 1 inch wider and 1 inch deeper than the old.

The actual process of repotting consists of the following simple operations: Place a layer of drainage material in the bottom of the new container. Slide the rootball out of the old container, and remove some of the drainage material that is stuck on the bottom; but do not loosen the soil around the sides of the ball. Hold the rootball in the center of the new container, and pack fresh soil in around it. Apply a little fertilizer, and water well.

If a plant needs repotting but you cannot find a larger container for it, slide out the rootball and carefully pick off about ½ inch of soil from all sides. Use a dull knife or a manicurist's orange stick. Trim off the exposed ends of the roots with a sharp knife or shears. Then replace the rootball in the container and fill around it with fresh soil.

Replacing soil. Sometimes a potted plant stops growing even though its roots still have plenty of room to grow. If nothing else seems wrong, the chances are that the soil has worn out.

Soil fatigue is a common problem for pot gardeners;

and in small containers especially it is rather difficult to prevent. But it is nothing to worry about. All you have to do is slide the plant out of its container; pry about half of the soil out of the rootball; and then repot the plant in fresh soil.

Fertilizing. Regular application of plant food not only keeps pot plants growing well but also eliminates one of the reasons why potting soil needs to be replaced.

The time to fertilize is when the plants are making growth, not when they are resting (in a dormant or semi-dormant condition). Make the first application in the early spring and repeat at two- to three-month intervals until growth starts to slow down. Light applications are better than heavy. Follow the directions of the fertilizer manufacturer.

Liquid fertilizers are no more nutritious than dry powders; but I prefer them for pot plants because they are easier to apply and the nutrients they contain are instantly available to the plant roots. You are also less likely to apply an overdose.

Watering. Ideally, plants growing outdoors in containers should be watered like house plants: Sometimes you apply water to the surface of the soil; sometimes you set the pot in deep water and let the soil soak up moisture through the bottom of the pot. But the truth is that bottom-watering outdoors is usually too much of a chore because there is no tub or basin in which to soak the plants and because some of the plants are too large to carry. So top-watering with a hose or watering can is the method you must use.

There are just two rules to follow: (1) Apply water as soon as possible after the soil surface dries out. (2) Water each plant until the water starts to trickle out the bottom of the container. Beyond this, it makes no difference what time of day you water. Neither does it do any harm to get the foliage wet so long as it has a chance to dry off before nightfall.

The frequency with which pot plants must be watered is a problem, however. Soil in pots dries out much more rapidly than that in a flower bed or shrubbery border. In hot, dry weather, in fact, outdoor pot plants often need to be watered every day and sometimes even twice a day.

What can be done about this? Not too much, but here are several points worth considering:

1. Potted plants exposed to wind dry out faster than those in protected spots.

2. Plants in the sun dry out faster than those in the shade.

3. If you group a number of pots close together, each plant helps to shade its neighbor to some extent and thus helps to slow evaporation of water.

4. Evaporation from the soil surface can also be retarded by covering the soil with a mulch of peat, sawdust, and so on.

5. By surrounding the sides and bottom of a container with some sort of insulating material, you can slow the loss of moisture through the container itself. One way to do this is to sink the container in the ground or in a box or planter filled with damp soil, peat, or sawdust. Another way is to set the container inside a larger container and fill the space between with moss, peat, excelsior, and so forth, which is kept moist.

Protecting pot plants against wind and cold. Once you have seen how easily wind can blow over a potted plant—and what a lot of work the accident can cause —you will realize more fully the importance of selecting nontippable containers for your plants. These are much your best protection against wind.

Cold protection is somewhat more difficult to provide. Plants in pots cannot survive very much below-freezing weather even though the same species would be perfectly safe if planted in the garden.

In areas where freezing temperatures are relatively rare, the best way to protect potted plants is simply to move them into a sheltered nook near the house or to cover them with burlap, polyethylene film, or even just newspapers. Burning Tree-Heet bricks under or alongside the plants also give excellent protection and with less work on your part.

In areas where the word "winter" stands for a long period of cold weather, the only way of carrying over perennial plants in pots is to bring them indoors into a sunporch, garage, or cold basement. Give evergreens some light; and water all plants only enough to keep the soil from drying out completely.

Another possible solution—but not so reliable—is to sink the containers in the ground outdoors. Mound soil up around deciduous plants. And surround the plants—both deciduous and evergreen—with canvas, heavy burlap, or tarpaper to break the winds and keep out the worst of the cold.

Protecting plants against insects and diseases. Pot plants are subject to the same ailments as garden plants, and should be protected in the same way. As I noted earlier, one of the advantages of container gardening is that diseased plants can be isolated easily.

Moving pot plants. It is almost inevitable that pot plants will be moved from one location to another—especially if you live in the North, where the plants need indoor protection in winter. This is when large plants become a problem. But here are five ways of solving it:

1. Slip a strong piece of canvas or a large coal shovel under the container and pull it.

2. Mount wooden containers on casters.

3. Mount casters on a piece of thick plywood to make a dolly for rolling containers here and there. Or buy a ready-made dolly of the same type.

4. To move a container across a lawn, roll it on three or four rollers made of short lengths of 2- or 3-inch iron pipe.

5. If you have a number of large pot plants, buy a small hand truck similar to that used by moving men.

Hanging plants. Hanging plants are charming but do not merit consideration when your main concern is to make gardening work simpler. They are double trouble to water. Because of their aerial position, the soil dries out with extreme rapidity; and to rewet it without standing on a ladder or without letting the plant down on a pulley calls for a contortionist.

Selected Plants for Potting

The list of plants you can grow in containers is long. Here are just a few of the best:

ANNUALS

Ageratum. Compact plants to about 8 inches, they are covered with blue flowers; grow in sun or light shade.

Dahlia. Plant dwarf types such as Unwin's hybrids. They grow to 18 inches, with flowers in various shapes and many colors; need sun.

Forget-me-not (Myosotis). Twelve inches tall with profuse blue or white flowers, most varieties grow in partial shade, but some are sun lovers.

Lobelia. Having lovely little blue flowers. Some varieties are compact and grow to 6 inches; others are trailing. They need partial shade.

Marigold (Tagetes). Use the dwarf types growing to

about 1 foot. The yellow pompon flowers are superb; also in orange and red; best in full sun.

Patience (Impatiens). These pink, orange, red, or white flowers are for shady locations. The commonest varieties grow to 18 inches, but there are also dwarfs.

Petunia. It is in a class by itself. There are many colors; many sizes up to about 15 inches. The compact dwarfs and balcony (trailing) types are probably the most useful in containers. Sun.

Phlox. Six- to 8-inch plants are covered with showy flowers in red, yellow, pink, or white. Sun.

Schizanthus. The flowers are like orchids or butterflies —in many colors and marked with contrasting colors. Foliage is fernlike; grows to 2 feet. Partial shade is suitable.

Sweet alyssum (Lobularia maritima). Covered with pink, rose, white, or violet flowers. In warm climates bloom lasts almost all year; grows up to 8 inches; needs sun or light shade.

Sweet pea (Lathyrus odoratus). The new dwarfs are only 1 foot tall and do not require staking. They start blooming earlier and keep on longer than older types. Many colors. Try them in large boxes in the sun.

Verbena. Red, pink, white, lavender, it grows to 1 foot and spreads much wider. Verbena needs sun; especially good for pots because of good resistance to drought.

PERENNIALS

Many perennials are delightful in containers; but most of them bloom for only a short period. This means that you might need two or three different potted perennials to keep a spot on your terrace bright with color through most of the spring, summer, and fall. And that, in turn, would mean extra work. Consequently, the list of perennials recommended here for container use is limited.

Begonia. The fibrous-rooted types are lovely and undemanding. They grow from about 1 foot up with pink, red, or white flowers; need partial shade. Tuberous begonias are among the most beautiful of all flowers—in many pastel shades. Some of the blossoms are huge. In cool, rather damp areas—as on the Maine coast or California's Monterey Peninsula—they are rather easy to grow. Just keep them in partial shade; give them a soil rich in humus; and fertilize and water regularly. But to get anything out of them in hot climates is a chore.

Coleus. A good foliage plant with varicolored leaves, it must be kept pinched to prevent it from getting leggy. Grows to 3 feet, but is usually lower. Needs partial shade.

Elephant's ear (Colocasia esculenta). Grow this for its huge, handsome red-marked leaves. It grows rapidly to 5 feet from a tuber. Needs partial shade and a rich, humusy soil.

Geranium (Pelargonium). Far and away the best perennial for pot culture, it blooms on and on and on; thrives in sun and heat; and is less demanding about moisture than many plants. Flowers are red, pink, salmon, and white and very showy. The common geranium grows to 3 feet. Some other types are larger; some are smaller. There are also trailers.

Hosta. The numerous flower stalks are pleasant; but hosta is grown primarily for its elegant foliage, which may be bright green, greenish blue, or delightfully variegated. Use the smaller varieties under 24 inches. Partial shade is recommended.

FERNS

Bird's-nest fern (Asplenium nidus). The undivided fronds are arranged in a clump resembling a bird's nest. It grows up to 3 feet and needs partial shade.

Chain fern (Woodwardia). A large fern to 6 feet with

soft green fronds, it usually grows in partial shade but tolerates considerable sun.

Cliff brake (Pellaea). This leathery fern with dark stalks grows to 2 feet; partial shade.

Holly fern (Cyrtomium falcatum). Tougher than many ferns and able to withstand more wind, it has glossy leaves shaped something like holly leaves and shaggy stalks. It grows to two feet; partial shade.

Maidenhair fern (Adiantum). Here is one of the prettiest ferns, with fronds to 2 feet. The stems are black; the leaflets are more or less fan-shaped and bright green. Partial shade is suitable.

Polystichum. It produces several evergreen ferns up to 2 feet. Popular names include Christmas fern, mountain holly fern, giant holly fern. Partial shade is recommended.

CACTI AND SUCCULENTS

These are topnotch container plants because they need somewhat less water and fertilizer than other plants. They look especially attractive in shallow containers. Grow them in a mixture of 1 part loam, 1 part humus, and 1 part sand; and be sure to put at least 3 inches of coarse drainage material in the bottom of the containers. Grow in full sun. Apply water in spring and summer, when the plants are growing, and when the soil dries out completely to a depth of ½ inch.

Among the many desirable types of plant for container culture are the following:

Agave. It has ornamental rosette-shaped plants, some very large. The century plant, for instance, has leaves 6 feet long. Use smaller species, obviously.

Aloe. Some of these are huge. Use the dwarfs. Leaves are arranged in rosettes. Flowers are red or yellow.

Crassula. Another large genus in many sizes, it has leaves that are fleshy and arranged in a cross shape on the stems. The jade plant is a familiar species. It is shaped like a picturesque tree and has pink flowers.

Echeveria. Hen and chickens is a well-known species. Plants grow to 2 feet in various shapes. All have beautifully colored or textured leaves, and some have nice flowers.

Euphorbia. A big class of succulents in many shapes. They have thorns, intricate flowers, and a milky sap. Crown-of-thorns, a 3-foot creeper with bright red bracts, is familiar.

Haworthia. They grow to 6 inches. Some form rosettes; some are column-shaped; some have windows in the leaves.

Sedum. These hardy succulents come in various shapes. Most are fairly small. Some are trailing. They have yellow flowers.

Sempervivum. The houseleeks are rosette-shaped and stemless, up to 1 foot tall. They spread widely. Flowers are white, yellow, pink, or purple.

Stapelia. The flowers are five-pointed and most beautifully colored. Plants grow to 9 inches. Some of them have an unpleasant odor.

SHRUBS AND TREES

The heights given are for plants growing in the garden (unless noted). In containers the same plants are generally much smaller.

Abelia grandiflora. The handsome foliage is evergreen in warm climates with flowers in white or pink clusters. The shrub grows to 5 feet in the sun.

Andromeda (Pieris japonica). This evergreen shrub grows to 8 feet with sprays of lovely white flowers like the lily-of-the-valley. Grows in light shade or sun.

Azalea. Azaleas grow to 15 feet. Use the smaller kinds in containers. The flowers get more brilliant with each passing year as new varieties are developed. Plants are either deciduous or evergreen. They grow in sun or partial shade. The new growth-retarding chemicals (see Chapter IX) work exceptionally well on azaleas.

Bamboo. The bamboos are woody grasses that are excellent in large containers because the containers keep them from running wild (as they often do in open ground). There are many kinds to choose from. All are slender and tall. *Bambusa multiplex* and *Phyllostachys aurea* are two especially recommended for container culture.

Banana shrub (Michelia fuscata). This evergreen has small, fragrant, magnolia-like flowers that are cream-colored and have a reddish or purplish edging. It grows in partial shade, to 15 feet.

Camellia. Here's a source of profuse, handsome flowers in reds and other colors. Plants are evergreen and can grow to 30 feet—but not in containers. Camellias need partial shade. You can grow them in containers as far north as New York City.

Chinese hibiscus (Hibiscus rosa-sinensis). The large flowers—singles and doubles—are in beautiful shades of red, yellow, orange, purple, and white. The leaves are evergreen and in various shapes. Plants grow to 20 feet or more, but there are many low-growing forms; need sun.

Citrus. Dwarf varieties of oranges, lemons, limes, kumquats, and tangelos are superb for pot culture. The trees have glossy, evergreen foliage; fragrant white blossoms; and delightful fruits. They grow indoors in winter almost as well as they grow outdoors in summer; need sun.

Dwarf hinoki cypress (Chamaecyparis obtusa nana). A dark green, mound-shaped evergreen with flat branches in layers, it grows to 5 feet in the sun.

Fatsia japonica. This evergreen shrub has handsome, large, deeply lobed leaves that are dark green and glossy. 15 feet. Grows in shade.

Fuchsia. This favorite shrub can reach 20 feet in the

garden, but is usually kept quite small in tubs. The lovely pendulous flowers are in various shades and combinations of red, purple, blue, and white. It grows in filtered sun.

Gardenia. This ever-so-fragrant evergreen shrub has glossy foliage and a profusion of waxy, white flowers that may be single or semidouble. It reaches 6 feet, needs sun.

Heavenly bamboo (Nandina domestica). Eight-foot evergreen shrub has canelike stems and delicate foliage that changes color several times during the year. Large white flower clusters are followed by red berries in the fall. Grow it in the sun for the best foliage effect.

Holly (Ilex). Many of the smaller varieties do well in large containers. Try the English, Chinese, or Japanese hollies. All are evergreen. The first two have red berries; the last, black. Holly grows in the sun.

Hydrangea. Deciduous shrubs to 6 feet with large leaves and great clusters of blue, pink, or white flowers. Sun or light shade is needed.

Japanese maple (Acer palmatum). Beautifully shaped deciduous tree with sharply cut leaves that turn from red to green to red again or are red the year round. Grows in sun, to 12 feet.

Juniper (Juniperus). These picturesque evergreens come in many types. Use those that stay under 2 feet—for example: *J. conferta, J. horizontalis, J. procumbens aurea* or *J. procumbens nana, J. squamata.* Grows in sun.

Lantana. These shrubs grow to 4 feet. They are evergreen or deciduous, with flower clusters of various colors; sun.

Loquat (Eriobotrya japonica). This evergreen tree has handsome, leathery leaves; fragrant white flowers; and edible yellow fruits. It grows to 20 feet in the sun.

Magnolia grandiflora. In a container this evergreen may reach 20 feet. The magnificent leaves are dark green and glossy. Large flowers are fragrant and white. It grows in sun.

Natal plum (Carissa grandiflora). Spiny, evergreen shrub to 15 feet, it has fragrant white flowers and edible red fruits.

Norfolk Island pine (Araucaria excelsa). A slim symmetrical evergreen tree with neatly tiered branches, it grows to about 10 feet in containers. Partial shade recommended.

Oleander (Nerium oleander). This is a poisonous evergreen shrub with fine white, red, pink, or purple flowers. Grows to 25 feet. Sun.

Olive (Olea europaea). This is an attractive evergreen with gray-green, willowy leaves and blackish fruits. It grows to 25 feet and often has a picturesquely gnarled trunk; needs sun.

Palm. Among the best palms for use in large containers are the sentry palms, pigmy date palm, and lady palm. The tallest reaches about 12 feet.

Peach. A variety named Bonanza grows only 4 feet tall if it is pruned annually, but bears a sizable crop of full-size, freestone fruits. The deciduous foliage is attractive; needs sun.

Pine. Pinus mugo mughus is a spreading pine that grows very slowly. It rarely exceeds 4 feet in a container. The Japanese black pine (*P. thunbergii*) is an upright but slow-growing tree that is a favorite for training as a bonsai. Both pines grow in the sun.

Pineapple guava (Feijoa sellowiana). A spreading evergreen shrub, to 12 feet, it has showy purple and red flowers and edible gray-green fruits. The foliage is gray-green on top, silvery underneath. Needs sun.

Pittosporum tobira. This 10-foot evergreen shrub has leathery foliage and clusters of white flowers smelling like orange blossoms. Grows in sun or partial shade.

Podocarpus. A very graceful conifer with pendulous branches and dense, willowlike leaves. It grows to 20 feet in sun or partial shade.

Pomegranate. For pot culture, use *Punica granatum*

nana. This is a deciduous shrub only 3 feet tall and bushy. It has small, inedible, orange fruits.

Rhododendron. The brilliant flowers of this familiar evergreen come in many colors. For pot culture, choose the smaller types. Plant needs filtered sun.

Rose. Grow the miniatures, floribundas, or polyanthas. They are beautiful and easy; need full sun.

Rosemary (Rosemarinus officinalis). This evergreen shrub has narrow, aromatic, two-colored leaves and clusters of small blue flowers. It grows to 6 feet and needs sun.

Skimmia japonica. A fine evergreen shrub to 5 feet. If you have male and female plants, you will have red berries in the fall. Grows in partial shade.

Spruce. The dwarf forms suitable for containers include *Picea abies gregoryana, P. a. maxwellii, P. a. nidiformis, P. glauca conica, P. excelsa pygmaea.* All spruces need sun.

Sweet bay (Laurus nobilis). A compact, cone-shaped evergreen tree, it grows to 8 feet in containers but much more in the garden. Sun.

VINES

Vines of all kinds can be grown in containers, but the annuals and small, fast-growing perennials are the best.

Asparagus. This variety is often called asparagus fern, but really is two forms of vine. Both have delicate, airy foliage on stems (up to 20 feet long) that may be trained upward or allowed to trail. Grows in partial shade.

Clematis. A deciduous or evergreen perennial with gorgeous flowers in many colors, it grows to 20 feet. Needs sun, but the roots should be kept shaded. It is cut back to the ground in the fall.

Cup-and-saucer vine (Cobaea scandens). Though this can be grown as a perennial in warm climates, it is best treated as an annual. It has bell-shaped violet flowers; grows to 25 feet in the sun.

Ivy (Hedera helix). This hardy perennial grows fast with dark evergreen foliage. Grows in part shade and also in considerable sun.

Moonflower (Calonyction aculeatum). This perennial is best treated as an annual. It is related to the morning glory and has white or purple flowers that bloom at night and stay open until the following noon. It grows in sun.

Morning glory (Ipomoea purpurea). Familiar annual with blue, white, or red flowers in profusion. Grows to 15 feet. Sun.

Quamoclit. Cypress vine is an annual with trumpet-shaped red-and-white flowers and fernlike foliage. It grows to 10 feet. Cardinal climber is very similar but a little taller. Both put on a wonderful display in the sun.

Wax plant (Hoya carnosa). This is an evergreen with elegant foliage and fragrant, waxy, white or pinkish flowers. It cannot survive frost, but since it grows to only 10 feet, it can be brought indoors in the winter.

XIV  Larger Paved Areas

Shortly after I finished my book *America's Great Private Gardens*, I asked a number of the landscape architects who had designed the gardens which maintenance-minimizing idea they advocated particularly. As might be expected, their answers varied, but all mentioned the use of paving.

Thomas D. Church of San Francisco was one of these. In his book *Gardens Are for People*, he says: "There is no doubt that more garden space can be covered with hard-surfaced materials and the results be both aesthetic and practical. The average driveway is too narrow, the parking space too cramped, the terrace too small and the paths too narrow; there are places in deep shadow where nothing will grow, and little used corners which can be paved and be the better for it."

Later on in the book, Mr. Church adds: "It may be the role of paving to remain calm—to be the common denominator and a foil for the excitement created by fences, steps, grass forms, brilliant flower combinations, foliage textures, and distant views."

These two statements by one of the world's leading

landscape architects and a masterful user of paving deserve close study. They say why paving is needed in today's garden, where it should be used, and how it should be handled. The statements make it perfectly clear that Mr. Church is a confirmed believer in paving; yet note the restraint with which he speaks.

Restraint is a virtue that many homeowners lack when they decide to increase the paved area of their garden. I have in mind a home just a couple of miles down the road from me. Several years ago, on a trip to town, I suddenly noticed that the entire backyard had been spread with bonewhite gravel. Of course it was instantly obvious what had happened: The owners had grown weary of trying to keep up the grass and flowers that formerly carpeted the yard; and they had taken the most drastic step they could think of (short of moving to the city) to simplify their chores. But they had failed to take two things into account: (1) The gravel would be pure torture to keep free of the leaves and twigs that dripped from the surrounding trees. And (2) the property was hideous. It may not have been a thing of beauty before; but now under its white shroud it was indescribably worse. It was totally lacking in form and logic.

Another residential property, also nearby, is almost as bad, but in a different way. In this case, the owner spread white gravel in neat but large circles and swoops under the trees and shrubs in his front yard. For some reason, the effect reminds me of one of those highway retail outlets with a front yard cluttered with graceless jardinieres, silver gazing globes, and pink flamingos.

These are but two of countless American gardens that have been flawed almost beyond repair (paved areas are rather difficult to obliterate) by unrestrained use of paving materials.

This indictment is, of course, intended for the garden owners, not the paving materials. I don't think all pavings

The startlingly beautiful concrete garden of Mr. and Mrs. Henry McIntyre.

are pretty. But when used by people with artistic skill, judgment, and restraint, even the severest or drabbest material can add to garden beauty.

The outstanding example of this is the garden of Mr. and Mrs. Henry McIntyre in Hillsborough, California. It is made almost entirely of concrete, and it is as large as many suburban lots. Yet it is one of the country's most beautiful and exciting gardens. In my book about great gardens I wrote of it as follows:

> Some gardens invite naming. This is one of them. But it defies naming, too. If I called it a concrete garden, you would be appalled at the picture that came to mind. If I called it a water garden, you would probably think of a garden built around and into a lake. If I called it a modern Moorish garden, you would know what I meant only if you had traveled abroad. Yet all these names are accurate.

Mr. and Mrs. McIntyre became entranced with Moorish water gardens during their visits to Spain. When they set out to build a new house in Hillsborough several years ago, they asked landscape architect Lawrence Halprin to explore the idea of developing a similar garden. A not-unimportant reason for their interest was their hope of having a garden that did not require a great deal of maintenance.

"The McIntyres hit us at just the right time," Mr. Halprin recalls. "It happened that we had been thinking along much the same line. We were interested in the use of water. And we were interested in gardens that are evocative to the people in them—but not because of their flowers. We worked closely with the McIntyres' architect, and the plan we eventually came up with suited the McIntyres almost exactly."

The magical effect of Mr. and Mrs. McIntyre's unlikely garden, with its 90-degree angles and flat, gray concrete surfaces, is traceable to a subtle combination of things.

No matter from where it is viewed—from inside the house, from the top of the surrounding hill, from the island in its center—the garden has a strong sculptural feeling.

It is filled with actual movement: water moving at various speeds; waving shadows cast by the eucalyptus trees that form towering hedges to east and west; the foliage of the few plants that are in the garden blowing in the breeze; birds coming for a drink or a bath. All this seems more apparent than in the usual garden because the background is so still.

The sound of water fills the air; and the tune changes as you walk from one part of the garden to the other and as the wind changes force. (The tune can also be changed by operating the fountains alone or in pairs instead of all three at once.) The large, thick fountain—the cornerstone of the water system—gives off a continuous, modulated roar. The steps down which the water tumbles in two directions from the big fountain are scooped out to produce a gurgling sound. The tall, single spout splashes irregularly into the pool below while the three small sprays patter like rain.

The end result of the garden's sounds and movement and sculptural qualities is somewhat surprising. At first sight, you are filled with excitement. Then this abates (but never totally disappears) to be replaced by a feeling of peace—clean and uncluttered.

Eight Rules for Using Paving

The contrast between the McIntyres' garden and the two gravel patches that my neighbors have created points up the most important rule about using paving in the garden:

Rule 1. If you don't have the counsel of a landscape architect, take it easy. In the long run, the appearance of your garden is far more important than any work you may save by paving it. There are plenty of easier and far safer ways to reduce garden maintenance.

Rule 2. Do not think for a second that paving invariably represents a 100 percent or even a 50 percent reduction in maintenance over an unpaved surface. No paved area is maintenance-free. It needs to be swept (far more often than a lawn needs to be raked, because things show up so clearly). It needs to be scrubbed. It may need drastic stain-removal treatment. And so forth.

Rule 3. Recognize that, in addition to creating their own work-making problems, most paving materials create a variety of other problems. For example, bricks and wood blocks are treacherously slippery when wet. Concrete, unless polished dangerously smooth, is abrasive to children's knees. Blacktop exposed to the summer sun is uncomfortably hot to walk on.

Rule 4. Remember that solid-surfaced paving shuts off water and air to plant roots and can result in unhealthy growth and even death.

Rule 5. When you use solid-surfaced paving in driveways and walks as well as in terraces and other areas, try to design it so that it does not funnel off your property an undue amount of the rain that falls. In other words, instead of slanting the driveway toward the street so that all the water runs into the storm drain, give it a crown so that the water runs off to the lawn and shrubs on the sides; or slant it toward a catch basin of some sort from which the water can be released underground into your garden soil.

Rule 6. To "look right," paved areas should serve a purpose in addition to contributing to ease of garden maintenance. Otherwise, they strike an upsetting, false note in the observer's mind. Example: One of the strongest advocates of paving, Mrs. Gertrude Kuh, a Chicago landscape architect, makes almost a specialty of building outsized, paved entrance courts and parking areas in order to reduce cultivated garden area. Yet because these are also needed to provide adequate off-street parking space, there seems to be nothing strange or out of place about them.

Rule 7. Paving should never be allowed to overwhelm a terrace or other outdoor living area in which it is used. Says Perry Wheeler, Washington, D.C., landscape architect: "One of the rules I follow in developing a terrace is to put in enough plant pockets and to use enough potted plants so that when you are sitting in the area you are at least as conscious of flowers and foliage as of paving."

Rule 8. Suit the paving material to the purpose of the paved area and to its situation in the garden. Situation factors to be considered include the nature of the surrounding area, the surrounding planting, and the amount of sun (which affects glare and heat absorption). Cost is another factor you are almost bound to consider, but you should try to avoid giving it top priority.

Paving with Brick

Characteristics. Bricks of all colors are strong enough to be used in all types of paved areas provided they are firmly bedded. The red and pink bricks are among the loveliest of paving materials—especially if they are laid without mortar, which makes the paving less rigid and severe.

As a rule, common bricks and textured face bricks are tops in beauty. They are also much less slippery than smooth face bricks. Used bricks (the genuine used bricks, not the newly manufactured "used" bricks") are delightful because of their uneven coloring and texture; but if they are not of uniform size, they are difficult to arrange in a tight, regular pattern. In winter some of them also have a tendency to spall and break.

Problems. (1) In shady spots, bricks quickly acquire a greenish coating of moss. When this is damp it is as slick as glass. (2) Being porous, bricks soak up considerable moisture; and in winter they often have a thin skin of ice long after other materials have thawed out. (3) Bricks are badly stained by oil, grease, and other things. The blotches are very hard to eradicate.

Construction. When laying bricks on sand, excavate the area to be paved to a depth of approximately 6 inches, which allows for a 4-inch sub-base. The bricks, which are 2¼ inches thick, should project slightly above the surrounding soil surface. The finished paving should have a slope in one or more directions of 1 inch in 8 to 10 feet.

Stretch strings to mark the outer edges and elevation of the paving. Then dig narrow trenches parallel with the strings. The bottom of the trenches should be 8 inches below the strings. Set bricks vertically into the trenches and tight against one another. Line them up exactly with

In a Washington garden soft pink bricks are laid on a sand bed so they will not look rigid and so they can be lifted out to form little plant pockets.

Granite blocks pave an entrance courtyard in the Boston area. Large flagstones are set in to add interest and to provide better footing for people getting in and out of cars.

the strings, and firm soil around them. The bricks can be laid with their wide faces parallel to the strings or perpendicular to them. (The reason for laying the edge bricks in this way is to prevent them from twisting out of place when they are stepped on.)

Now tamp the soil in the excavated area, and fill in with 3 inches of bank-run gravel and 1 inch of sand or crushed stone or with 4 inches of crushed stone. (Use 6 inches of crushed stone under driveways and parking areas.)

Lay a 2by4 across the edge bricks on the long sides of the paved area, and trim it to this length. Then notch the ends to fit over the bricks. The notch should be 2 inches deep so that the wood above the sub-base hangs 2 inches below the tops of the edge bricks. This is your sand leveler.

Sprinkle the sand with water so it will pack slightly. Level it with a rake in the area where you will start laying brick. It should be spread to within about 1¾ inches of the tops of the edge bricks. Then lay your leveler across the edge bricks and pull it forward about a foot. The sand base behind it is now ready to receive the bricks.

Whatever your paving pattern, lay the bricks tight together. The quarter- to half-inch space that used to be recommended is not only unnecessary but is a dangerous heel-catcher. Firm each brick as you lay it. Then when you finish a row, lay the leveler over it, wide side down, and tap with a hammer or brick until the entire row is level.

After laying three or four rows in this fashion, rake another strip of sand smooth and repeat the process. Check every sixth to eight row to make sure the rows are perpendicular to the edge bricks. Use a carpenter's square and/or a folding rule.

When the entire area is paved, sweep sand into the joints between bricks and water it in with a hard spray.

Sealing the bricks with an oil sealer made for use on

masonry surfaces helps to keep out water and prevent spalling. It also makes the brick much more resistant to staining.

Paving with Granite Blocks and Cobblestones

Characteristics. Granite blocks are rectangular chunks of stone ranging from 2¾-inch cubes up to blocks 12 by 5 by 5 inches. They differ from cobblestones only in that the corners are squared off. Cobblestones are somewhat rounded. Both are durable in the extreme, handsome, and fairly resistant to staining; but the blocks, being flattened on all sides, are more comfortable underfoot, and water runs off them better.

Problems. (1) Even the blocks are a little too rough for wide expanses of terrace. (2) Sweeping is difficult, especially if you use cobblestones.

Construction. Lay like bricks on sand or, better, crushed stone. Blocks are usually laid with ½-inch joints.

Paving with Fieldstone

Characteristics. Flat fieldstones produce a ruggedly handsome paving but are not often used because they are so rough and irregular. They are generally heavy enough to be laid directly in the ground for stepping-stones or a walk of casual design. But they are better laid in cement mortar.

Problems. (1) The extreme roughness can be avoided by careful selection of stones; but if selection is not careful, the paving is hard to sweep and rake and is somewhat hazardous to the shuffling type of walker. (2) Grease and oil stains are difficult to remove because of the rough surface (though they may not actually penetrate to any extent). (3) Shale is soft and spalls badly and for this same reason, of course, should not be used; but it is tempting because of its flatness.

Construction. Lay fieldstones with mortar. Excavate at least 4 inches deeper than the thickness of the stones. Pour in a 4-inch layer of bank-run gravel and firm well. After brushing the stones free of dirt, imbed them firmly in the gravel and make sure all are set at the same level by laying a 2by4 across them. (Of course, the entire paved area should be sloped—about 1 inch in 8 feet, no less—to provide drainage.)

Space the stones ½ inch or more apart. Then, after a large section has been laid, trowel a semistiff mortar made of 3 parts sand and 1 part Portland cement into the joints. Work it down so that it fills the spaces completely. Strike it off with the edges of the stones—or higher if necessary—to eliminate puddled areas and to assure good drainage. Trowel smooth. If any mortar joints are unusually wide because of the irregularity of the stones, press smaller stones into them. These not only help to fill the joints but add to the beauty of the paving.

Scrape excess mortar from the stones and wipe off mortar stains with a damp rag. After the mortar has set, cover the paving with damp burlap for six days to allow the mortar to cure slowly. Any stains that remain can be removed later with a solution of 1 part muriatic acid in 10 parts water.

Paving with Flagstones

Characteristics. Flagstones are suitable only for surfaces that are not required to bear very heavy loads. They are ideal for walks, terraces, and pool areas because they produce a very attractive, very flat, nonskid surface.

Both rectangular and irregular flagstones are available. Using stones of different dimensions eliminates any feeling of monotony that might be expected with rectangular stones. Large areas paved with irregular stones can have the fragmentary, jumbled look of a cracked automobile windshield if the stones are not selected and arranged with considerable care.

Problems. (1) Flagstones stain rather easily and permanently. (2) They are also expensive.

Construction. If you use rectangular stones of different dimensions (the usual practice), give the stone dealer the overall dimensions of the area you are paving and ask him to figure out what size stones are needed and give you a numbered plan showing where each stone is to be laid. This service adds about 10 percent to the cost of the stones, but saves you time, exasperation, physical labor, and a pile of cut stone chunks.

If you use irregular flagstones, you should order enough to pave the area plus 10 percent to allow for waste in cutting. A stone can be cut along a straight line by scoring it heavily with a cold chisel and snapping it downward over a piece of L-shaped iron. To cut along a curving line, score the stone on both sides with a cold chisel until it breaks.

When laying flagstones on sand use stones of 1½-inch thickness. Thinner ones are likely to crack. Slope the paved area 1 inch in 10 feet.

Excavate the area to a depth of 5½ inches and firm the soil well. Then fill with 3 inches of bank-run gravel and 1 inch of sand or crushed stone, or with 4 inches of crushed stone. Rake smooth; then level and firm the sand with a long 2by4. Lay in the stones, setting them tight together. Firm well and check the level again with your 2by4. Then sweep fine sand into the joints and water it in.

In a lawn area flagstones should be set just slightly higher than the surrounding soil surface. But if the paving abuts a plant bed, there is a possibility that the outer stones will slide sideways into the bed; therefore, you should place steel curbing, redwood boards, or some other type of curbing tight against the outer edges of the stones.

Laying flagstones directly in the ground is done in walks and sometimes in terraces. It saves work because you simply scoop out the soil to a depth of 1½ inches and set in the stones. The stones are spaced 1 to 2 inches apart, and the joints are filled with soil in which grass or small ground covers will grow.

This type of paving should be avoided, however, because in order to keep the grass from spreading over the stones, you must hand clip it frequently. This is not easy maintenance.

When laying flagstones in mortar use 1-inch-thick stones. Have the dealer supply you with rectangular stones laid out to a numbered pattern.

Excavate the area to be paved to a depth of 4 inches. If drainage is poor, excavate to 6 inches and pour in 2 inches of gravel. Tamp the base well. Pour in 2½ inches of concrete mortar, as for a poured-concrete walk, and level it with a long board. Let this set for 24 hours. Then make a grout of ½ sack Portland cement in 3 gallons water and brush a thin layer onto a section of the concrete. Then trowel on ½ inch of a fairly stiff 1:3 mortar. Tap the flagstones into this with a hammer, making sure all are at the same level. Space the stones ½ inch apart. Do not step on the stones; work from a plank suspended above the stones. After the stones are in place, you can trowel mortar into the joints and strike it off flush with the surface of the stones; or you can wait up to 24 hours before doing this. When the mortar in the joints has set, cover the paving for six days with damp burlap. Remove lingering mortar stains with muriatic acid solution.

Paving with Slates

Characteristics. Slate for paving is available in a number of colors. The surface is flat and has an interesting, variable texture (you should use only natural-surfaced slate for paving). The stones are available in sawn squares and rectangles or in irregular chunks. An area paved in rectangular slates has a somewhat formal appearance. Where irregular pieces are used, the effect is informal, and it is sometimes difficult to tell whether the paving is slate or flagstone.

Like flagstones, slate lacks the strength to be used in heavy traffic areas. But it is more resistant to staining.

Problems. (1) Individual slates—especially irregular pieces—sometimes shiver in cold weather. (2) The color of some slate changes with weathering. This is generally nothing to worry about, but the problem can be avoided by using nonfading slate. (3) Black slates and other very dark types absorb sun heat and feel hot underfoot.

Construction. Follow directions for laying flagstones. Use 1-inch-thick slates when laying them on sand; ¾-inch slates in mortar.

Paving with Tiles

Characteristics. Quarry tiles come in large, brick-red squares; patio tiles in squares and rectangles and in several colors. Both are smooth, stain-resistant, and very attractive for terraces, pool areas, and walks.

Problems. (1) Tiles are somewhat slippery when wet. (2) They crack if they do not rest evenly on a firm subbase or if given a hard whack. (3) The expense is considerable.

Carefully cut slates laid on sand pave a terrace outside Chicago. Special metal edges keep the stones from sliding into plant beds.

Cypress block terrace in a Chicago-area garden is pleasantly resilient and cool, but slippery when damp.

Construction. To lay tiles on sand, handle them like flagstones. Plan the paved area to accommodate the tiles without cutting. If cutting is necessary, ask the tile dealer to do it for you; or score on both sides with a cold chisel until the tile cracks in two (this is not easy).

To lay tiles in mortar follow the procedure for flagstones. Before bedding tiles in concrete, soak them for 15 minutes or longer in clean water. Allow to drain well (but not dry) and then set in place. Because tiles are not so large and heavy as most flagstones, you may accidentally dislodge them if you try to fill the joints immediately. Better wait for 18 to 24 hours. Take care to wipe off mortar stains with a damp rag as they occur.

Paving with Wood Blocks

Characteristics. Redwood and cypress are preferred because they resist decay, but other woods can be used if they are pressure-treated with a preservative. The blocks are usually 4- to 6-inch cubes laid tight together in terraces. The end grain is exposed. If allowed to weather naturally, the blocks soon blend into the garden as well as the trees from which they came. They are pleasantly resilient underfoot.

Problems. (1) Even the most decay-resistant wood may eventually become spongy and rotten. (2) When damp, the blocks are slippery. This is especially a problem when they are laid in shady spots.

Construction. Laying wood blocks on sand is the same as for bricks, but it is not necessary to brush sand into the joints if the blocks are set close enough together. The edge blocks should be about 8 inches long and set on end so that they do not twist outward when stepped on.

Ogden, Utah, poolside shelter is floored with thick planks laid out in herringbone pattern. (John D. Eccles)

Paving with Wood Planks

Characteristics. Strictly speaking, a planked surface is a deck or a platform. But in many gardens it serves the same purpose as paving.

Decks are commonly built to provide usable flat space for sitting, games, and the like, on sloping land or on other undesirable land; to provide walkways across swampy land, beaches, and such; to provide a change in elevation on flat land; and so forth.

Decks are made of decay-resistant redwood or cypress or of other woods that have been pressure-treated with a preservative. The wood is usually stained or left to weather naturally.

Problems. (1) Because the deck boards are spaced ¼ to ½ inch apart to allow for drainage, women in spike heels find walking hazardous. (2) Splinters are a threat to bare feet. (3) Decay is possible if decay-resistant wood is not used or construction is faulty.

Construction. This process varies too much for me to give any more than a few rudimentary facts that are generally applicable to most decks:

Support posts are generally 4by4s anchored to masonry piers that are 6 to 8 inches across at the top. The piers should rest on masonry footings 12 to 16 inches across and set below the frost line. The tops of the piers should be above ground and should slope slightly so that water will not soak into the bottom ends of the posts.

The spacing of posts depends on the size of the beams they support, or vice versa. For instance, if beams are 2by10s, posts cannot be more than 10 feet apart. Joist sizes depend on the space they span and on how closely they are set together. If you employ an architect or competent builder, he will figure these things out for you.

Decking material can be 2by4s, 2by6s, or 2by8s. The top edges should be beveled slightly to minimize splintering. As noted, the boards should be spaced no less than ¼ inch apart.

As a further guard against decay, the space under the deck should not be closed in.

Paving with Blacktop and Other Asphaltic Materials

Characteristics. Depending on the construction and final surface treatment, asphalt paving ranges from gray to black in color. It is not attractive enough for anything but driveways, walks, and play areas (where its comparative softness makes it extremely desirable). Its appearance can be improved, however, by spreading a thin layer of screened gravel or crushed stone on top.

Problems. (1) Asphalt paving soaks up heat, feels uncomfortably hot underfoot, and on very warm days is easily indented by heels. (2) It prevents water and air from reaching roots that extend underneath. (3) If not properly designed, it sluices valuable rainwater from your garden. In some situations, this concentrated runoff may be responsible for serious erosion of ground at a lower elevation than the paved area.

Construction. Packaged blacktop is the only asphaltic material that the amateur can easily install himself. Excavate the area to a depth of 5½ or 6 inches. Fill with bank-run gravel and roll it well. Spread on a 1½- to 2-inch layer of blacktop, rake smooth, and tamp or roll until it is compacted.

Because of its smoothness, the paved area need not be sloped more than 1 inch in 10 feet. To prevent the edges from cracking or crumbling, place steel curbing, cobblestones, or something similar against them.

If asphalt paving is laid near trees, allow a 12- to 24-inch space between it and the tree trunks. Do not pave over more than 50 percent of the root area. These precautions are necessary to assure that adequate moisture and air reach the tree roots.

Paving with Gravel or Crushed Stone

Characteristics. As opposed to the bank-run gravel that is used as a sub-base under many paving materials, the gravel used as a finish paving material is free of dirt and screened to uniform size. The individual particles are more or less round, as a rule. Crushed stone, such as bluestone, consists of clean, uniformly sized, angular particles that are produced by crushing large rocks.

Gravel and crushed stone (including marble chips) of various colors and sizes are readily available at moderate cost. Except when the colors are badly chosen, a graveled surface has an attractive, pleasantly natural look. It is an excellent foil for other paving materials that are used with it. It retards runoff of water and allows it to soak in to reach roots of trees and shrubs.

Problems. (1) Gravel and crushed stone must be raked frequently to look their best. This is a chore. (2) Furthermore, it is very difficult to rake leaves, twigs, cigarette

Small, white gravel in terrace area is kept out of the grass by wide blocks of limestone which form a mowing strip.

butts, and other refuse out of gravel. (3) The gravel scatters easily from the paved area onto the surrounding lawn and shrubbery areas, where it is hard to rake up and may damage the lawn mower. In snow country, the scattering done by plows and snow blowers is a first-class headache. (4) Fine gravel gets into your shoes, while coarse gravel is unpleasant to walk on. (5) Unless precautions are taken against them, weeds come up as easily as if the gravel were beautiful garden soil; and they are hard to eradicate.

Construction. Excavate the area to a depth of 5 to 6 inches. Pour in 4 to 5 inches of rock or bank-run gravel that consists mainly of stones. Compact heavily with a steamroller or bulldozer. Then spread 1 inch of fine, screened gravel or crushed stone, or 1 to 2 inches of coarse gravel or crushed stone. (Establishment of a very firm, rocky sub-base is necessary to keep screened gravel from disappearing into the ground in wet weather. In cases where the natural soil is full of clay or the area to be paved is low or marshy, it may even be necessary to excavate to a depth of 12 to 18 inches and to build up from there first with large rocks, then with coarse bank-run gravel, then with finer bank-run gravel, and finally with the finish gravel.)

To keep weeds from coming up through gravel, some landscape architects cover the sub-base with heavy polyethylene film that is slit here and there to allow water to sink through. The screened gravel is spread directly on the film.

Another way to keep down weeds is to treat the graveled area with a herbicide, such as AMS. Follow the manufacturer's directions carefully (see Chapter X).

To minimize scattering of the gravel, surround the paved area with raised curbs of steel, brick, stone, concrete, or redwood. Or you can surround the area with wide mowing strips (see Chapter III).

Semishaded section of a Phoenix garden is paved with coarse gravel and large rectangular slabs forming a walkway.

Paving with Gravel in Combination with Solid Slabs

Characteristics. In this type of paving—which is designed to relieve the monotony of a large gravel-surfaced area (but rarely a driveway) and to make walking easier—slabs of concrete, flagstone, slate, tree trunks, and the like are set into the gravel in a studied pattern. The solid paving slabs can be circles, squares, rectangles, hexagons, and so on of varying sizes. They can be arranged in any way that suits the gardener.

Problems. The solid paving materials present the same problems as when they are used alone. The problems with the gravel are also the same as if gravel alone is used; however, walking is easier, and relatively little raking is required to smooth gravel that has been mussed.

Construction. Provide a sub-base, as for ordinary gravel paving, and top with a ½- to 1-inch sand cushion where solid paving pieces are placed. Set the solid paving pieces first; then fill in around them with screened gravel or crushed stone. Use the same weed-control and scatter-control methods as for gravel paving.

Paving with Chopped Tree Bark

Characteristics. Chopped bark is a mulching material made of small chunks of dark brown bark. As a paving material, it is used primarily in walks and paths. It is delightfully soft and quiet underfoot, and is very attractive in wooded and other informal garden areas.

Problems. (1) The bark gradually decomposes and therefore must be added to occasionally. (2) It is easily scattered onto surrounding surfaces (but tends to disappear from sight and cannot damage mowers). (3) It can be washed away on a slope. (4) It also feels slippery on slopes.

Construction. Scoop out an inch or two of soil; firm the base, and pour in the bark. A raised curbing of redwood, cypress, or steel helps to keep it in place.

Paving with Ordinary Concrete

Characteristics. In the hands of an artist who appreciates its plasticity, concrete has great beauty. But the nonartist must struggle—usually to no avail—to relieve its harshness and stiffness.

From a practical standpoint, however, concrete is an excellent paving material because of its great durability and ease of maintenance. It can be given a variety of textures—a fact that allows you to suit the paved surface exactly to your needs and aesthetic goals.

Problems. (1) Concrete is tiring to stand on. (2) It is rather dangerous for children to play on. (3) It stains badly. (4) It deprives roots underneath of water and air. (5) It exaggerates the runoff of water. (6) Large expanses of ordinary, light gray concrete are glary.

Construction. If the soil is well drained, excavate it to a depth of 3¾ inches and firm the bottom well. If the soil is not well drained, excavate to a depth of 6 inches or more and fill up to the 3¾-inch level with bank-run gravel, firmed well.

The concrete paving should be sloped in one or more directions 1 inch in 10 feet. The top of the paving should be ¼ inch above the surrounding soil. If using concrete close to trees, do not pave within 12 to 24 inches of the trunk, and do not pave over more than half the area; otherwise the trees may die for lack of air and moisture.

Build forms of wood around the edges of the paved area. Use 2by4s for straight forms and hold them in place with stakes spaced about 4 feet apart. For curved edges, use thinner wood and stake it every foot. The tops of the forms should be at the height of the finished slab. The stakes should be cut off to the same height. The forms must be thoroughly greased or oiled so the concrete will not stick to them.

Concrete for paving should be made with either ordinary Portland cement or Type 1A Portland cement. The latter is recommended for use in cold climates and for paving on which salt may be used to melt snow. In either case, the mortar should consist of 1 sack cement, 2 cubic feet sand, and 2 cubic feet coarse aggregate. If colored concrete is desired, use white Portland cement instead of the usual gray, and mix in mineral oxide pigments according to the manufacturer's directions. Generally, 7 pounds of pigment added to one bag of cement give a strong color; 1½ pounds give a pleasing pastel color. Extra time and care must be taken when mixing pigments into the dry concrete ingredients to make sure of a uniform color in the finished concrete.

Use concrete within 30 minutes after it has been mixed. Pour it into the excavation between forms and spade and tamp it well to settle it and eliminate air pockets. Then lay a straight "strike-off" board across the forms and saw it back and forth while moving it sideways across the paved area. This strikes off the concrete even with the tops of the forms.

When the moisture on top of the concrete starts to disappear, smooth the concrete with a float—a flat board or metal blade with a handle on one side. This produces a good nonskid surface. A rougher finish is made by dragging a stiff-bristled broom across the surface. For a smoother surface, let the floated concrete set until it is quite stiff and then finish it with a steel mason's trowel. Edging is done at this time with a special tool that rounds off the edges.

When the concrete sets to the point where it does not show fingerprints, cover it with damp burlap and keep it covered and wet for six days. The alternative is to cover tightly with polyethylene film.

There are two ways to make the contraction joints that are required in all sizable concrete surfaces: (1) Place redwood or cypress boards on edge between the forms and level with them. Space the boards 4 to 6 feet apart. Pour the concrete between them. (2) After smoothing the concrete with your float, cut grooves across the concrete at 4- to 6-foot intervals with a T-shaped "jointer" (which can be obtained from a masonry supplies dealer) held against a straight board.

Several methods of producing a patterned concrete finish have become popular in recent years. For example, in order to develop a random flagstone pattern, bend an

18-inch length of ½-inch copper tube into a flat S-shape, and slightly flatten one end. Use this to tool joints into the concrete after it has been struck off. Then, when the moisture disappears, go over the surface with a float and run the tube down the joints again to smooth them. The joints may be left as is or filled with contrasting mortar when the slab dries.

A geometric pattern can be created by pressing sharp-edged molds into the concrete after it has been smoothed. Use tin cans of various sizes to make circles. Large cookie cutters and odd-shaped tin cans can be used to create other designs.

Delicate, fossil-like leaf impressions are made by pressing fresh leaves into concrete right after it has been floated and troweled smooth. The leaves must be embedded deeply enough so that you can pass a trowel over them without dislodging them, but must not be covered with mortar. Remove the leaves after the concrete has set.

To make a travertine-like "keystone" finish, strike off and float the concrete in the usual way and then roughen the surface with a broom. Mix 1 sack white cement, 2 cubic feet sand, and ¼ pound colored pigment with enough water to make a soup with the consistency of thick paint. Dash this grout vigorously onto the slab with a large brush, such as a wallpaper-paste brush. This makes an uneven surface with ridges up to ½ inch high. Allow the surface to harden until you can kneel on it with a kneeboard. Then flatten the ridges with a steel trowel. This leaves a surface that is smooth in some parts, coarse-grained and holey in others.

Paving with Exposed Aggregate Concrete

Characteristics. This is an ornamental concrete in which the surface is more or less covered with small pebbles or stone chips that may be of a single color, such as black, or of mixed colors. Since the pebbles project slightly above the concrete, the surface feels and looks rough, and is skidproof. The effect is very decorative.

Exposed aggregate is as durable as ordinary concrete but is generally used only in terraces, walks, and pool areas.

Problems. These are the same as with ordinary concrete. In addition, exposed-aggregate concrete is rather difficult to sweep clean.

Construction. The procedure is the same as for ordinary concrete. Contraction joints are commonly made with redwood or cypress lumber, or they are cut into the concrete with a power saw four to 12 hours after the concrete is placed.

The coarse aggregate finish is made with marble chips, granite screenings, or other colored rock materials of ½- to ¾-inch diameter. Scatter the aggregate evenly over the

Paving in Arizona sunshine becomes blistering hot, so this homeowner paved his pool area in Kool Deck. (Arizona Photographic Associates)

Exposed aggregate concrete laid in large redwood-edged squares produces a handsome, skidproof, and relatively glareproof terrace in an Ogden, Utah, garden. (John D. Eccles)

surface as soon as the concrete has been floated. Then press the material below the surface of the concrete with your strike-off board.

When the concrete is firm enough to support the weight of a man kneeling on a wide board, go over the surface with a magnesium float to make sure that all bits of aggregate are completely embedded and surrounded by concrete. Then, just as soon as the concrete starts to harden, brush the mortar away from the top portion of the aggregate with a stiff brush. Spray the surface gently with water to flush off the mortar. Take care not to dislodge the stones.

Cure under damp burlap or plastic film for six days.

Paving with Concrete Patio Blocks

Characteristics. Patio blocks are 1½-inch-thick concrete rectangles without cores. Some resemble ordinary concrete blocks in texture; others are covered with pebbles or stone chips. They are available in various colors and sizes up to 16 by 16 inches. Paving made with them lacks the rigidity and severity of poured concrete.

The blocks are generally used only in terraces and walks. They are not strong enough to support heavy traffic.

Problems. (1) The blocks are readily stained with oil and grease, although they can be sealed with a clear coating. (2) They are not so durable as flagstones.

Construction. When laying blocks on sand, handle them like flagstones. As far as laying blocks in mortar is concerned, you can do it, but don't: You wind up with a surface that is as rigid as poured concrete.

Paving with Kool Deck

Characteristics. Kool Deck is a special material used around swimming pools because it is cooler underfoot than other paving. It also provides a nonskid, stain- and mold-resistant surface. The material is combined with white cement and sand to form a concrete-like surface resembling coral rock. It is available in five colors.

Although it is used primarily in hot climates, where the sun heats paving to a point almost unbearable to bare feet, Kool Deck is also used in the North. It does not soak up moisture to an appreciable extent and therefore resists damage by freezing.

Problems. (1) Cost. (2) It must be installed by professionals who follow directions exactly. (3) The color may change, though not to an appreciable extent.

Construction. Kool Deck is laid in a thin layer on a concrete slab constructed in the usual way. Application is made before the slab dries completely. The material is dashed onto the concrete with a large brush and is then troweled.

XV  Proper Watering Is Easy Watering

The most important single job the gardener has to do is to keep his garden watered. It is a time-consuming chore—especially when it is done improperly.

And that, unfortunately, is the way most gardeners do it. They don't apply enough water at a slow enough rate for the ground to absorb it. As a result, they must drag out their hoses several times a week during dry weather to redo their work.

Your aims in watering the garden should be: (1) to apply enough water to wet the entire root system of each plant; (2) to prevent loss of water through runoff, excessive evaporation, and excessive transpiration; and (3) to do the entire job with the least possible effort. In parts of the country where the soil and/or water are very alkaline, an additional aim should be to prevent an excessive build-up of alkaline salts in the soil.

To Help Soil Absorb Water

When you apply water faster than the ground can soak it up, you waste considerable water. And in order to give each plant what it needs, you must stand over it with your hose for a longer time than is really necessary.

There are several things you can do to prevent this double loss:

Terracing sloping land. Chapter XI gives several reasons for terracing a sloping lot. Here is another: It makes better use of water.

When you water plants on a slope, some of the water flows downhill, where it may not be needed. True, the amount of runoff is reduced if the slope is covered with grass or other plants. Nevertheless, loss of water is inevitable.

On terraced land, however, the loss is negligible because there is only one place for the water to go—straight down into the ground.

Making a soil percolation test. Every gardener knows that sandy soil absorbs water faster than loam and that loam absorbs it faster than clay. But do you know exactly how absorbent your garden soil is?

There is a very easy way to find out: The next time you have a two- or three-week dry spell, make a percolation test.

Place a sprinkler in a flat area of your lawn; and place near it, on the ground, a flat-bottomed glass jar. (The jar should be marked on the side to show a 1-inch depth.) Turn on the water to full speed, and notice whether the drops disappear quickly into the soil or begin to form puddles. If the water disappears, fine: Keep sprinkling at the same rate. But if there are puddles and they continue to form after the sprinkler has been running for about ten minutes (which is enough time for the soil to have softened), it is an indication that your soil is relatively nonabsorbent. You should then gradually reduce the flow of water at the faucet until puddling stops.

Continue sprinkling until the jar holds 1 inch of water.

Then turn off the water and note exactly how much time has elapsed since you first turned on the sprinkler. Wait for about two hours for the water in the ground to settle. Then dig a hole next to the jar and measure the depth to which the water has penetrated.

You now possess several pieces of valuable information about your soil:

1. You know how fast you should run your sprinkler in order to put every drop of water into the ground where you want it. Thus, when you water a slope in the future, you can minimize the loss of water through runoff. You can also reduce the erosion that even light runoff causes.

2. You know approximately how long it takes to apply 1 inch of water with the sprinkler that you used in the test. (But remember that another sprinkler may work faster or slower.) This will help you in the future to tell— simply by looking at a clock—whether you have watered an area of your garden adequately.

3. You know how deep 1 inch of water will wet your soil in a certain length of time; or putting it in another way, you know how long it takes to wet your soil to a certain depth. This will enable you in the future to form a reasonably accurate opinion about whether you are satisfying the moisture requirements of your plants. (If 1 inch of water does not penetrate deeply enough, you can apply 2 or 3 inches in order to double or triple the depth to which the soil is wet.) You also have a pretty good idea about how porous your soil is. (By way of comparison, irrigation experts have learned from tests that, as a rule, if a soil is sandy, you need to apply ¾ inch of water to wet it to a depth of 1 foot; if a soil is loam, you need 1½ inches of water to wet it to a depth of 1 foot; and if a soil is clay, you need 2½ inches of water to wet it to a depth of 1 foot.)

Improving soil porosity. As I just indicated, once you have tested your soil's porosity, you should know how to water it efficiently—without waste of water or your own time. However, if the soil is so dense that it takes you an inordinate amount of time to water it, you should find it worthwhile to change its composition.

The cheapest and best way to do this is to mix in sand and small gravel or crushed rock as discussed in Chapter II.

Adding humus also increases soil porosity. So does gypsum if the soil contains sodium salts.

To Help Soil Retain Moisture

Water escapes from soil by two routes: Some is evaporated from the surface. A lot more is taken up by plant roots and given off through plant leaves by the process known as transpiration.

It is evident from this that the speed with which soil dries out depends on weather conditions (intensity of the sun, temperature, humidity, and wind) and on how fast moisture is taken up by plant roots. It also depends on the composition of the soil. Clay soil loses moisture more slowly than loam; and loam loses it more slowly than sandy soil.

Some of the things you can do to make your soil more moisture-retentive should be obvious:

Adding humus to porous soil. Humus is like a sponge; and when mixed into sandy soil—and even into loam—in sufficient quantities (see Chapter II), it makes the soil more spongelike.

Applying mulch to bare soil. A mulch acts as an insulating blanket that holds moisture in the soil, out of reach of the elements that are trying to steal it through evaporation.

Increasing space between plants. Every plant needs a certain amount of water during each 24-hour period. It stands to reason, therefore, that if two plants are growing close together in a plot of soil that contains, say, a gallon of water, they will use up the water much faster than either plant by itself. Moral: If you place plants far enough apart so that they don't all draw on the same source of moisture, the soil will retain its moisture over a longer period (and you will not have to water the garden so often).

Providing space between plants to retard water withdrawal from the soil does not necessarily mean that your garden must be sparsely planted (even though this has some work-saving advantages). But it does mean that you should not crowd shrubs, flowers, and so on as closely as you might if you lived in a very rainy climate. And it also means that you should not plant grass, ground covers, and other small plants under trees and large shrubs, because even the smallest mouse of a plant steals moisture from the big plants alongside.

How Often Should You Water and How Much?

Occasional deep waterings do more good for plants than frequent shallow waterings because they stimulate deep rooting. They also save you work because water is not lost from the soil so rapidly through evaporation.

But how do you know when a plant needs a deep watering? And how can you tell whether you are applying enough water?

Answer: Consider the condition of the soil within 6 to 48 inches of the surface. This is the area in which plant roots are most active (yes, even small grass plants send roots deep into the ground). It follows that if the soil in this area contains moisture, the plants do not need watering. But when the moisture level drops to 12 to 18 inches below the surface of the soil, you should apply enough water to dampen the dry space again completely.

One way to find out about your soil's moisture supply is to dig a hole. Another way is to buy a soil probe. All you do is drive this deep into the ground, pull it out, and examine the soil core that comes up with it.

But the most accurate way of determining whether soil contains enough moisture is to install a tensiometer. This is an instrument that is permanently sunk into the soil to measure how much moisture is available to plants. Simply by reading the gauge at the top of the instrument you can tell at any time whether the soil contains enough moisture; and when water is needed, you can also tell when you have applied enough.

Tensiometers are widely used by western farmers and park and golf course superintendents. They are available in 6-, 12-, 18-, 24-, 36-, 48-, and 60-inch lengths. Although you can get by with a single instrument—especially if you own a small lot with uniform soil—two give you a more accurate picture. One instrument should be a short one (probably 12 inches) that measures the moisture in the soil at one-quarter of the depth of the plant roots; the other instrument should be a long one (36 inches) that measures the moisture at three-quarters of the depth of the roots. Because roughly 90 percent of the moisture requirement of plants are obtained from the upper three-quarters of the root zone, the two tensiometers combine to tell you what the conditions are through most of this critical area.

Water Distribution

Most gardeners give little thought to the mechanics of watering beyond complaining that they do not like pulling hoses around the garden and bemoaning the absence of a faucet at the far end of the lawn. Actually, watering is a chore in good part because of inadequacies in the water distribution system (and these are not limited to lack of outdoor faucets).

Improving your house piping. Several years ago, when I was interviewing U.S. Department of Agriculture water experts at Beltsville, Maryland, a man who works closely with Maryland homeowners made the statement that most garden-watering problems trace back to poorly designed piping systems inside the house. His fieldwork showed him, he said, that most hose bibbs (outdoor faucets) are served by the same pipes that lead from the water meter to the bathrooms; and that, to make matters worse, the pipes and attached fittings are much too small. The result is that, even when a gardener turns a hose on full, the loss of pressure is so great that the hose does not deliver a full stream of water.

When I asked this man how he would correct the situation, he gave the following answer:

1. Install hose bibbs on a line separate from that serving the other outlets in the house.

2. Use 1-inch pipe and fittings in the line (or lines) to the hose bibbs.

3. Insist that your plumber install hose bibbs that pass the maximum amount of water (many are seriously constricted).

4. Insist that your plumber design the garden-watering lines to give at least 30 pounds of pressure *at the sprinklers* in the garden.

Installing plenty of outdoor faucets. One is not enough. Two are not enough. Probably not even three are enough.

Ideally, every spot in a residential lot should be within at least 50 feet of a faucet; and each outdoor faucet should have its own 50-foot hose. To hold down cost, as many of the faucets as possible should be installed on the outside walls of the house. But you should not hesitate to run pipes through the garden to remote faucets. Such piping can be done easily and inexpensively with lightweight, flexible plastic tube. This is so tough that it is not damaged by freezing; consequently, it can be laid within a few inches of the soil surface (provided that it does not run through cultivated areas where you might cut it with a spade or fork).

Hose dimensions. Use 50-foot lengths of ¾-inch hose. Fifty-foot lengths are preferable to 25s because they halve the number of connections between lengths and thus reduce friction loss. Three-quarter-inch hose is better than ⅝ or ½ because it carries more water at higher pressure. Thus you can apply more water faster than with smaller hoses; or if you are using a sprinkler you can apply more water over a larger area.

Flexibility of hoses. Choose them with this in mind regardless of cost. Whatever size hose you use, avoid the cheap plastics. One type has such thin walls that it can be tied in water-stopping knots like a piece of spaghetti. Another type, made of clear plastic, is so stiff and cantankerous even in fairly moderate weather that it cannot be pulled straight or wrapped in a neat coil.

My personal preference is the unreinforced neoprene hoses. These are manageable at all times and durable. Probably the best hoses—at least from the standpoint of durability—are the reinforced rubber types. The large sizes, however, are a bit too heavy to handle with ease.

Installing hose guides around the garden. Mrs. Pendleton Miller of Seattle invented the best of these. She is dedicated to the idea that gardening should not be too much work (more about her in Chapter V).

Hose guides like this are used throughout Mrs. Pendleton Miller's Seattle garden.

Some years ago Mrs. Miller decided that something had to be done to make it easier to pull hoses through her garden without lifting them around corners to avoid damaging her plants. She came up with the idea illustrated on this page. It consists of a ship's belaying pin that revolves on a steel rod stuck into the ground. Mrs. Miller uses these gadgets wherever a garden path turns a corner or wherever a hose being dragged along behind her might become snagged on a tree or corner of the house.

Hose spindles based on Mrs. Miller's design are now on the market. They are neither so sturdy nor so attractive as hers. But they help to make it easier to pull hoses around the garden.

Storing hoses. Always use reels or racks. If you do not have enough outdoor faucets, reels that hold from 150 to 400 feet of hose and that can be rolled around the garden are a definite labor saver. They keep your hoses reasonably neat and certainly improve their portability—though I must confess that I have found the reels exasperating on various occasions.

Inexpensive racks that screw to the wall near a faucet are just the ticket if you have plenty of faucets and the hoses to go with them. I know of no other way to keep a stored hose from getting into atrocious snarls.

Portable Sprinklers. These take much of the work out of watering lawns and other open areas. And you can increase their convenience by attaching a timer to the faucet or by buying a sprinkler with a built-in timer. The timers can be set to deliver water for any length of time up to four hours and then to turn the water off.

If your lawn is large, smooth, and relatively flat, a traveling sprinkler that automatically marches up and down the lawn eliminates the necessity for moving an ordinary sprinkler from place to place.

Nontraveling sprinklers should be selected: (1) for the coverage that they give (which ranges from roughly 1,000 to 5,000 square feet); (2) for their sprinkling pattern (square, rectangular, or round); and (3) for the rate at which they lay down water. The last point is the only one that you cannot determine at the time you make your purchase; and you should therefore have an understanding with the dealer that if the sprinkler is not right, it can be returned.

The problem is this: Some sprinklers throw out water at a much faster rate than others. This means that if you unknowingly buy a high-rate sprinkler and your soil happens to be dense, the sprinkler may supply water faster than the ground can absorb it and you may then have a runoff problem. Closing the faucet to reduce the flow of water will correct the problem, but at the same time it reduces the coverage that the sprinkler gives. Under the circumstances, the only sensible solution is to exchange the sprinkler for one with a slower sprinkling rate.

Porous hoses. These can put water exactly where you

want it. Types made of canvas—called soakers—ooze water into the soil directly underneath. They operate so slowly that even clay soil has time to soak up almost every drop. This is a great advantage when you are watering on a hillside or when water is in short supply. On the other hand, because a soaker wets only a very narrow strip of soil, you must move it frequently.

A flat, three-tube plastic sprinkler hose with tiny perforations on one side is more useful. When you use it perforated side down and run the water at slow speed, it is like a canvas soaker. If you use it perforated side up and turn the water on hard, it distributes water along its entire length in a strip about 6 feet wide.

Like most watering equipment, the three-tube sprinkler hose is a portable device that you move around the garden as necessary. A somewhat similar device you can make yourself consists of a thick, rigid, or flexible plastic tube with perforations or small spray nozzles that is permanently installed in a hard-to-get-at part of the garden that needs frequent watering. In Florida, for instance, an acquaintance of mine made an installation of this kind in a long shrubbery border in front of a wall. The tube was laid on the ground near the back of the border, and the water was directed diagonally upward to either side of the tube through nozzles spaced about 15 inches apart. Without this kind of installation, the border would have been difficult to water.

Another kind of permanent spray-tube installation is used in a Hawaiian garden—also to water a long, straight shrubbery border. In this case, the tube is perforated and is mounted on poles just above the tops of the shrubs. It is not attractive (though, because there are trees behind the shrubs, it is not very noticeable); but its aerial position is made necessary by the fact that the shrubs are so dense that they can be watered satisfactorily only from above. At ground level, the spray would be largely wasted.

Underground sprinkling systems. Although they are designed mainly for watering lawns, you can—by proper selection of sprinkling heads—use them to water other garden areas as well. Thus you take all the work out of watering. There are no hoses or sprinklers to move; not even faucets to turn on and off. All you do is set the automatic timing device that controls the system. This turns on the sprinklers at the desired time, lets them run for the desired period, and then turns them off.

Sprinkling systems are made by a number of companies, but all are essentially the same. They consist of a time control; a network of pipes or tubes laid underground; and a variety of sprinkler heads—some that are exposed, some that are hidden below ground level, some that give a round, fountain-like spray, some that rotate, some that oscillate back and forth, some that spit out water over long distances in jets. The cost ranges from a couple of hundred dollars into the thousands, depending on the size and complexity of the system.

The best way to buy an underground sprinkling system is to ask representatives of several firms to visit your garden, study your needs and problems, and then make recommendations. If you are a do-it-yourself enthusiast, you might also investigate the possibility of making your own installation with the Toro Manufacturing Company's Moist O'Matic system.

Some of the problems involved in putting in underground sprinkling are covered by Robert M. Hagan of the University of California in the U.S. Department of Agriculture's *1955 Yearbook of Agriculture:*

> Before investing in sprinkler equipment, one should study its operating characteristics, including discharge capacity, area covered and distribution of water over the wetted area. An important specification is the pressure required at the sprinkler. To obtain the distribution pattern for which the sprinkler was designed, a certain minimum pressure is required at the sprinkler head. When the pressure is too low,

the drops are large; more water is thrown to the outside edges of the area covered. A typical example of inadequate pressure is the doughnut pattern—an area near the head receives little water and soon dries out. When the pressure exceeds the design pressure, the spray is broken up into very fine drops, or "fog," so that much of the water is deposited near the sprinkler head in still air or is carried away if it is windy. Variations in pressure affect the patterns of some sprinklers more than others. Pressure also affects the discharge capacity of the sprinkler. If the pressure is doubled, the discharge is increased by a factor equal to the square root of 2. Thus the discharge is increased by 41 per cent.

Eight steps in planning and installing an underground sprinkler system are: Determine the available static water pressure; make a sketch of turf area; select and locate the control valves; select and space the sprinkler heads; determine the number of sprinkler heads on one line; select the size of pipe on the basis of friction loss in pipes and resistance of water meters, valves and fittings; install the system, allowing for settling of the soil; and adjust the sprinkler heads as needed.

Available static pressure should be measured by attaching a pressure gauge to any faucet. The test should be made at an hour when most of the sprinkling is done in the neighborhood to obtain the minimum pressure.

A sketch of the yard showing location of house, walks, drives, lawn areas, gardens, water-supply lines and available connections should be made on a scale of not less than ¼ inch per foot. The system then can be completely mapped out on paper and the correct sprinklers, fittings and pipe selected.

Control valves should be selected and located with particular care. The ideal valve is of rugged construction, offers little resistance to flow and does not leak when it is closed. Angle valves are most satisfactory for sprinkler installations, and they should be provided with a union connection. Locations next to walks or porches, and far enough away from the nearest sprinkler heads to avoid the spray, are most desirable.

The sprinkler heads must be placed close enough to cover

the entire area as uniformly as possible. Sprinklers may be arranged in a square or triangular pattern. The latter arrangement allows a greater spacing between heads with a given sprinkler type. Sprinklers having a cone-shaped pattern (where the amount of water applied decreases steadily from the head outward) are most suitable for overlapping to give a nearly uniform application over the irrigated area. With such sprinklers, it is best to place them at distances equal to the radius of the area wet by each head. That means that the spray from one just reaches the head of another. Half-circle heads are available for installation along walks and borders and when properly spaced may be used to wet corners so that quarter-circle heads need not be installed.

The maximum number of heads to be installed on a line under one control valve depends on: Available pressure at the main, total resistance or pressure loss in the supply line between main and sprinklers, the capacity of sprinkler heads (see the manufacturer's data table) and the arrangement of sprinklers—whether on a single, continuous line or in two or more branch lines. When too many heads are installed on one line, the pressure at the sprinklers will not be adequate for proper distribution, coverage will be reduced and dry spots will appear between heads. Although no harm results from installing fewer heads on one line than is feasible, greater economy is obtained by arranging the layout so as to require a minimum number of valves. In sparsely settled areas in which new homes are being built, however, it may be wise to plan the system on the basis of a considerably lower pressure in the main than may now be available.

Friction loss in pipelines must be considered. The smaller the pipe and the higher the water velocity through it, the greater the friction loss and the greater the pressure drop. For a given flow of water, each foot of ½-inch pipe will have as much resistance as 12.5 feet of 1-inch pipe. Friction loss tables are available for different pipe sizes. Resistance offered by a pipe depends not only on size but also on roughness of the inner surface. When a pipe corrodes on the inside, frictional resistance is increased. Copper tubing has a smooth inside surface, which corrodes slowly and will maintain a high water-carrying capacity. Non-corroding, smooth plastic and rubber pipes also are available. Water meters, valves and fittings also cause a loss in pressure. The losses for them vary considerably with different manufacturers. Friction losses are most conveniently expressed in terms of an equivalent length of 1-inch pipe. For example, a 1-inch angle valve has a resistance equal to 8 feet of 1-inch pipe; a 1-inch globe valve has a resistance equivalent to 30 feet of 1-inch pipe. One-inch elbows have an equivalent resistance of 2 feet of 1-inch pipe; a side outlet tee is equivalent to 3 feet of 1-inch pipe.

The actual procedure for determining the proper pipe sizes and numbers of sprinkler heads on given lines is rather complicated.

Good workmanship during installation pays dividends in the long run in lower losses of pressure and absence of leaks, which may be hard to locate. On new lawns it is difficult to set sprinkler heads at exactly the right elevation. Often the ground settles and the heads are left too high. To permit later adjustment after the soil has settled, sprinklers are commonly put on long nipples, so that they extend about 4 inches above the soil. After the grass is well established and the soil settled, the nipples can be easily removed because they extend above the grass, cut to proper length, and reinstalled. That avoids both sunken heads and high heads, which are hazardous and interfere with mowing. Where there is danger of freezing damage, each sprinkler line should be laid to a waste valve.

Even a well designed and installed system may not work well unless some care is given it during operation. For proper performance, grass must be kept from interfering with the spray from heads set flush with the surface. As the turf becomes older, the sod may thicken and leave the heads too low. When this occurs, the sprinklers should be removed and longer nipples installed. Sprinkler heads may become clogged with foreign matter and fail to distribute water evenly. It may be necessary to remove the heads and clean them. If the water pressure falls too low for proper operation of the sprinklers when they are all turned on at once, fewer heads should be used at one time. Low water pressure will reduce the diameter covered by a sprinkler head and cause an uneven distribution pattern. Wind may so distort the distribution as to leave dry spots between heads and along the windward edge. One should do no sprinkling when it is windy.

Using tensiometers. It is a mistake to think that, just because a garden has a sprinkling system, the moisture requirements of all plants are fully satisfied. They should be, but they rarely are. The reason for this is that the person who sets the control that turns the sprinklers on and off cannot be sure what the condition of the soil will be on any given day in the future. He can only guess; and he is likely to guess wrong, because any number of things may occur to change soil conditions.

Tensiometers take the guesswork out of sprinkler system control. They constantly measure the amount of moisture in the soil; and when the soil in the root zone becomes dry, they tell the sprinklers to turn on and refill the soil with water.

All types of sprinkling systems can be controlled by tensiometers. The number of instruments needed varies according to soil composition, plant moisture needs, and the size of the garden. You might need two instruments in a small garden, four in a very large one. They would add about $125 to $500 to the total cost of a sprinkling system.

How To Water

Lawns. The way you sprinkle your lawn has a lot to do with the amount of work you must put into lawn maintenance. Overwatering is bad because: (1) the soil is more easily compacted by traffic when it is wet and this, in turn, causes thin, weedy turf; (2) poorly drained soil becomes water-logged, and this prevents grass roots from taking up fertilizer nutrients; (3) fertilizer is leached out of porous soil before it can release all its nutrients; (4) diseases, insects, and weeds flourish.

Of course, underwatering causes problems, too. But tests indicate that grass generally does better with too little water than with too much. The secret to success is in applying enough water when you do water to wet the soil deep down and thus to force the grass to develop deep roots. This allows grass to survive prolonged periods of relative dryness. And this, in turn, allows you to reduce lawn maintenance operations.

The question of when to water your lawn is answered by Dr. Hagan:

> In many places it makes little difference. One should realize, however, that the time selected for watering may influence both irrigation efficiency and condition of the grass. Highest irrigation efficiencies [meaning that most of the water goes into the ground and is not lost through evaporation] can be attained when temperatures are low and humidity high. The most uniform distribution of water can be expected when water pressures are ample and there is no wind. As for the grass, it makes little difference when turf is irrigated except in summer, when fungus diseases may be serious. Watering lawns in full sunlight during the heat of the day very seldom harms grass. Occasionally some injury appears in turf grown on tight, slowly draining soils if they are permitted to become nearly saturated during very hot weather. Then the grass and its roots may be damaged—a condition called scalding. Watering early in the day permits the grass to dry rapidly and may reduce the disease problem. An ideal time to water is near sunrise. Watering is less desirable during the afternoon, when temperatures are high, humidities low and winds may be strong. Water pressures are often low during the late afternoon and early evening. When lawns are irrigated at that time, the grass will remain damp all night—an encouragement to disease if nights are warm.

Flowers. Like other small plants flowers are best watered in the morning so that any foliage that is accidentally dampened will have plenty of time to dry before nightfall.

You should try as much as possible to apply water only to the soil immediately around the plants. Plants in straight rows are most easily watered with a canvas soaker or a three-tube sprinkler hose laid perforated side down. Plants that are casually spotted through a border can also be watered with a soaker, and those in a sloping bed must be watered in this way; but it takes an unnecessary amount of time to weave the soaker around the plants. (The three-tube sprinkler is even more difficult to use because it does not bend sideways.) An easier way to care for casually arranged flowers in a *flat* bed is to build a small dike of soil around the edges of the bed and to pour in water directly from a slow-running hose until the soil is wet way down.

Vegetables and small fruits. Water in the morning with a canvas soaker or three-tube sprinkler hose laid down each row at the base of the plants. An alternate method— if your garden is flat—is to make a furrow down each row with a hoe and to fill this with water from a hose. This, however, prevents use of a mulch.

Trees. In watering trees (as well as shrubs and vines), it is important not only to apply enough water to wet the soil deep down but also to apply water over the entire root zone. Since tree roots grow outward from the trunk in all directions as far as the tips of the branches and even beyond, applying water only at the base of the trunk does very little good. You should, instead, apply a more or less even depth of water over the entire area that is overhung by branches. Here are four ways to do this:

1. Coil a three-tube sprinkler hose, perforated side up,

in a loose spiral around the tree. If the ground is sloping, however, use the hose perforated side down. Or use a canvas soaker.

2. If a tree is on flat ground, build a small dike of soil around it under the tips of the branches and fill the saucer with a hose. If the saucer is filled with a mulch that is disturbed by a direct hose stream, tie the hose to a branch and apply water through a fine-spray nozzle pointed downward.

3. If a tree is on sloping land, drill holes with a soil auger at 18- to 24-inch intervals around the tree under the tips of the branches and scatter more holes throughout the circle. The holes should be 24 inches deep. Insert sections of 3-inch perforated drainpipe in the holes. Fill the pipes occasionally with water by flooding the area or by holding a hose in each pipe. (The trees can also be fertilized through the pipes.)

4. Attach a water lance—a hollow, needlelike tool used to carry water to deep plant roots—to the end of a hose and stick it into the soil at 24-inch intervals throughout the tree's root area. (Note that the usual directions to stick the lance deep into the soil at the base of the trunk are inadequate because water does not travel sideways in soil; therefore, a single insertion of the lance does no more good than applying water at the base of a trunk with a hose.)

Shrubs and vines. Water by flooding a saucer in the soil or with a three-tube sprinkler hose or canvas soaker. Hedges are especially easy to water with a sprinkler hose.

(To help satisfy the moisture requirements of valuable shrubs when you are away on vacation, water them thoroughly and then spray with a plastic antitranspirant such as Wilt-Pruf. Retarding transpiration reduces the shrubs' craving for water and thus makes the supply of water in the ground last longer.)

Ground covers. Water in the morning with a portable sprinkler set above the tops of the plants so that the foliage cannot interfere with the spray. On flat or slightly sloping land it is also possible to build an earthen dike around the planted area and to flood the saucer with a hose.

Removing excess salts from soil. This problem exists in parts of the country where the soil is alkaline and the water may be, too. It is also a problem if the water used in your garden has been softened (as it often is in cities in hard-water areas). In both cases, the salts may accumulate in the soil to such a degree that they kill the plants and clog the pores of the soil so that water has difficulty passing through.

The problem can be prevented by making unusually heavy applications of water every two or three months. This washes, or leaches, the salts deep into the earth out of the reach of plant roots.

XVI  Those Wonderful Mulches

There are many gardeners who are convinced that mulching is far and away the greatest of all labor-saving ideas. It may well be—although I don't know how anyone can make such a measurement. But this is certain: No other really great labor saver affects the traditional appearance of gardens to such a limited extent. In other words, unlike many of the ideas discussed in this book, mulching does not mean giving up or restricting use of flowers, reducing lawn areas, planting small-size trees, or the like. On the contrary, it allows you to garden just the way you have always gardened; and yet it saves you an enormous amount of work.

Mulching greatly reduces the need for watering plants by slowing down the loss of water from the soil through evaporation.

Mulching eliminates weeding by keeping the life-giving sun from weed seedlings.

Mulching practically does away with cultivating because it protects the soil from the sun and thus keeps it from baking hard.

Mulching minimizes erosion by slowing the flow of

water across the land and by keeping the soil underneath in a spongelike condition. Thus it spares you from repairing the damage done by erosion.

Mulching eliminates the necessity for resetting or replacing plants that are heaved out of the soil by frost because it prevents the soil from thawing and freezing repeatedly in fall and spring.

Mulching simplifies disease-control work to some extent by preventing water from splashing up from the soil onto plant foliage. This helps to keep at least some of the dangerous microbes and spores that lurk in the soil from getting on leaves and stems.

Mulching with organic material minimizes a variety of gardening chores by adding valuable humus and nutrients to the soil and thus promoting more vigorous plant growth.

Mulching—in a word—is wonderful.

What to Mulch and When

Almost all trees, shrubs, vines, flower beds, and vegetable gardens benefit from being mulched. In the case of the first three, the mulch should be maintained the year round; and ideally it should cover the entire area in which roots grow (roughly from the trunk out to the ends of the branches). In flower beds, the mulch is maintained from the time the plants start to grow until they die down in the fall. Vegetable gardens are mulched in the same way, or you can maintain a year-round mulch if you pull the material away from the rows from the time you sow seed until the plants are well up. Both vegetable gardens and flower beds should be completely blanketed with your mulching material.

Perennial plants of all kinds are often mulched in the winter to protect them from extreme cold and to prevent them from being frost-heaved. The mulch is applied after the soil freezes in the fall and is removed—or pulled back from the crowns of the plants—just before growth starts in the spring.

Which Type of Mulch?

There are two basic types of mulch—the organics and the inorganics. The main advantage of the plant-derived organics is that, as they decompose, they add humus to the soil. This process, as I said earlier, makes for more vigorous plants. And they, in turn, require less work.

On the other hand, the main advantage of the inorganic mulches—including plastics, stones, or a combination of the two—is that they do *not* decompose. This means you do not have to replace them as often as the organics. And that, in turn, eliminates work.

Which type of mulch is the better? I doubt if anyone can say for sure.

When it comes to specific mulching materials, however, the choice is somewhat clearer. But each gardener must make his own. He will be influenced by the availability of the materials; the cost; the appearance of the material in use; how long it lasts; whether or not his soil needs humus; special needs the mulch must fulfill; and so on.

Here is an alphabetical rundown of most of the available mulches:

Buckwheat hulls. They are of uniform, small size and add much to the beauty of a rose garden or flower bed. But they are so light that they are easily scattered by wind and feet.

Chopped tree bark. This mulching material is one of the best for use in your prettiest garden areas. It is clean, stable, very attractive and decomposes rather slowly.

Cocoa bean hulls and pecan shells. Here are two other

attractive, clean, stable mulching materials that are slow to decompose. Cocoa bean hulls, however, must be mixed with sawdust (2 parts hulls to 1 part sawdust) to prevent formation of a mold that is often caused by oil in the hulls. You should also avoid using the hulls around rhododendrons and azaleas because they have a high potash content that may damage these plants.

Coffee grounds. They are an excellent mulch and soil conditioner; but you will probably have trouble getting hold of enough to treat many plants.

Corn cobs. Relegate them to out-of-the-way areas. They are effective but unsightly.

Fiberglass insulation. It is used to give winter protection to plants whose crowns are susceptible to rot: delphinium, chrysanthemums, and the like. Fiberglass does not become soggy with water as organic mulches do.

Grass clippings. They need to dry before they are used; otherwise, they become mildewed and matted. They are improved by mixing with some other mulching material.

Hay. If you know anyone who has a hayfield but who does not keep horses or livestock, make friends with him at once: He owns one of the finest supplies of mulch you can hope to find, and even if you have to pay for mowing the field, it is worth the expense. Hay is an excellent mulch that decomposes quickly and cleanly. Use it in vegetable gardens and wherever else that its slightly unkempt appearance will not bother you.

Salt hay, cut from ocean marshes, lasts two or three times as long as ordinary hay.

Leaves. They make a good mulch after they have decomposed somewhat. But fresh leaves give off unwanted heat during decomposition; they often pack into slimy or flaky layers; and they sometimes form a barrier against the passage of rain. Furthermore, if any of the leaves are diseased, they will transmit the disease to the plants being mulched.

Oak leaves, however, are a top favorite for mulching rhododendrons, azaleas, camellias, and other plants that require an acid soil because they increase soil acidity.

Peanut shells are lightweight and rather unattractive until they have weathered.

Peat. A favorite organic mulch, peat is slightly acid. But it has one drawback: After it has been wet and dried several times and has settled, water has difficulty in passing through it. So instead of hoarding the moisture supply in the soil, the peat keeps moisture out of the soil. This problem can be minimized, however, by mixing sawdust with peat.

Pine needles. They are a top choice for mulching acid-soil plants. They decompose more rapidly than oak leaves.

Polyethylene film—black. This material is widely used by farmers to mulch row crops. You can use it to good advantage in your vegetable garden, around roses and individual trees, and in shrubbery borders. If not abused, it lasts for several years. Of course, since it is completely watertight, polyethlyene must be laid so that moisture can get through but will not then escape too rapidly from the soil. When plants are in a row, two strips of film can be laid on either side of the row, or a single strip can be laid over the row and slit down the middle for the plants. In other kinds of plantings, pieces of film are simply laid rather loosely on the soil, and occasional cuts are made through them. In either case, enough water to supply plant needs seems to get through.

The main trouble with black polyethlyene—as with all plastic films—is its appearance. It is difficult to keep in place and flat in windy locations. And it may activate undesirable fungi in the soil (though agricultural scientists discount this as a serious problem).

Polyethylene film—white. White is better than black film because it transmits the sun's rays and thus raises soil temperature. This quality, in turn, promotes earlier and more vigorous growth of perennial plants in the spring. The heat also minimizes soil fungi problems. On the other hand, weeds grow under the film, although they do not get large enough to cause trouble.

Polyethylene film—green. It is much like the white film.

Polyethylene film with a pebble or chopped-bark covering. This does everything that uncovered plastic mulch does and looks good besides. The covering of pebbles or bark need be only thick enough to conceal the film. If you use white film, the pebbles can be pushed aside in the early spring so that the sun can heat the soil.

Sawdust. Among the advocates of sawdust are the horticulturists at the Brooklyn Botanic Garden, which adds up to a handsome recommendation. However, sawdust has the strange faculty of depleting the nitrogen supply in the soil, so you should apply a nitrogenous fertilizer before using it and annually thereafter.

Seaweed. A good mulch, it should be allowed to dry before you use it; otherwise it forms a slimy mass. It contains some potash.

Stones, pebbles, and shells. In permanent, ornamental plantings around shrubs and trees they are very good looking. And they are surprisingly effective in holding in moisture. But the larger the stones, the thicker you must make the layer in order to keep down weeds. Oyster shells should be crushed somewhat before they are applied.

Straw. It is not so attractive as hay but otherwise has the same qualities for mulching. It decomposes a bit more slowly.

Sugar cane. The ground-up stalks are increasing in popularity as a mulch in those areas where they are available. They have very good water-holding capacity.

Tobacco stems. They are available only in a few areas. It is thought they help to control insects to some extent.

Wood chips. There not many things better for

mulching plants on slopes, because the chips are large enough, coarse enough, and heavy enough to stay put even in heavy rains. And they cost nothing if you can talk the tree-trimming crews of your electric utility or telephone company into giving them to you, or if you have to take down trees on your own property. But they are somewhat unkempt looking, especially as they come from the chipper.

The best chips are from hardwood trees, because they rot more slowly. Soil to be mulched should first be given a dose of nitrogenous fertilizer; and you should add more of the same fertilizer annually thereafter, because, like sawdust, the chips draw nitrogen from the soil.

How Much to Use

Between 2 and 4 inches of an organic mulch or pebbles are usually enough to prevent weed growth and retard moisture loss. As the blanket decomposes, new material must, of course, be added; but you rarely have to do this more than once a year. (If you use a chemical weed killer to treat the soil that is mulched, less mulch is required. See Chapter X.)

In applying organic mulches around small plants care must be taken not to cover the crowns of the plants. And as noted before, when polyethylene film is used, you must allow some open space around the crowns so that water can enter the soil.

If your property is a haven for mice, you should also pull an organic mulch away from the trunks of fruit trees. Thus deprived of protective covering, the little pests are less likely to gnaw on the tree trunks.

XVII 🌿 Work-saving Tools for Purchase or Rent

There is one problem with modern garden tools: They make work so easy that it is difficult to resist buying more tools.

If I encourage moderation, it is not to save you money. Rather, it is to remind you that tools need maintenance, too; consequently every new one you buy adds to your work while subtracting from it.

What's the conclusion? Simply that when you set out to buy another tool, you should bear two points in mind: (1) The more ruggedly dependable a tool is, the less attention you must give it. In short—shop for quality. (2) Since engines generally require more service than other tool parts, you may do yourself a favor if you buy one or two multipurpose power tools with interchangeable attachments instead of a number of single-purpose power tools.

A final question to ask yourself just before you tell the tool dealer, "I'll take it," is whether you really need the tool in question so much that you must buy rather than rent. To me, the convenience of letting someone else maintain and store the less frequently used garden tools far outweighs either the pleasures of owning my own tools or the occasional annoyances caused by rented tools that are not in first-class working order.

As you can see from this statement, I am not a garden-tool-collector. But this does not mean that I am not a garden-tool-using enthusiast. I am. If I knew how to measure the progress we have made in reducing garden maintenance over the past 20 years, I am sure I would find that new kinds of tools have contributed most.

Which Tools for You?

From the time man first used a pointed stick rather than his fingers to cultivate soil, all garden tools have helped to save work. But I shall not insult your intelligence by talking here about rakes and hoes and spades. Let's stick to the newer garden tools and equipment and some of the older items you may not have thought too much about.

Which of these you need is for you alone to decide. I emphasize this in the light of a brief conversation my wife had with a friend of ours—a widow. Dropping by our new house for the first time, she was, I guess, pleased to find that the meadow that surrounds us is more or less a duplicate of the one around her home. "I hope Stan has a riding mower," she said to my wife. "I can do my whole place in an hour. It's the best tool we ever owned."

I have no doubt she is right. Another friend with a meadow says the same thing. But it so happens that, while I have no enthusiasm for mowing, I look upon it as a good way to get the exercise that a sedentary occupation denies me during the week. In other words, no riding mower for me.

Whether you are interested in mowers, cultivators, pruning tools, or what not, you should not be a copycat either. Listen to what friends and experts have to say about the equipment that is available; but let the final decision about acquiring it be your own.

High-wheel rotary mower. (Locke Manufacturing Companies)

Rotary mowers. Rotaries have always been the first choice of gardeners who have rough grass to cut; but in recent years, their cutting action has been so greatly improved that they are now considered excellent for fine lawns. As a rule, cutting height can be adjusted from 1 to 3½ inches; but there are machines that will cut a little lower or a little higher. In theory, the width of the cutting swath is the stated width of the mower; that is, an 18-inch mower theoretically cuts a swath 18 inches wide. In actual fact, however, the width of the swath is slightly less than the stated mower width; and the difference is greater on large mowers than on small.

Self-propelled rotaries obviously require less effort to use than push types. But one drawback of some self-propelled units is that they go slower than you may like to walk. In this situation, you should choose a model that lets you operate at any speed up to about 3½ miles per hour. The alternative—if you have a smooth, flat lawn—is to use a push-type mower.

For cutting over rough ground and sandy soil, the so-called high-wheel rotary is recommended. This has two large, rubber-tired bicycle wheels in the rear that make it exceptionally easy to roll. Some of the machines have 6- and 7-horsepower engines to permit easy cutting of coarse southern grasses. An additional feature is a cutting unit that swivels with the contour of the ground and thus ensures against scalping of high spots.

Most rotaries are gasoline-powered and have two-cycle or four-cycle engines; but electric mowers have been gaining in popularity for gardens not exceeding 10,000 square feet and require less maintenance than gas mowers. They are also quieter, and most models have a handle that swings over and thus eliminates the need for turning the machine at the end of each cut. On the other hand, electric mowers have a 100-foot power cord that you must contend with; all models are of the push type; and damp grass causes clogging.

All rotaries require somewhat less maintenance than reel mowers. The supervisor of park operations in Kansas City has made the statement that "rotaries run much longer than the reel type before needing blade adjustments or sharpening, and they're relatively maintenance-free and rugged."

Reel mowers. They are recommended for cutting very fine lawns and also irregular ground which rotaries may scalp. Cutting height can be adjusted from about ½ to 2¼ inches. Cutting width is the actual width of the blades.

Both self-propelled and push-type models are available. Because reel mowers weigh more than rotaries, self-propelled reels are even more desirable than self-propelled rotaries—provided they move at a speed you consider comfortable. On level "putting-green" lawns, however, push models are easy to use. Most reel mowers are gasoline driven, but a few electrics are to be had.

Grass catchers. Many rotary mowers are equipped with a large bag to catch grass clippings. All reel mowers can be equipped with an open cloth or plastic hopper serving the same purpose.

Do you need a grass catcher? Yes and no.

On Bermudagrass, bentgrass, and zoysia lawns that are kept cut very short, you do.

On other lawns, grass clippings under ¾ inch in length do no harm if they are left where they fall; but longer clippings may bring on a variety of problems. It follows that when grass is growing very rapidly in the spring, you need a grass catcher if you do not intend to mow the lawn more than once a week; otherwise the lawn will be smothered under clippings that are unhealthily long. At other times of the year, however, when grass is growing more slowly, you can get by without a grass catcher.

Why not use a grass catcher all year round? Because it is a chore to cope with; and there is no sense in letting it complicate mowing at times when grass-clipping removal is unnecessary. Furthermore, there is evidence that short clippings left on the lawn in the summer help to slow the release of nitrogen from fertilizer and thus indirectly help to simplify fertilizing operations and lawn maintenance.

Riding mowers. You should consider a riding mower only if your health is poor or if you have about half an acre of open, unobstructed lawn that allows plenty of room for maneuvering. Even then, I think you will do better with a garden tractor.

Riding mowers are gasoline powered, and most are

rotaries. When mowing, they should not operate at much more than 3½ miles an hour; but they can cover a lot of ground in a short time because they cut a wide swath.

Units with between 3½ and 6 horsepower are the right size for most gardens. You need a more powerful engine if your lot is hilly. Attachments include carts, lawn sweepers, spreaders, aerators, rollers, and snowplows.

Garden tractors. If you have a large garden, a midget tractor or even a small farm tractor can save you more work than any other tool. With an assortment of attachments, it can be used for mowing, rolling, aerating, raking, sweeping, vacuuming leaves, spreading, plowing, disking, rotary tilling, cultivating, harrowing, trenching, small-scale bulldozing, loading, sweeping pavements, spraying, snowplowing, and so on.

Garden tractors are generally riding units, but there are walking types which can in most cases be converted to riding units. They have gasoline engines of from 6 to 12 horsepower; and even larger units will probably be produced in the near future.

Edgers. This tool you will not need if you rim your lawn with mowing strips (Chapter III) or spray the edges in the spring with maleic hydrazide (Chapter IX). But if you don't do either of these things, then an electric or gasoline edger is almost an essential. Some models are used only for cutting sharp edges. Others operate in vertical position for edging and in horizontal position for cutting clumps of tall grass.

Cleanup machines. If you have not yet investigated these, I predict that it will not be long before you do. They are the perfect answer not only to annual leaf-raking drudgery but, in some cases, to various other garden cleanup problems.

Lawn sweepers are large, hand-propelled or gasoline-engine-driven carts with revolving wire brushes that whisk up leaves and other trash in a swath 20 to 30 inches wide.

Lawn vacuums are oversized vacuum cleaners that will clean up to 30,000 square feet of lawn and open garden space per hour. Although they do not handle small branches and stones as easily as lawn sweepers, they are better for cleaning paved areas. Much of their present sales-doubling growth, in fact, is attributable to their popularity for cleaning up around swimming pools.

Leaf blowers resemble rotary mowers set on edge. They generate a blast of air that blows leaves and other trash into piles for burning or collection. (An ingenious system for disposing of leaf piles is used in the city of West Allis, Wisconsin. A metal gangplank, or ramp, with high sides is laid from the ground up to the open end of a garbage truck; and a jeep with a snowplow blade pushes the leaves up this into the truck. A somewhat similar system might be used on large residential properties.)

Rotary tillers. Most gardeners have use for a rotary tiller—which thoroughly chops up and turns over soil to a depth of about 8 inches—only when they are remaking a lawn or developing a large flower bed. For such purposes a rental unit is all you need. But if you have a vegetable or berry garden, a tiller of your own will soon prove to be a good investment. It not only makes light work of weeding but also simplifies spring garden preparation and fall plowing and helps to keep the soil in good tilth at all times.

Aerators and lawn renovators. The first punch holes in the lawn to let in oxygen. The second have revolving vertical knives that dig out the dead grass (thatch) and at the same time scarify the soil. Both are used to maintain beautiful turf; but since you need them only once or twice a year, you should rent rather than buy.

Spreaders. For small properties, the original V-shaped spreader is more than adequate for applying fertilizer, insecticides, herbicides, and grass seed. But for large properties, buy or rent a rotary spreader with a horizontal propeller underneath the hopper. It spreads fertilizer and so on in 8-foot swaths and allows you to cover as much as two acres an hour.

Hedge trimmers. The ones that operate on electricity or a battery are of doubtful value if you use maleic hydrazide and/or B-Nine (see Chapter IX) to control the growth of hedges and shrubs. But if you do not use these chemicals, by all means buy a trimmer—preferably one with two cutting edges. In making your purchase, test the weight of the available models to determine which is easiest for you to handle. Note also that there is some variation in operating speeds.

Pruners. These tools are certainly not new; but despite the fact that they greatly help to make pruning easier and faster, few people seem to have them. One tool I recommend is a lopping shears for snipping off branches as large as 2 inches in diameter. The tool is similar to an ordinary hand pruner but has a larger cutting throat and handles from 20 to 34 inches long.

The other essential pruning tool is a pole pruner that allows you to cut wood high in trees and vines while standing safely on the ground. The pruning head, operated by a rope, severs branches up to 1½ inches across. It is mounted at the end of a slender wood pole 8 to 12 feet long. Buy the longest.

A slim, curved pruning saw at the end of a long pole is another useful tool.

Chain saws. This is another tool that most gardeners

should rent. Purchase is advisable only if your property is large and well wooded.

Chain saws are powered either by gasoline or electricity. Use of the latter type is limited unless you have a portable generator that allows you to work beyond reach of the power lines.

Brush chippers. A chipper is the tool that utility crews use to chop up the branches that they prune out of trees. An excellent coarse mulching material results.

Rent a chipper the next time you have a great deal of wood to cut out. It will make the business of disposing of the trash easier, faster, and safer than burning.

Brush and weed cutters. These portable, gasoline-powered tools are designed mainly to keep down brush and weeds on large properties. They are carried over the shoulder and have a long, curving tube with a revolving blade that enables you to mow down brush without bending, to get in under low-hanging trees and shrubs, even to reach down into holes.

Trash burners. Burning garden trash in the open is a time-consuming chore because you have to stand by to watch out for sparks, to keep the fire from creeping out at the sides, and to push unburned material into the center of the blaze. A good trash burner makes this unnecessary.

Newest types are pyramid-shaped and have sides of solid steel. A cap permits burning even in the rain, while well-designed louvers in the base create a draft that makes even green wood burn. Capacities range from 2 to 20 bushels.

Note, however, that more and more states and cities are passing laws forbidding all open-air burning—even with trash burners.

Sprayers. If you have an orchard or a lot of trees,

shrubs, and roses, a gasoline- or electric-powered sprayer that rolls on rubber-tired wheels will give you faster and more complete protection against insects and diseases than you can possibly achieve with a small sprayer; and in the long run it will save money over the employment of tree-spraying services.

Power sprayers for home use range from about 10 to 30 gallons in capacity. Ask for the longest possible hose.

Soil augers. These tools are worth your consideration only because they are so inexpensive that it makes little difference whether you use them frequently or not. But they do come in handy from time to time.

The auger is a 1¼-inch bit that fits any ¼- or ⅜-inch electric hand drill. With it you can make holes up to 18 inches deep in any kind of soil. It's useful in feeding trees or planting bulbs.

Garden carts. Mounted on two large, rubber-tired wheels, they are easily pushed or pulled over any ground, yet hold more than most wheelbarrows. The bottom is flat so that flowerpots and the like will not topple. Best of all, by lifting the handle high, you can tip the front of the cart to the ground so that it becomes a giant dustpan into which you can quickly sweep garden debris.

Hand trucks. Gardeners are often faced with the necessity for moving large, heavy loads around the garden: sacks of fertilizer, bales of peat, shrubs in tubs, balled-and-burlapped plants, and so on. Although a wheelbarrow is usually large enough for such loads, the problem of getting a load into and out of the wheelbarrow sometimes proves stupendous. A lightweight, tubular-steel hand truck similar to that used by moving men and truckers is a good, inexpensive answer. You load it simply by slipping the tongue at the bottom of the truck under the load. Two rubber-tired wheels make the truck comparatively easy to roll across fairly rough ground.

Using Power Tools

Since each type and make of power tool is different, it is impossible to give directions for keeping them in good operating condition. But in all cases, four rules should be observed:

1. Keep the manufacturer's "use-and-care" booklet in an easy-to-remember, easy-to-refer-to place—and use it.

2. Take the time to clean each tool thoroughly after every use. It will require less service if you do.

3. Store the tool in a dry place—not under a plastic sheet that holds in moisture, but in an airy spot under a roof.

4. Put the tool "to bed" in the fall in accordance with the manufacturer's directions. If it is conditioned properly at this time, it should be ready to start right up in the spring when you need it again.

XVIII ❧ Anticipating Trouble from Insects and Diseases

Spraying (or dusting) is one of those gardening chores you cannot avoid if you want to keep a garden going. And there is not much you can do to make it a great deal easier.

This is not to say that antipest work today is not less time-consuming that it was before World War II. Thanks to the development of increasingly effective insecticides and fungicides, we have, on the contrary, made great progress. But until some genius comes up with a way to prevent all insect and disease damage by the single application of a single spray on, say, March 1 of every year, large additional labor savings simply are not in the cards.

In other words, I promise no sensational news or advice in this chapter. But if you are looking for every possible crumb of help in the work-reducing line, perhaps a reminder about some of the old but always good insect- and disease-prevention practices will stand you in good stead.

Disease- and Insect-free Plants, Seeds, and Bulbs

Here is one of the simple precautions that smart farmers take to make sure entire crops are not wiped out. It is an equally good and simple precaution for the home gardener.

If you are buying plants from a distance, deal only with firms that have a solid reputation for quality and that fully guarantee their products. If you are buying locally, inspect the plants carefully before taking delivery, and reject any that look suspicious.

Never ask a friend to send or bring you plants from any distance until you have checked with your state Agricultural Extension Service about plant quarantines. Though these rules may strike you as a nuisance when you cross a state line and are stopped by a waiting roadside official and told to open your automobile and baggage for inspection, they are for your garden's protection.

A final good rule to follow is to insist on "certified" plants, seeds, or tubers when these are available. Certification means that the fields from which the plants come have been officially inspected and found to be free of the troubles that commonly affect these plants.

Plant varieties tolerant of, resistant to, or immune from common diseases. In one of its recent vegetable seed catalogs, Northrup King gives the following definitions of these three terms:

Tolerant: Capable of sustaining a disease without serious injury or crop loss. A tolerant variety may become affected by a given disease, but to a lesser extent than a susceptible variety. Normally, the damage to a disease-tolerant variety is less than to a susceptible one under the same conditions.

Resistant: Able, to a certain degree, to suppress or retard the activity of a given pathogenic organism or virus. Capable of defending itself against invasion or overcoming the effects of invasion.

Immune: Exempt from a given disease; having qualities which do not permit infection. Immunity is absolute. A plant may be slightly susceptible, moderately resistant, extremely susceptible or extremely resistant [to a disease]—but not moderately immune or highly immune.

Chapter VI includes a long list of vegetable varieties that are resistant to or tolerant of certain diseases. Given a choice between these and others that are not resistant to disease, it is a good idea to choose the former.

Rotating crops. When you plant the same kind of plant in the same location year after year, the pests to which that species is susceptible may accumulate in the soil to the point that they eventually overwhelm the plants. It is, therefore, a wise precaution to plant each kind of annual flower, vegetable, and summer bulb in a different spot each year. (It isn't a bad idea to move perennials once in a while, too.)

An adequate system of rotation, as a rule, calls for moving plants from location A the first year to location B the next year and then back to location A the third year. But if it is convenient to allow two years between use and re-use of the same soil for the same plants, you gain further assurance against trouble.

Concentrated plantings of related species. It is wise to avoid these because different plants in the same family are sometimes attacked by the same pests (example: the striped cucumber beetle may attack all members of the cucurbit family, including cucumbers, squashes, melons, and so forth). Consequently, if you make a very large planting of such plants in one corner of the garden, you may create a more inviting target for their enemies than if you set out fewer plants or space them much farther apart.

Keeping the garden clean. Cleaning will remove many of the places in which microbes and insects lurk.

Rip out and destroy diseased plants, leaves, stems, and fruits as soon as you notice them. Keep trash out of flower beds, vegetable gardens, and shrubbery borders. Eliminate weeds in and around the garden because they may harbor diseases that can attack closely related cultivated crops.

Watering plants carefully. Moisture helps to spread diseases through a garden. Obviously, there is little you can do to prevent rain from causing trouble in this way; but there are two sound precautions to take when you water the garden yourself. First, apply water early in the day so that any water that may get on the foliage can dry before nightfall. Second, try not to get water on the leaves—especially if they show signs of mildew, blackspot, or other disease.

Picking flowers and vegetables when dry. If they are covered with rain or dew, you may accidentally transmit disease from plant to plant just by touching or brushing them. Beans, for instance, are susceptible to a bacterial blight that is often spread in this way.

Fertilizing sparingly. Although fertilizer helps to prevent plants from contracting diseases by promoting vigorous growth, too much fertilizer causes such lush, rank growth that leaf spot diseases may be encouraged. This is a common cause of lawn troubles.

Suiting the soil's pH content to your plants. The soil's acidity or alkalinity sometimes influences the severity of garden disease problems. For example, clubroot of cabbage is more serious if the soil is acid than if it is neutral. Conversely, potato scab is worse in neutral soil than in acid soil.

Disinfecting seeds before planting. Or you can plant in a sterile medium, such as sphagnum or vermiculite. This helps to prevent the seedlings from being killed by the damping-off fungus disease. The usual and simplest way to treat seeds that are planted directly in the garden is to put a pinch of a seed disinfectant, such as Spergon, into the seed packet and shake well until the seeds are coated.

Soaking seeds in hot water or a solution of bichloride of mercury may also be recommended for some plants; but this kind of treatment is more commonly reserved for iris tubers and gladiolus corms. To prevent soft rot, the former are dipped in a solution made of 1 tablet of bichloride of mercury (a deadly poison) in 1 pint of water. Gladiolus corms are soaked for two hours in the same solution to prevent scab.

Sealing tree wounds. Diseases often enter trees and other woody plants through scars left when branches are cut off or broken. To seal off these points of entry, trim branches close to the trunk. Scrape out unsound wood. And paint wounds over 1-inch across with prepared tree paint or any good exterior house paint.

Insect traps. Don't use them. True, they catch a lot of bugs, but some of them are good bugs that help to keep down the bad ones. Furthermore, traps attract to your yard a great many insects that would otherwise be perfectly happy to remain next door.

Effective use of sprays and dusts. Modern insecticides (including miticides and nematocides) and fungicides are your best means of controlling small garden pests. But their effectiveness depends partly on how well they are used. Here are six points to note:

1. Chemicals applied by spraying are generally effective for a longer time than those applied by dusting. Dusting,

however, is an excellent method of application in a number of situations.

2. Spray chemicals should be purchased in the form of concentrated liquids or wettable powders. The latter dissolve in water better than ordinary powders.

3. Unless a chemical is designed to kill a pest upon direct contact, sprays should be applied so that they cover all surfaces of the plants you are protecting. Be sure to spray the undersides of leaves, in other words.

4. Although rain does not necessarily wash a spray chemical completely off a plant, the best time to spray is after a rain. Make additional applications after each succeeding heavy rain.

5. Follow the manufacturer's directions for using an insecticide or fungicide.

6. Sprayers must be cleaned thoroughly after each use, and a new batch of spray should be made up for each subsequent use.

Inasmuch as many insect and disease problems are not treatable until they actually arise, it is inevitable that you must drag out your sprayer occasionally throughout the growing season to cope with them. This is the unavoidable part of the pest-fighting chore. Other problems, however, are preventable by advance application of chemicals.

How can you accurately predict such problems? One thing not to do is to borrow trouble and spray every plant in sight "just in case." A far more sensible course is to keep a mental record of problems that have cropped up regularly in the past. This is a good indication that they are likely to arise again. The other way to anticipate—and ward off—trouble is to ask your state Agricultural Extension Service what new or aggravated insect and disease problems are expected for your area in the summer ahead. Local nurserymen may also be able to advise you about this.

Here are a number of common insect and disease problems that can usually be avoided by *preventive treatment* of the target plants with the indicated chemicals:

Insects

Asiatic garden beetles. These ½-inch, oval, cinnamon-colored beetles are found mainly east of the Mississippi River. They eat the foliage of many flowers, vegetables, trees, and shrubs; also attack lawns. Dusting lawns in the spring with chlordane kills many of the grubs.

Cankerworms. Also called inchworms or measuring worms, these widespread pests are easily identified by the way they inch along the ground and lower and raise themselves from trees on threads. They do serious damage to many shade and fruit trees by devouring the foliage. Spray with Sevin or lead arsenate as soon as the leaves develop in the spring.

Cutworms. They are large, fat, smooth caterpillars that chew on the stems, leaves, or buds of tomatoes, cabbages, and various other vegetables and flowers. They are in many parts of the country. You can usually discourage them by wrapping 4-inch-high collars of cardboard around the stems of young plants. The collars should extend an inch below the soil line.

Elm bark beetles. Very small and reddish-black, they transmit the Dutch elm disease. Spray methoxychlor on the trunk and branches of trees in the spring before the leaves come out.

Elm leaf beetles. The beetles themselves are ¼ inch long, yellowish, and have a black stripe on each wing. The grubs are ½ inch, yellow with black stripes. Both beetles and grubs eat leaves of elm trees. Spray with methoxychlor when the leaves are open halfway, and repeat the application three weeks later.

European chafers. These eastern beetles are oval, ½

inch long, tan with dark wing bands. The grubs are white and have brown heads; ¾ inch long. They chew through grass roots, causing brown patches in the lawn. To kill the grubs, dust the lawn in the spring with chlordane.

Japanese beetles. They are a dreadful scourge east of the Mississippi River but can be kept fairly well under control by dusting the lawn in the spring with chlordane. This treatment kills the grubs, which are 1 inch long, whitish, and have brown heads. The beetles are handsome fellows, about ½ inch long, with coppery wings. They feed on grass, flowers, fruits, trees, and so on.

June beetles. Sometimes known as May beetles, they are large, black, or reddish-brown beetles that feed at night on deciduous trees and grass. To control them, dust chlordane on the lawn in the spring.

Mites. These infinitesimal sucking insects are found throughout the country and attack many kinds of plants. They cause rusty discoloring of leaves, which may then drop. Ordinarily, mites do not do widespread damage, because beneficial insects prey on them. But when malathion or Sevin are used extensively in the garden, many of the mite-eating insects are killed, and the mite population swells and causes alarming trouble. It follows that the best way to prevent mites from getting out of hand is to mix a miticide such as Aramite, Dimite, or Kelthane with malathion or Sevin when using the last two chemicals.

Nematodes. Here is another widespread group of microscopic insects that attack many plants—mainly flowers and vegetables. Since they lurk in the soil, the best way to control them is to treat the soil before planting with a fumigant such as chloropicrin, Nemagon, D-D Mixture, or Vapam.

Scales. These insects are small, white or gray pests that cover the stems and leaves of various plants. They suck the plant juices, thus causing the leaves to turn yellow and fall. Some of the most injurious scales are the euonymus, oystershell, scurfy, San Jose, pine needle, and juniper scales. These types can be kept under control by spraying plants in the early spring with a dormant oil spray.

White-fringed beetles. A pest in the Southeast, these are gray-brown beetles with white wing edges. The grubs are ½ inch long, dirty-white, legless, and curved. Both eat many different plants. Dusting chlordane on the soil in the spring before planting your garden kills the grubs.

Wireworms. They are like little, hard, coiled springs. They live in the soil and attack seeds, seedlings, and older plants of various kinds. Working chlordane into the soil in the spring prevents their depredations. An alternative is to fumigate the soil with D-D Mixture.

Diseases

Camellia flower blight. It causes the blossoms on camellias to turn brown and drop and is a common problem wherever camellias are grown; but it can be prevented by applying Terracolor to the soil in the winter.

Clubroot. This disease attacks cabbages and related plants almost everywhere. It causes the leaves to turn yellow and wilt on hot days. Roots are often misshapen. The disease can be largely prevented by applying enough lime to the garden before it is planted to bring the pH up to 7.2.

Crown rot. Most common in the North, this disease of delphiniums, iris, and other plants causes stems to rot or break off at the ground during hot weather. To prevent its recurrence in a garden where it has been a problem, fumigate the soil with chloropicrin.

Damping-off. As noted earlier, you can usually prevent this disease by treating seeds before planting with Spergon. Or plant the seeds in a sterile medium. Or fumigate the garden soil with formaldehyde.

Dutch elm disease. See elm beetles, above.

Snow mold. A white, cottony mold that develops on the leaves of grass (primarily bentgrass), it causes them to turn brown and stick together. It occurs almost everywhere. To prevent it, keep the lawn cut in the fall and don't apply high-nitrogen fertilizers. Spray with Dyrene before the first lasting snow and once again if the snow melts before spring finally arrives.

Southern blight. It resembles crown rot (which see) and is prevented in the same way.

Tulip fire. A widespread disease, it causes spots and then a brown-gray mold to develop on the leaves, stems, and flowers of tulips. Avoid planting bulbs with yellow lesions on the outer white skin. Fumigate the soil in which diseased tulips previously grew with Vapam.

Special Note About Roses and Fruits

Because roses and fruit trees are subject to attack by many insects and diseases, you can raise them successfully only by instituting and maintaining an extensive preventive spray program. This involves considerable work, but there is no alternative.

Roses should be sprayed with an all-purpose rose spray or (my favorite) with Phaltan and Isotox Garden Spray mixed together. Make the first application when the plants begin to leaf out in the spring; and repeat applications weekly thereafter until frost.

Fruit trees should be sprayed according to a schedule recommended for your area by your state Agricultural Extension Service.

XIX  Four Ways to Simplify Fertilizing

Fertilizing, as I said earlier, is one of those gardening duties you cannot escape. But there are several ways to make it somewhat simpler:

Using a spreader. Whether you use the conventional V-shaped, drop design or a rotary (see Chapter XVII), a spreader will save you time and energy. Properly used, it will also spread the fertilizer more evenly and at the correct rate and will thus guard against burning of the grass.

Theoretically every fertilizer package carries instructions for how to set the various makes of spreader in order to distribute that particular brand of fertilizer at the proper rate. Some packages, however, tell you nothing at all. Consequently, to use your spreader effectively with them, it is necessary to make a test to see how it should be calibrated. Here is the method suggested by the Diamond Alkali Company:

Procedure	*Example*
Step 1: On the fertilizer package, note how much coverage the fertilizer should give. (If this information is not printed on the package, ask the garden supply dealer.)	25 pounds will cover 2,000 square feet

Step 2: To determine the amount of material to cover 100 square feet, add two zeros to the weight.

$$2,500$$

Step 3: Divide this number by the number of square feet printed on the package. This gives you the number of pounds of material to cover 100 square feet.

$$2,000 \overline{)\,2,500.00}^{\,1.25}$$

Step 4: To convert this number to pounds and ounces, remember that the numbers to the left of the decimal point stand for pounds and that those to the right stand for ounces. Multiply the latter by 16.

$$.25$$
$$\times\ 16$$
$$\overline{4.00}\ \text{or}$$
1 pound 4 ounces for each 100 square feet

Step 5: To determine the distance that the spreader should travel to cover 100 square feet, measure the width of the spreader drop and divide this figure into 100.

Width of Spreader	Distance to Travel
18 inches	66 feet
21 inches	57 feet
24 inches	50 feet

Step 6: Establish a place where fertilizer dropped can be retrieved for weighing purposes. If the basement or garage floor is not long enough for the distance to travel, cut the measurement in half and go over the area twice. If you do not have an area from which you can retrieve the fertilizer, suspend a box top under the spreader to catch the material.

Step 7: Set the spreader opening to give you what you think is the correct distribution rate; pour some fertilizer into the hopper; and roll the spreader across the test area as in Step 6. Then sweep up the fertilizer and weigh it.

Step 8. Open or close the spreader opening as the test indicates. If necessary, make a second test.

Even though you may always use a fertilizer that gives instructions for setting spreaders, it is wise to test your spreader in the above manner occasionally to make sure that it has not slipped out of adjustment for some reason.

Using slow-acting fertilizers. Commercial fertilizers vary in the speed with which they make nutrients available to plants. Fast-acting fertilizers dissolve quickly in water; are taken up through plant roots almost immediately; and soon dissipate their energy. Slow-acting fertilizers, on the other hand, are slow to dissolve and therefore release their nutrients gradually over a long period of time.

Despite the speed with which they work, the two kinds of fertilizer are equally beneficial to plants. But from the standpoint of the weary gardener, the slow-acting types are the more desirable in certain cases because you do not need to apply them so often.

Among the more common slow-acting fertilizers are urea, bonemeal, and cottonseed meal. Urea—an excellent source of nitrogen—is available in balanced lawn fertilizers containing phosphorus and potash. A typical lawn food with urea has an analysis of 22-8-4. Applied in the spring, a 20-pound bag of this formula will take care of the nutritional requirements of 5,000 square feet of grass growing on fertile soil until fall, when a second application should be made. (On poor soil or sandy soil, you should use 40 pounds of the fertilizer.) What's more, because the fertilizer is a slow-release type, there is little danger of overstimulating the grass and producing succulent growth that requires frequent mowing and that is unusually susceptible to fungus diseases.

Bonemeal is used primarily in perennial gardens and around woody plants. Cottonseed meal is a favorite for feeding rhododendrons, azaleas, and other plants that prefer an acid soil. In both cases, one application in the early spring satisfies the requirements of most plants; however, you also need to apply a fast-acting fertilizer if you want to give flowers a "shot in the arm" at a certain time. (Vegetables generally do best when fed a steady diet of fast-acting fertilizer.)

Fertilizing as you water. One of the most beautiful gardens I have seen is fertilized in this way; and a minimum of effort by the gardener is required. Don Estep, a landscape gardener in South Laguna, California, invented the system.

He buys high-nitrogen liquid fertilizer in half-gallon bottles. When the system is in operation, water enters a bottle from a faucet via a small tube; diluted fertilizer flows out through a second tube and is sprayed on the plants along with water from a watering hose. The bottle is drained in 10 minutes, but watering is continued for as long as necessary thereafter to slake the plants' thirst and to flush the fertilizer (it is not a foliar spray) off the foliage and into the ground.

Mr. Estep says that the system requires some effort to install (the exact method is his secret), and he does not recommend it for a small place. But for large properties and those with difficult terrain, the system is a definite work saver.

Employing a lawn spray service. Such services are provided by fuel oil dealers who want to keep their tank trucks and personnel busy during the summer. The first service was started in the early 1950s; but it is only within the past few years that others have become available in more than a handful of communities.

A typical service is that of the Troy Oil Company in Indianapolis. During the spring, it fills its tank trucks with a 15-10-5 liquid fertilizer and chlordane and sends them out to spray the lawns of homeowners requesting help. Gardeners can buy as many or as few treatments as they think necessary; but Troy recommends three: One application of fertilizer mixed with a strong chlordane solution before May 15; another application of fertilizer mixed with weaker chlordane in June; and a separate application of 2,4-D (made from a special tank and with a special applicator) between May 10 and June 15. The cost of a single application is $6 per 2,000 square feet, plus $1.50 for each additional 1,000 square feet. For three or more applications, a 10 percent discount is allowed.

Prices charged by other services, the fertilizers and other chemicals they use, and the treatments they offer vary; but they are worth investigation. Before signing up for a service, however, you should find out what kind of fertilizer is being used and at what rate, and who is the authority for that rate of application (it should not be the oil dealer alone unless he is recognized as a knowledgeable gardener). Make certain, too, that if a feed-and-weed spray is used, both the fertilizer and the herbicide will be timed to give maximum results (in some cases, separate applications at different dates may be preferable). Your state Agricultural Extension Service can advise you best about this.

XX What to Do About Outdoor Lighting and Pool Maintenance

Gardening today is taking on new dimensions. There is a definite trend toward garden lighting. There is an equally strong trend to use water for its visual and audio effects.

Although both elements—light and water—add vastly to a garden's appeal, they also, alas, inject new maintenance problems of sufficient importance to merit attention here.

How To Simplify Lighting System Maintenance

The following section was written for me by the man I consider to be the country's leading authority on outdoor lighting—John Watson, of Dallas. He has illuminated everything from his own superb little garden to large estates, golf courses, industrial parks, and Canada's magnificent Victoria Park overlooking Niagara Falls.

Most outdoor lighting installations do nothing but create maintenance headaches—headaches that are occasionally so bad that homeowners are discouraged from using their lighting systems ever again. It is for this reason that I today give almost as much thought to the maintenance aspects of a lighting installation as to its ultimate effect. There have even been cases where I allowed the design of the lighting to suffer somewhat in preference to creating a maintenance problem.

In residential installations, the same kinds of maintenance problems tend to crop up so frequently that it is easy to set down a number of hard-and-fast rules for guarding against them:

1. Don't place outlets in grass areas where you must mow and hand-clip around them. Another drawback of outlets located in such areas is that wires must run on the ground from them to the lights in flower beds or trees; and these are not only in constant danger of being damaged but must also be picked up every time the lawn is mowed. If at all possible, outlets should be located in flower beds or shrubbery borders—preferably back against a wall or a tree where they will not be in the way of anyone working in the beds.

2. Install all cables from the fuse box to the outdoor outlets underground, and protect them carefully. Underground cables are installed in two ways: Some are run through conduits (pipes). Others are made with very tough insulation which permits them to be buried directly in the ground.

I prefer—and some communities require—conduit installations because they cause fewer troubles and, if large conduit is used, it is possible to snake additional wires through it at a later date if you decide to change or enlarge your lighting system. There are, however, two kinds of conduit. The one that should be used outdoors is called rigid conduit, because it is made of heavy, hard-to-bend steel that lasts many years even under adverse conditions. The other, called thin-wall conduit, is the kind that should be used indoors only. But it is often used outdoors in cut-rate installations. Here it invariably causes trouble—sometimes within two or three years—by rusting away and exposing the wires to moisture, soil chemicals and accidental damage by spading. Replacement is costly and involved.

Although direct-burial cable is generally safe to use underground, I always advise running it through rigid conduit in flower beds and similar areas where there is a possibility of driving a spade or fork through the wires.

3. Use watertight fixtures and fittings. Although I stress the importance of this rule in connection with fixtures that are buried in the ground, it also applies to those above ground. Moisture has an insidious way of working its way into electrical fixtures; and when it does, maintenance problems are bound to arise.

4. Control all garden circuits with switches. This is for both safety and convenience. For one thing, there is always a danger that a wire running through the garden may be cut; and if it happens to be "hot," someone is likely to be hurt. Furthermore, if you happen to plug a light or appliance into a live circuit when the ground is damp, you may be elecrocuted.

From the convenience standpoint, switch-controlled circuits make it unnecessary to go out into your garden every night to plug in your lights. Thus you eliminate one other little maintenance problem that could in time spoil your enjoyment of your lighting installation.

5. Wire lighting fixtures directly into outlet boxes whenever possible. Then there will be no plugs to come loose at unpropitious moments.

6. Use bulbs that will not break when water strikes the hot glass. The proper lamp for outdoors is the PAR series made of tempered glass. The 75-, 100-, and 150-watt sizes, which are most commonly used in the garden, are completely weather-resistant; but the 300- and 500-watt sizes need to be protected with a glass and metal cover or should be installed well up under sheltering eaves.

Smaller bulbs that can be used outdoors without protection are ordinary household lamps in the 15- and 25-watt sizes. These do not generate very much heat and can therefore survive exposure to rain or snow. If larger household bulbs or indoor R-type (reflector) bulbs are used outdoors, they must be completely enclosed.

7. Use long-life bulbs to reduce relamping problems. The long-life bulbs sold for indoor use are not suitable. But if

you have a substantial budget, mercury lamps that are rated for a life of 10,000 hours are excellent.

In areas which are affected by great fluctuations in voltage, the life of many household bulbs is shortened by the heavy surges of power. To protect against this problem, use 125- or 130-volt lamps. These may last twice as long as standard 110-volt lamps, yet cost no more.

8. Put glass covers or screens on lights focused up into trees and shrubs. Years ago I gave a garden party that taught me the necessity for covering lights that are aimed upward. That evening the June bugs were out in force; and as more and more of them fell into the lights and began to burn, the odor that permeated the garden almost destroyed the delightful party atmosphere.

Admittedly, June bugs are not a problem all the time; but once you have tried to clean them out of a light fixture, you will never fail to take steps to keep from from falling in.

The same steps are also needed to keep leaves out of fixtures. When these are dry, the heat of the bulb can cause them to burst into flame which then damages the fixture, the wiring, and nearby plants and buildings. When leaves are wet, they may cause rusting of the fixture.

9. Avoid fixtures mounted on stakes. They are easily knocked over; and when that happens, it takes time to set them into proper position again.

10. Secure all fixtures firmly. Fixtures that are poorly mounted on trees, buildings, and the like are just as likely to come loose and swing out of focus as stake lights. And resetting is even more difficult—especially when you have to climb a ladder to get at them.

How to Reduce Garden Pool and Fountain Maintenance

Several years ago, on a trip to Phoenix, I came up with one of those odd bits of information that have a way of sticking in the mind. I found that—not surprisingly—

many of the people in that hot, dry climate enjoy the sight and sound of running water in their gardens. But unfortunately, because of the dust that sometimes fills the air and because of the high concentration of alkali salts in the water, the fountains are so prone to clogging that in the opinion of one expert gardener, "Anyone's crazy to bother with them."

No doubt, this is an odd problem. But it points up the fact that even things as pristine and innocent as a little stream of water can add to the gardener's work if he doesn't watch out.

Keeping fountains going. All fountain kits require a certain minimum depth of water to operate properly (and they are also recommended for use only in pools of certain minimum diameter). You should not, therefore, build a pool without first checking the requirements of the fountain kit, or vice versa.

Continued fountain operation depends on making sure that electricity gets through to the pump. (In other words, the same kind of sealed, underground wiring system needed for an outdoor lighting installation is needed for a fountain.) And the water must be kept clean.

In the instruction and maintenance manual that comes with one of its small fountain kits, Kim Lighting and Manufacturing Company gives the following directions: (1) Regularly remove trash from the pool to keep it presentable and to prevent clogging of the suction screen on the pump. (2) Drain pool and replace with fresh water periodically. (3) Control algae (see below). (4) Remove and clean pump suction screen at least once a month. If this becomes clogged, the pump is starved for water and may be seriously damaged. (5) If spray nozzles become clogged with minerals or trash, use a probe to break the clog open. Clean out spray rings by means of flush-out plugs. (6) Close the fountain down in winter. Drain the pool and fountain equipment, and remove and store the pump, spray rings, piping, light, and so on.

Draining garden pools. You can save work here if you put a drain in the bottom of the pool when you build it. The drain opening should be within easy reach of the side of the pool. In a wet climate, screw an overflow pipe the depth of the pool into a female pipe coupling that constitutes the drain opening; when you unscrew the pipe, the drain is opened. In a dry climate, where rain is not likely to overflow the pool, you can use a threaded plug screwed into the female pipe coupling as the stopper. In either case, there must be a pipe leading from the drain opening to a storm sewer, dry well, or some low spot on your property.

If you do not have a drain in a pool, the easiest way to empty out water is to siphon it off through a hose. Stretch the hose from the pool to a spot lower than the bottom of the pool. Then connect another length of hose to a nearby faucet and hold the open end of this hose to the pool end of the siphon hose (do not connect them). Turn on the water until the siphon hose is running full; then, while still running water through the hoses, lower the butted ends into the pool. You can now turn off the faucet. The siphon hose will continue to run, sucking the water out of the pool until only a fraction is left in the bottom.

Keeping water clear in a reflecting pool. If there are no plants or fish in the pool, use any of the chemicals used to kill algae in swimming pools. Leaves, twigs, grass clippings, and the like need to be picked out by hand or with a swimming pool vacuum cleaner.

Keeping water clear in a fish pool or lily pool. This kind of pool requires little maintenance if you establish a proper balance of animal life and aquatic plants in the first place. They work together to keep the water clean and pure.

Goldfish destroy insects and insect larvae. Aquatic scavengers, such as ramshorn and coral, eat algae and green scum. Tadpoles devour decayed matter. Mussels act as filters. Exactly what and how many of these varied creatures you need depends on the size of the pool and the water supply. A good tropical fish dealer should be able to advise you.

The plants most needed in the pool are the oxygenators that supply oxygen to the water while absorbing the impurities in it. Arrowhead, anarchis, ludwigia, and vallisneria are a few of the most desirable. They are grouped in small pots which are placed at the bottom of the pool. Other plants—such as water lilies, umbrella plants, and water hyacinths can also be planted in the pool but should not be in the same pots as the oxygenators. To keep the goldfish from stirring up the soil in pots and tubs, cover it with an inch of sand or pebbles.

Protecting pools in winter. If a concrete pool has a drain, you can leave it empty through the winter; but it will look better, be less of a hazard, and come through just as well if it is full. Tossing in a log or two to relieve the pressure of ice against the sides is advisable if the concrete is not reinforced.

Plastic pools should be kept full (no logs are needed); otherwise the water pressure in the ground may float them right out of their holes.

Appendix of State Offices of the Agricultural Extension Service

Many of the state services also have county offices. State Agricultural Experiment Stations are usually at the same address as the state headquarters of the Extension Service.

ALABAMA	Alabama Polytechnic Institute, Auburn
ALASKA	University of Alaska, College
ARIZONA	University of Arizona, Tucson
ARKANSAS	College of Agriculture, University of Arkansas, Fayetteville
CALIFORNIA	College of Agriculture, University of California, Berkeley
COLORADO	Colorado State University, Fort Collins
CONNECTICUT	College of Agriculture, University of Connecticut, Storrs
	Connecticut Agricultural Experiment Station, New Haven
DELAWARE	School of Agriculture, University of Delaware, Newark
FLORIDA	University of Florida, Gainesville
GEORGIA	College of Agriculture, University of Georgia, Athens

HAWAII	University of Hawaii, Honolulu
IDAHO	University of Idaho, Moscow
ILLINOIS	College of Agriculture, University of Illinois, Urbana
INDIANA	Purdue University, Lafayette
IOWA	Iowa State College of Agriculture, Ames
KANSAS	Kansas State College of Agriculture, Manhattan
KENTUCKY	College of Agriculture, University of Kentucky, Lexington
LOUISIANA	Agricultural College, Louisiana State University, Baton Rouge
MAINE	College of Agriculture, University of Maine, Orono
MARYLAND	University of Maryland, College Park
MASSACHUSETTS	College of Agriculture, University of Massachusetts, Amherst
MICHIGAN	College of Agriculture, Michigan State University, East Lansing
MINNESOTA	Institute of Agriculture, University of Minnesota, St. Paul
MISSISSIPPI	Mississippi State University, State College
MISSOURI	College of Agriculture, University of Missouri, Columbia
MONTANA	Montana State College, Bozeman
NEBRASKA	College of Agriculture, University of Nebraska, Lincoln
NEVADA	College of Agriculture, University of Nevada, Reno
NEW HAMPSHIRE	University of New Hampshire, Durham
NEW JERSEY	Rutgers University, New Brunswick
NEW MEXICO	College of Agriculture, State College
NEW YORK	College of Agriculture, Cornell University, Ithaca
NORTH CAROLINA	State College of Agriculture, University of North Carolina, Raleigh

NORTH DAKOTA	State Agricultural College, Fargo
OHIO	College of Agriculture, Ohio State University, Columbus
OKLAHOMA	Oklahoma State University, Stillwater
OREGON	Oregon State College, Corvallis
PENNSYLVANIA	Pennsylvania State University, University Park
PUERTO RICO	University of Puerto Rico, Box 607, Rio Piedras
RHODE ISLAND	University of Rhode Island, Kingston
SOUTH CAROLINA	Clemson Agricultural College, Clemson
SOUTH DAKOTA	South Dakota State College, College Station
TENNESSEE	College of Agriculture, University of Tennessee, Knoxville
TEXAS	Texas A. and M. College, College Station
UTAH	College of Agriculture, Utah State University, Logan
VERMONT	State Agricultural College, University of Vermont, Burlington
VIRGINIA	Virginia Polytechnic Institute, Blacksburg
WASHINGTON	State College of Washington, Pullman
WEST VIRGINIA	West Virginia University, Morgantown
WISCONSIN	College of Agriculture, University of Wisconsin, Madison
WYOMING	College of Agriculture, University of Wyoming, Laramie

Index